The Enjoyment of Scripture

Books by Samuel Sandmel

A Jewish Understanding of the New Testament

Philo's Place in Judaism

The Genius of Paul: A Study in History

The Hebrew Scriptures: An Introduction
to Their Literature and Religious Ideas

We Jews and Jesus

Herod: Profile of a Tyrant

We Jews and You Christians: An Inquiry into Attitudes

The First Christian Century in Judaism and Christianity

The Several Israels

Two Living Traditions

Editor: Old Testament Issues

The Enjoyment of Scripture

THE LAW, THE PROPHETS, AND THE WRITINGS

SAMUEL SANDMEL

New York   OXFORD UNIVERSITY PRESS   1972

Copyright © 1972 by Oxford University Press, Inc.
Library of Congress Catalogue Card Number: 76-86303
Printed in the United States of America

To my secretary, Mrs. Sam November,
unique in skill, unique in devotion
to her family, to mine and me, and
to the Hebrew Union College

Contents

Book of Amos: His words, the redactor's work, and the possibility of interpolations. Judges: From compilation into unified accomplishment. The long narrations: Pentateuch; Joshua-Judges-Samuel-Kings; Chronicles-Ezra-Nehemiah.

ousy and madness. David's reign. Bathsheba. Absalom. The portrait of David here and in Chronicles. 5. Solomon: His wisdom. The building of the Temple. 6. The Divided Monarchy: Reheboam. The treatment of the prophets. Elijab and Ahab. Elisha. The Deuteronomist's manner.

VI *The Laws*, 182
Pre-Hebrew codes. The quality of Biblical Laws. Their range. A Wilderness origin? From secular to religious law.

VII *Verse and Poetry: Canticles, Lamentations, and Psalms*, 188
Distinction between verse and poetry. Hebrew meter. Aspects of Hebrew grammar. Parallelism: its form and import. Verse, as in Proverbs. Figures of speech. Some types of poems. Canticles: Love poetry. Lamentations: Disaster. Psalms: The emotional impulse in religious poetry. The oldest psalms and folk-lore. The ritual procession. Man's despair; his confidence in God. Thanksgiving. Historical Psalms. The righteous life.

VIII *Wisdom Literature: Proverbs, Ecclesiastes, Job*, 208
What is wisdom? Proverbs an anthology. "Prudent" living. Ecclesiastes: The realities of life. Lack of an afterlife. What does a man's life mean? The author a spectator. What *yitron* is there? His inquiries. The enjoyment of youth. Job: The meaning of misfortune as God's injustice. Job not a Greek drama. The prose prologue. The poem: The sharing of Job's emotions. The dialogue. The thrust of the book: Can man understand misfortune? God's response and Job's concession. Elihu. The epilogue.

IX *The Literary Prophets*, 237
Contrast with the Deuteronomic prophets. The transmission of prophetic texts. Tacit presuppositions: The covenant, fidelity to Yahve, and social ethics. The form of prophetic books. The prophet's authority. The call: Amos, Isaiah, Jeremiah, Hosea.

Amos and Hosea: Social justice and fidelity. Isaiah: Complexities in the Book of Isaiah. The Song of the Vineyard. The acting out of a figure. Symbol. Social justice and fidelity. Assyria only Yahve's tool. Micah: The essence of religion. The response to an unpopular message. Zephaniah: God and the future. Nahum: Poet rather than prophet. Habakkuk: The challenge to God.

Jeremiah: His experiences. His poetic qualities. His disdain of the Temple. His inner compulsion. The meaning of the disasters of 597 and 586. The new covenant. Ezekiel: Individual responsibility. Repentance. Symbolism. The valley of dry bones.

Second Isaiah: From denunciation to comfort. Fullest monotheism. God and history. Israel as God's witness. The second Exodus.

Post-Exilic prophets: Haggai, Zechariah, Malachi, and Joel. Scattered poems of hope.

Daniel: Assurance in distress. The manner of Apocalypse.

The uniqueness of prophetic literature.

A Note on Translations and Transliteration

The translations from the Hebrew are my own. A portion of these were prepared for my *The Hebrew Scriptures: An Introduction to their Literature and Religious Ideas*, and are here reproduced by permission of the publisher, A. A. Knopf Company.

An asterisk (*) indicates that the translation rests on some minor alteration in, or correction of, the underlying Hebrew. All modern translations have encountered this necessity.

Pronouncing the transliterated Hebrew

Pronounce consonants as in English, except for:

ḥ, equivalent of German *ch*;

', once a gutteral, but now soundless; it represents the letter aleph;

', a deep gutteral, is sounded by Oriental Jews, but treated as soundless by most European Jews; it represents the letter *ayin*.

Pronounce vowels, for practical use, as follows:

a	as in father
ā	as in father, but longer
e	as in met
ē	like the a in fate
i	as in did
ī	like the ee in deed
o	as in hope, but short
ō	as in hope, but longer
u	as in rude
ū	as in rude, but longer

A Chart of History and Literature

The purpose of this chart is to enable the reader to coordinate the history and the literature. It is not possible to be precise about the dates of the literature, nor does a suggested date rule out the possibility for additions to completed books (as attested to in the additions to Daniel and Esther in the Greek versions).

History	Literature
1. The Patriarchal Age (2000*-1300* B.C.)	
2. The Age of Moses, Joshua, and Judges (1300*-1000* B.C.)	Judges V 1100*
3. Samuel, Saul, David and Solomon (1050-931)	Oldest of the Psalms and other poetry 1200-950*
4. Preexilic Period: 931-586	Oldest prose parts (J?) of the Pentateuch (950-850* B.C.)
a. The Divided Monarchy:	Amos 760-750*
b. The Assyrian Destruction of the Northern Kingdom 722/721	Hosea 745-725* Isaiah 740-701* Newer stages (E) of Pentateuchal prose 850-750 Early prose parts of Joshua-Judges-Samuel-Kings 800-700* Micah 725-690*
	Additional Psalms (dates unknown) Zephaniah 630-625*
c. Reign of Josiah 640-609 B.C.	Habakkuk 625-600* First Edition of Deuteronomy and Deuteronomic Writings
d. The Fall of Assyrian Nineveh to the Babylonians 612 B.C.	Nahum 612-610* Jeremiah 626-586*
e. The Babylonian Invasion of Judah 598	Passages in Jeremiah
f. Destruction of Judah and the Exile to Babylonia 586	
5. The Exilic Period 586-538 B.C.	Passages in Jeremiah Ezekiel 593*-560*

a. Persian conquest of Babylonia 538	II Isaiah 538-520*
b. The Return from Exile 538*-516	Further compilation of Pentateuchal materials (late J-early P) 550-530*
6. The Post-Exilic Period 530*-150	
a. Persian Period 538-332	Haggai 520
	Zechariah 520-518*
	Second Edition of Deuteronomic Writings 510*
	Assembly of older Ritual Psalms 500*
b. Careers of Ezra and Nehemiah 450*	Malachi, Joel, Obadiah 490-450*
	Third Isaiah (?) 500-450
	Priestly Completion of the Pentateuch 450-400*
	Completion of Book of Deuteronomy 400*
	Compilation of Proverbs 400*
	Job 450-350*
	Additional Psalms 550-450*
	Compilation of Book of Psalms 450-375*
	Jonah 425*
	Ruth 425*
	Ezra-Nehemiah-Chronicles 375-250*
c. Greek Period 332*-150	Compilation of Prophetic Books
	Ecclesiastes 375*-350*
	Canonization of Pentateuch 400-300*
	Translation of the Pentateuch into Greek 250*
	Daniel 166-165*
	Canonization of Prophets and Psalms 200-100*
7. Maccabean Period 150-63 B.C.	
8. Roman Period 63 B.C.-5th century A.D.	Canonization of The Writings 90-100* A.D.
a. Destruction of Temples in Jerusalem 70 A.D.	

* Indicates approximate dates.

Abbreviations of the Biblical Books

Am.	Amos	Jos.	Joshua
Cant.	Canticles	1 Kings	1 Kings
1 Chr.	1 Chronicles	2 Kings	2 Kings
2 Chr.	2 Chronicles	Lam.	Lamentations
Dan.	Daniel	Lev.	Leviticus
Deut.	Deuteronomy	Mal.	Malachi
Est.	Esther	Mic.	Micah
Ex.	Exodus	Nah.	Nahum
Ezek.	Ezekiel	Neh.	Nehemiah
Ezra	Ezra	Num.	Numbers
Gen.	Genesis	Ob.	Obadiah
Hos.	Hosea	Prov.	Proverbs
Is.	Isaiah	Ps.	Psalms
Jer.	Jeremiah	Ruth	Ruth
Jg.	Judges	1 Sam.	1 Samuel
Joel	Joel	2 Sam.	2 Samuel
Job	Job	Zech.	Zechariah
Jon.	Jonah	Zeph.	Zephaniah

The Enjoyment of Scripture

Introduction

As far as I know, there does not exist a book quite like this one. Others have written (as I myself have) about the history, the religious ideas, and the important externals of the literature, where and when it was written. No one, however, has hitherto tried to present a purely literary appraisal. Necessarily, for reasons of reasonable length, this book is limited to writings found in the Hebrew Bible, the collection which Christians call Old Testament, and Jews Tanak; this latter is an artificial word, the consonants standing respectively for *Torah* (The Law), *Nebi'im* (The Prophets), and *Ketubim* (The Writings). Appraisals of individual books, or of portions of Scripture do exist, especially appraisals of Job. Most of the literary appraisals are, however, apt to be incidental and are invariably laudatory, and often laudatory in the extreme, to the point that one sometimes gets the impression that critical faculties have been suspended or not called on at all. I too can join in the high admiration which some, indeed much, of scriptural literature merits, but at the same time there is some of it which I find tedious and pedestrian (such as the legislation for the animal sacrifices in the Book of Leviticus); some of Scripture I must candidly say I find no less than abhorrent[1] (such as the hymn of hate which is the substance of Nahum). Passages are written in such a way as to condone the cruelty, vindictiveness, and even mayhem being described, and such passages offend me, as I shall note at the appropriate place. I have heard, and read, such opinions from others and agree with them. There is still another unfavorable opinion, but one which in my judgment is unsound. It ascribes to the Hebrew writings a corporate, a national, sentiment that is extremely self-centered and selfish, and marked by a disdain for people who are not Hebrews. I concede the presence of such disheartening sentiments in Scripture, but there is also to be found a concern quite the reverse, and as heartening as it is generous in spirit. I am persuaded that in quantity the concern for all men balances the self-concern, and that at their best these writings exhibit a solicitude for all men and all nations which more than counterbalances the admittedly infelicitous sentiments and passages.

This is a book of judgments on the literary method and quality of the various writings found in the Tanak. Above I indicated my dissent from a blind worship of Scripture. I should say that this book exhibits another dissent, this from the technical Bible scholarship in which I was trained, achieved reasonable competency, and was for a long time as misguided as my predecessors. That technical scholarship is known as the Higher Criticism, and it is learned and scientific and thorough. It is also dull and unimaginative. Mind you, the biblical scholarship is not incorrect; it is only pedantic, unperceptive, and, worst of all, has recently turned gushingly pious. And some of it is so oriented to linguistic dexterity, calling into play the accrued knowledge of Semitic languages, that it has made the Book of Psalms, a collection of 150 poems, a textbook in Hebrew grammar, and the devil with the poetry. Some of the scholarship reflects a desperate effort to trace alleged developments in ideas or attitudes, so as to recover social or traditional antecedents, with the consequence that a passage can lose its force and value through the sacrifice of context to hypothetical background.

One might have thought that the main thrust of biblical scholarship would have been to deepen the comprehension of, and the emotional response to, some striking literature. One need only consult the standard handbooks to discover the real preoccupation: to deduce prudently when and where something was written, or to guess recklessly about these where sufficient decisive information is not available. How often idiosyncratic theories have been presented as if they are incontrovertibly demonstrated! Let me give one single example: There is a theory that *originally* the episode at Mount Sinai was not at all connected with the exodus of Hebrew slaves from Egypt. I doubt the correctness of what is a tortuous theory as its author presents it; anyway, what we encounter in the Bible is the depiction of a direct connection between the two, and that which is actually found in the Bible is infinitely more important than sheerest speculation about an original disconnection. What is important is what the Bible came to say, not the guess about the remote background to what it says.

Most preposterous of all has been the scholarly quest for unshakably reliable history. For religious conservatives to ascribe historical inerrancy to Scripture is natural, and even commendable; for critical scholars to do so, in the name of scientific scholarship, is less intelligible and less laudable. Nineteenth-century scholarship, especially in Germany, had the merit of presuming the absence of *precise* historical reliability in scriptural accounts. Perhaps these scholars were overly skeptical about the *general* reliability of Scripture. The pendulum has swung, however, to the point that now precise historical reliability is attributed to materials which cannot possibly merit such a claim, and also to materials imbedded in longer writings—and there so deftly interwoven with legend and theological beliefs that it is quite impossible to separate history from non-history. Yet every quarterly published in the field of Bible these days seems to have at least one article in every issue defending as historical that which nineteenth-century scholars gave up on. My opinion is that the problems of precise historical reliability cannot be usefully solved because we lack full information and because we cannot objectively separate in writings not designed to be accurate history what is accurate history and what is not.

Worst of all has been an enslavement to the Bible, as if its sanctity should exempt it from that scrutiny which a natural interest in aesthetics should prompt. One must here record a startling fact that one would scarcely know from reading the scholars: some of the psalms are rather poor poetry (though some are remarkably worthy), some of the narration clumsy and inept (though most is quite skillful), and some of the ideas not only not exalted but downright offensive to any sensitive, thinking person. It does not seem to me that Scripture is enhanced by a less than straightforward approach to it. In general literature, there is not always a matching of great ideas and great writing; at times splendid thoughts are expressed in ordinary writing, and at times extraordinary skill can be discovered in writings in which the thinking is scarcely to be admired. So, too, in Scripture, we should reasonably expect to find samples of great ideas haltingly expressed, and reprehensible attitudes brilliantly articulated. What is striking about Scripture, though, is the great number of marriages of exalted writing and exalted thought.

This is primarily a book of judgments. I have no expectation that all my readers will agree with all, or any, of my opinions. My main concern, however, is not to persuade the acceptance of my own ideas, but rather to open up, as widely and as broadly as I can, the whole question of how the biblical writers wrote, how they thought, and how well they did their job of writing. A craftsman is a master of techniques; an artist is the craftsman whose imagination and intuition carry him beyond the techniques. Some biblical writing does not rise above the level of craftsmanship; there is enough of such writing in Scripture for us to be able to discern some of the characteristics of the craft of the Hebrew writer. I shall devote, especially initially, a good bit of attention to the evidences of craftsmanship, and, even when proceeding to higher levels, I shall occasionally revert to the matter.

The subtitle speaks of "The Law, The Prophets, and The Writings," reflecting the three divisions standard in the Jewish transmission of Scripture. These divisions represent three stages at which the many writings—thirty-nine titles—were assembled and were then invested with a special sanctity. The normal term by which one speaks of the attainment of such sanctity by a biblical book is *canon*, "measuring rod." There survive from the late biblical age, in whole or in part, a good many books which were not deemed to merit the special sanctity that has attached to these thirty-nine. Obviously, a book which became canonical had to have been written, and circulated, prior to its coming into the canon. We know from passages in the ancient rabbinic literature that there were disputes over certain books, arguments about whether to admit them into the sacred list or not, for example, Ezekiel, Esther, and Ecclesiastes. Apparently, "The Law" (also called The Five Books of Moses) was the first to achieve the status of canon. How early this took place we cannot know; it happens that The Five Books of Moses was translated into Greek —something most unusual for writings other than royal decrees— about the year 250 B.C. Necessarily, The Five Books (in Greek, the *Pentateuch*) was then held in high veneration. Let us guess, as modern scholars have, that the Pentateuch was accorded this high veneration at least a century prior to the "canonization," since only a book venerated for a good many decades would have been translated. To guess about the attainment of veneration does not tell us when The Five Books was written; it tells us only when The Five achieved the status of being canonical.

The second division, "The Prophets," appears to have been selected no later than 100 B.C. The earliest prophetic book is Amos, who lived in the eighth pre-Christian century; hence, about six hundred years elapsed between the time of Amos and the attainment of canonicity by his book; perhaps this statement makes all the clearer the distinction between the writing of a book and its attainment of canonicity. As a matter of fact, that division called "The Prophets" consists of nineteen books, if we treat I and II Samuel and I and II Kings each as a single book. Four of the nineteen are called "The Earlier Prophets": Joshua, Judges, I and II Samuel, and I and II Kings; three are called "The Major Prophets" (major because they are relatively long books): Isaiah, Jere-

miah, and Ezekiel; the remaining twelve are called "The Minor
Prophets" (minor because they are short): Amos, Hosea, Micah,
Zephaniah, Habakkuk, Nahum, Haggai, Zechariah, Joel, Malachi,
Obediah, and Jonah. The justification for including Joshua,
Judges, Samuel, and Kings, which are narrative, quasi-historical
books, among "The Prophets" is that in them the unfolding of incidents frequently leads to the narration of the appearance of
some prophet who comments on what is taking place. If we were
to date Amos, the earliest, and Jonah, the latest, at 750 B.C. and
450 B.C., respectively, then the prophetic literature comes from a
span of at least three hundred years. Within that span some very
important historical events took place: Israel, the northern kingdom, was destroyed in 721, its population was deported to some
eastern region, and that population disappeared through assimila-
tion and amalgamation; some eastern peoples were transported
into the northern area, where they later became known as Samaritans. Again, in 586 Judah, the southern kingdom, was overrun, the
holy Temple built by Solomon was destroyed, and the population,
with their monarch, was transported to Babylonia; the exiled
Judahites did not disappear, but maintained their identity, and
some seventy years later were permitted to return to Judah—this
when the Persians had conquered the former conquerors, the
Babylonians. Under the Persians, monarchy was not restored; instead, the self-government permitted by the Persians was assigned
to priests, the chief of whom was the high priest. The restored
community had to face poverty, struggles with Samaritans, and
conflicts with neighboring peoples. The three hundred years,
then, were not centuries of tranquility but of great upheaval. We
can marvel that so much writing was preserved, and we can
wonder—we have no direct information—how the preserved writings managed to be transmitted; we can also wonder with what
fidelity and accuracy they were preserved and copied.

The third division, "The Writings"—for which the Latin word
Hagiographa, "sacred writings," is often used—is a quite miscel-
laneous collection. Five short books are called *Megillot*, "scrolls":
Ruth, Esther, The Song of Solomon, Lamentations, and Ecclesi-

astes. Two books are compilations: Psalms, and Proverbs. Quite unique, and each perhaps in a class by itself, are Job and Daniel. Three historical books are present; possibly they were once a single, long account: Ezra, Nehemiah, and I and II Chronicles. Most scholars agree that Daniel was written about 150 B.C. (though the material in it is older); some of the Psalms undoubtedly go back at least to 1200 B.C. The canon of the Hagiographa was finally fixed about 100 A.D., though the Psalms seem to have become canonical about the same time as the Prophetic books. In any case, the Hagiographa are varied in form and content, and represent the widest possible range of times of writing. Perceiving that The Law, The Prophets, and The Writings are diverse, we are led to the sensible conclusion that the Bible is not a book, but a veritable library, representing different ages and different authors, and, because it represents different men, it also reflects different minds. The difference in minds is not alone a result of the events or crises that prompted certain oral utterances which became committed to writing, or which spurred writing without the traversal of an oral period; the difference in minds is the product of the individuality of men, in their style and in their personal responses to situations, for an event which can cause one man despair can awaken within another a passing or an abiding hope.

Prior to its canonization, a piece of writing could be copied with enough inattention by the copyist to furnish the normal mistakes which turn up, say, when you and I copy: repeating certain words, omitting certain words, telescoping two separate short words into one abbreviated long word, and the like. Once a writing became canonical, however, it was copied with such relentless fidelity that even the inherited mistakes and the omissions and the telescoping were retained: this we know from the presence of self-evident errors. If an English sentence were written, "Tha man came," in reading it we would automatically alter *tha* into *the*; comparable errors are possible in the Hebrew; the text was transmitted without correcting such errors. Moreover, ancient translations, such as the Greek, also contribute to our modern ability to correct of some of the mistakes inevitable in all copying. The canonical writings, however, elicited so careful a copying that a chain of sages, the *Masoretes* ("traditionalists"), not only did their work with painstaking devotion, but ultimately assembled and bequeathed elaborate notes, still extant, about the text. The Hebrew text preserved from ancient times by Jews is called, out of deference to these traditionalists, the Masoretic Text.

But let us for a moment jump ahead into the fifteenth Christian century, when the printed Bible first appeared from the press of Johann Gutenberg. This text was set in type from a manuscript, of course; that manuscript in turn was a copy of an earlier manuscript. The oldest surviving complete manuscript of the Hebrew Bible goes back only to the tenth Christian century, no earlier. In our printed Bibles, we deal with copies of copies of copies of copies; we do not possess the original, or holograph, of a single biblical book. Moving backward to the three stages of the canonization, discussed above, we discover that even in the year 100 A.D. people possessed only copies, not holographs. As we try to move even farther back, we can become aware of the possibility of accidents beyond faulty copying. For example, parchment pages which were once bound together might have become unsewn, and then the pages resewn in a different order. Or else a scribe, having prepared ten sheets of parchment, might have discovered that the text he was copying required only nine and a half sheets; perhaps he might have filled the last half sheet with material from an entirely different manuscript. Disarray, disorder, omissions, diversity of content—all these things seem present, so much so that modern scholars, whose bent is independence and disagreement, often are forced to agree on such matters, though at times some make assertions about disorder and disarray without gaining full agreement.

But we must go on, back from copyist to author. Just as Shakespeare could use older material out of which he drew his plots or his characters, so differences in style and differences in viewpoint in Scripture suggest that certain writings were based on earlier materials, the authors sometimes paraphrasing what they were using, sometimes simply quoting the material. Throughout I and II Kings we are repeatedly told that for fuller information about a particular king, we should consult the "Book of the Account" of that king. Later I shall speak in some detail about the way in which the longer books emerged from a long process involving the use of sources and then of writing and rewriting.

But a certain prudent principle must guide us. Suppose we came across the following:

> I wish de war was over, and mah white folks would come back, and git de farm workin' again. It good to be free, de way you hear we gonna be, but I'm hungry, and I don't want to starve a freeman; mah white folks was allus nice to me.

Suppose that we are told nothing about the author, about when he wrote, or about where. Would it be too hard to infer that the author was a black slave, more apt to be old than young? Would we not conclude that this was written after the beginning of the Civil War, but before its end? And would we not infer that it was written in a slave state, and therefore in the South, but that there seems little way to decide precisely what state it was written in?

Much of what we find in the Bible is somewhat comparably anonymous. Happily, we are given in the Bible enough historical information so that often we can make from anonymous documents reasonable inferences kindred to those that can be made from the passage given above. This sort of study has been done with consummate skill by biblical scholars for almost two hundred years.

But surely there are questions about the little passage that could and should be asked, questions go beyond when and where and by whom it was written. For example, what kind of man is revealed in the style and the content? Patient or impatient, calm or impetuous, reasonably experienced and wise or inexperienced and naïve? It is respecting these more subtle and profound matters, in which style reveals the mind and heart of a man, that the scholarship has been mostly silent, and precisely what the scholarship has been silent on is what I wish to speak about. I would like to give my understanding about the kinds of minds and hearts revealed in the biblical writings, and about the craftsmanship and the artistry which are disclosed.

Since the Bible is a library, I must omit some things. I trust my omissions are judicious. The material is vast, and I have tried to determine how best to lead the reader into the material without overwhelming him. I try to take him from the particular to the more general, to lead him from the more simple to the complex. Here and there I deliberately repeat myself.

We shall go from some short examples of narrative prose to longer examples, and then to artfully written short pieces. Thereafter we will proceed to the very lengthy prose works. Necessarily we shall look at some of the laws. Last of all we shall inquire about verse and poetry, to find the pinnacle of biblical writing. Three constant questions will be before us. How did the Hebrew writer write? How does style and content reveal the mind and heart of the writer? How well did the writer succeed in his endeavor?

Which Bible should the reader consult for his further reading? I recommend especially two modern translations,[2] the (American) Revised Standard Version (1946) and the (British) New English Bible (1970). Both can be readily understood. The chief difference between them is in their objectives. The RSV provides, in our own speech, a most reliable translation. It is pre-eminently literal, however, even to the point of preserving the manner of the Hebrew: "The sons of God saw that the daughters of men were fair; and they took to wife such of them as they chose" (Gen. VI:2). Anyone who knows the Hebrew language could translate this sentence back into the biblical tongue and actually approximate what is in the Bible, so closely does the Revised Standard Version follow the Hebrew. The New English Bible is just as reliable, but it is not designed to be literal. In the NEB Gen. VI:2 reads: "The sons of the gods saw that the daughters of men were beautiful; so they took for themselves such women as they chose." This is faithful, but it is not literal, and one who would try to translate this back into Hebrew would not so readily approximate what is in the Bible. For the reader who knows some Hebrew, I recommend the RSV, but for him who knows none, I unhesitatingly recommend the NEB, for its English is more fluent than that of the RSV.

But another word is necessary. Since the Bible is so old and was written so far away, there are places mentioned in it and customs cited in it which need some quick clarification. I recommend the use of a Bible printed with brief explanatory notes, such as the splendid Oxford Annotated Revised Standard Version or the soon to be published Oxford Annotated New English Bible, with helpful introductory materials, helpful explanations, and excellent maps. The Jerusalem Bible has many virtues, though its size and weight may be impediments to some. An annotated Bible is surely what a reader should use.

I record with deepest gratitude the devotion with which Mr. Wilbur D. Ruggles and Miss Caroline Taylor of Oxford University Press have assisted me in the translation from manuscript to printed form. Their collaboration towards this book, as for previous books, has been a veritable pleasure.

I

Narrative Prose

A very poignant episode illuminates how a Hebrew author told his story:

> There was a man from Ramathaim Zofim, of the hill coun-
> try of Ephraim, and his name was Elkanah, the son of Yero-
> ham, the son of Elihu, the son of Tohu, the son of Zuph, from
> Ephrata. He had two wives. The name of the one was Han-
> nah, and the name of the second was Peninna. Peninna had
> given birth to many children, but Hannah had none. From
> time to time the man would go up from his city to worship
> and sacrifice to the Lord of Hosts at Shiloh (*where there
> were two sons of Eli, Hophni and Phineas, priests to the
> Lord*). Elkanah would make his sacrifice on the proper day,
> and then give portions [of the meat] to Peninna his wife and
> to all her sons and daughters; to Hannah, however, he gave
> only one portion, even though he loved Hannah whose womb
> the Lord had closed up. Peninna, Hannah's "foe," provoked
> Hannah profoundly, in order to distress her at her being
> childless. This would happen year after year: when Hannah
> went up to the Temple of the Lord, Peninna humiliated her,
> so that Hannah would weep and not eat. Elkanah her husband
> would say to her, "Why do you weep and why do you not
> eat? Why is your heart distressed? Am I not better to you
> than ten sons?"

One day Hannah arose and went to the sanctuary. Eli the priest was seated at the doorway. In the bitterness of her soul, Hannah prayed to the Lord, and she wept piteously. She vowed, saying, "Lord of Hosts, if you will pay regard to the affliction of your servant, and bear me in mind and not forget me, and if you will give your servant a male child, then I will give him to you for all his life, and no razor will come upon his head."

It so happened that as she prolonged her prayer before the Lord, Eli was looking at her lips. Now Hannah spoke in her heart; only her lips moved, but her voice was not to be heard. He thought she was a drunkard. He said to her, "How long will you be a drunkard! Put the wine away!"

Hannah said, "No, your excellency. I am a woman of distressed spirit, and I have drunk neither wine nor strong drink, but am only pouring out my soul before the Lord. Do not consider me some wicked woman. I have been speaking from the abundance of my lament and distress."

(I Sam. I:1-16)

This is a most moving story, deeply sympathetic to the heartbreak of an unhappy woman. The obtuseness of the priest provides a sharp contrast, increasing our identification with Hannah through our revulsion at the discourtesy she encounters.

Perhaps by our standards the story seems a bit naïve, in that it is told with extreme simplicity; but this is more apparent than real. If we read in the right way, we can share in Hannah's heartbreak, and we, like her, can be offended by the callous words of the priest.

We should notice, first of all, the brevity of the story. This is in part a result of the author's abstention from detailed description; characteristically, he tells us nothing of Hannah's appearance, such as the color of her eyes or her way of walking. He provides us, indeed, with only one essential, that Hannah was without children, while the "co-wife" had many. In Hebrew narration, characterization emerges from what the people say and do, and not from any extended description of them, for the author does not directly intrude. The narrator reveals the inner feelings of the characters through their actions and reactions; he will almost never disclose the inner psyche for its own sake. Accordingly, we are told concrete things, that is, that Peninna vexed Hannah, not that Hannah was a vexed woman; we are not told that Eli was a condescending person, but instead we see him acting in condescension. We must notice this preference for the concrete, since it permeates all of Hebrew narration. Indeed, the Hebrew language is not rich in abstract nouns. The narrator tells us *about* the characters only so much as will make their actions comprehensible. It is enough for him that Eli was a priest; what kind of a person he was emerges through what happens.

As to the style, Hebrew prefers short, simple sentences, and only rarely uses involved, complex ones. A legacy from the older translations is the anomalous (and incorrect) use of *and*, even in beginning a new topic. There is a Hebrew prefix, the letter *vav*, which indeed at times does mean "and"; however, at other times the *vav*'s function is to determine the time factor in the peculiar way Hebrew uses its tenses. In old translations, every *vav* was rendered as "and," and this led to improper translation.

The consequence of such factors as the absence of description, the lack of inquiry into the inner mind, and the preference for short, simple sentences, is that a Hebrew narrative moves at a very fast pace, especially when compared with the leisureliness of modern narration. There is a concomitant directness in the narration, with the result that the impact of the events, coupled with the perception and the insight, can be far stronger than a leisurely, extended account would be. The dramatic encounter between the suffering woman and the callous priest is all the more compelling because it has proceeded to its strong climax after a relatively terse setting of the scene.

When, through study, we increase our knowledge of the ancient Hebrew environment, we can sense an even deeper facet of the emotional content of this episode. To the ancient Hebrews, as we learn from other biblical passages, no blessing was as great as having children. The Psalmist (Ps. CXIII:9) speaks of God as "He who makes the barren woman dwell in her house as a mother of children, and happy." Hence the statement that Hannah was childless is more than a fact; it is an invitation for us to pity her. We know, too, of the eminence of Shiloh in those times, and hence we realize that the dramatic incident took place at an important sanctuary, not at some obscure temple.

Though this is a thoughtful little story, its appeal is emotional, not intellectual. We can generalize about Hebrew narration that, however thoughtful a story might be, and whatever lesson, familiar or fresh, or trivial or profound, it might intend to teach, its primary intent is to work in us some response in our feelings. Our sympathies are from the first directed to Hannah, and it is with her that we identify ourselves. Therefore, we cannot fail to notice, and cannot fail to respond to, the contrast between the insensitivity of Eli's rebuke and the pathos of Hannah's response. We must notice too the sweetness, but, in context, the misdirection, of Elkanah's loving words, "Am I not better to you than ten sons?"

We should observe, too, the mention of the *two sons of Eli,* which I have put in italics. The sons play no part at all in this concentrated episode; rather, they are mentioned here so as to prepare us for some developments which ensue later. The Hebrew narrator was especially gifted at foreshadowing, at preparing us for future events.

The episode of Hannah presents primarily a single emotion, pity for a distressed person. Many brief episodes with a single emotion are found in Hebrew narration, though there are, to be sure, more complex narratives, and we shall look at them. We shall see some samples of horror, of forlornness, of heart-rendering sorrow, of awe, and of ribaldry.

No horror story in literature, to my knowledge, is as hideous in its gruesome details as the narrative in Judges XIX. It is related there that long ago, before the Hebrews had completely conquered Canaan, a certain Levite—in this context Levite probably means "priest" rather than a member of a particular tribe—was returning northward to his home in the hill country of Ephraim, accompanied by his concubine. She had left him; he had persuaded her to return with him.

They arrived at a place which was then known as Jebus—later it became known as Jerusalem—at that time in the hands of the Cananite Jebusites.[1] The priest preferred to lodge in an Israelite city. They arrived at sundown in Gibeah, in the territory of the Israelite tribe of Benjamin. An old man hospitably brought them into his house. In the midst of the hospitality, some base men of the city surrounded the house, and they demanded of the old man that he lead out the Levite so that they could have homosexual relations with him. The old man pleaded with the men to shun this evil, and to abstain from the wickedness of injuring a guest in his home. He offered, instead, to bring out for them both his virgin daughter and also the concubine. The old man was unable to persuade the crowd; the Levite then led his concubine out to them, "and they knew her, and abused her, all night until the morning." Towards dawn they let her go, and then the ravished woman staggered to the door of the house; there she fell to the ground.

In the morning, when the Levite, preparing to go on his way, opened the door of the house, he found the concubine lying dead, with her hands grasping for the threshold. He put her on one of his asses, and returned to his home in Ephraim. He took up a knife, and cut up the body of the concubine, limb by limb, into twelve pieces; these he sent to each of the tribal areas, summoning them to vengeance on the tribe of Benjamin.

Even today, as we read the story, the grim and gory details shock us. The narrator spares us few of those details, and he has us share his own preoccupations with the terrible deeds. Again, as in the story of Hannah, the narrative is laconic; again, we are given no description of the characters; again, it is incident which commands our attention. The story is very primitive in its crudity; the author tells us where and when the incident took place for precisely that very reason, for he deliberately describes how chaotic conditions were in the early days before there was a monarchy.

In a different vein is the pathetic story of Jephthah's daughter (Judges XI:29-40). Earlier in the long account, we have been introduced to Jephthah, a coarse but courageous man who had a capacity for leadership. He had been sired by his father Gilead out of a harlot and was driven from the home by his scornful half-brothers. Jephthah went eastward to a place called Tob, where he gathered about him a group of ruffians.

The Ammonites, a Gentile people who lived near by, began to harass the Gileadites. His kinsmen now implored Jephthah to save them. Jephthah set as a condition for his return to his native place that he be named the chief of the Gileadites. When he went off to war, he made a vow to sacrifice to the Deity "whoever comes forth from the doors of my house to meet me, when I return victorious from the Ammonites." Jephthah won his victory, and on his return to his home it was his own daughter, his only child, who came out to meet him. In her joy at his victory, she came out to him "with timbrels and dances." Jephthah, stricken with great sorrow, said to her, as he tore his garments, "Alas, my daughter, you have truly rendered me *prostrate*,[2] and you have occasioned me *distress*. For I have opened my mouth to God, and I therefore cannot take back my vow." She said to him, "Do to me what came out of your mouth, now that God has taken vengeance on your enemies, on the Ammonites."

The narrative does not depict Jephthah telling his daughter what his "distress" is; presumably it seemed to the narrator unnecessary here to repeat the substance of the vow since the auditor or reader obviously has been made aware of it already.

The daughter—she remains nameless throughout the account— went on to say, "Let this be done for me: let me be left alone for two months, so that I may descend"—their home was on the *Mitzpah*, the peak—"into the mountains, and there bewail my virginity, I and my companions." At the end of two months she returned to her father. He lived up to his vow.

The narrative ends: "She died a virgin. It used to be a custom in Israel for the women to go annually, four days a year, to lament the daughter of Jephthah the Gileadite."

This narrative is so ancient that it does not pause to condemn Jephthah for his implied willingness to offer human sacrifice, a practice which later came to be regarded as an abomination unsuited to Israel and suitable (II Kings III:27) only for Gentile peoples. The story, again, is terse, and it moves quickly to its climax, for it is but a single episode.

The gamut of emotions which the scriptural stories run should make us suspect that they would include humor. They do, indeed, and richly. The humor is coarse when it has to be, and genteel when it can be. But our generation is curiously impeded from seeing any humor in Scripture, unquestionably because of a set of mind which persuades us, wrongly, that humor and sanctity cannot be together. The case could be made, moreover, that in the immediate past centuries religion has exiled humor, and given it to the irreligious. We become long-faced as soon as we find ourselves in any contact with religion; in fact, to smile in a sanctuary has, lamentably, come to be considered a near desecration.

Nothing is so perilous to laughter as to tell someone that he is now going to hear something funny, and perhaps the humor presently to be pointed out will have disappeared through this advance labeling. But let us look at some minor samples to see the kinds of things which the Hebrews could laugh at.

Our first example is one single sentence (II Kings XIX:35). The context is this: the Assyrians laid siege to Jerusalem, during the reign of King Hezekiah, around the year 690 B.C. A disaster struck the Assyrian troops in the night, possibly, as some scholars have suggested, a form of bubonic plague. Here is the verse: "That night, the angel of Yahve went forth and, in the camp of the Assyrians, smote 185,000; they arose in the morning, and behold they were all dead bodies." This is broad humor, dependent on the incongruity of the situation, and also upon exaggeration. We will meet incongruity and exaggeration from time to time.

Still another example involves a pun, but entails much more than that. *Nabal* means "fool"; it is a name borne by a sheep-herder in southern Judah, an area in which David was active when he was in flight from King Saul. David sent some of his men to ask Nabal to supply food for a feast. Nabal refused. Thereupon David led four hundred men to seize the food. Nabal's wife, Abigail, learning of Nabal's refusal, prepared food for David's men without her husband's knowledge, and rode out to David, to intercept him and keep him from raiding their property. Meeting David, and prostrating herself, she spoke, among other words, these (I Sam. XXV:25): "Let my lord pay no attention to this coarse man Nabal. Like his name, so is he; Nabal is his name, and folly is with him."

Sarcasm, plain ordinary sarcasm, is frequent. Cain, having killed Abel, on being asked by Yahve, "Where is your brother?" replied, "Am I my brother's keeper?" When Joseph, who had told his brothers of his great dreams in which they all were subservient to him, set out to visit them, and they saw him coming, they said (Gen. XXXVII:19-20), "Here comes that dreamer now! Let us kill him, and throw him into one of the pits . . . and see what happens to his dreams!"

Or the humor can be sly, as in the case of the hypocrite, Laban, from whom the Patriarch Jacob departed surreptitiously, this after Laban had mercilessly cheated him. When Laban pursued and overtook Jacob, he said (Gen. XXXI:27): "Why did you run away secretly, and cheat me, and not tell me? I would have sent you away with mirth and songs, with tambourine and lyre!"

Even slier is the humor in a delicious scene in which Abraham buys a burial cave from Ephron. Ephron presumably wants to give it to him, for he says (Gen. XXIII:14): "A piece of land worth four hundred *shekels*, what does that amount to between you and me?" Thereby Abraham learns Ephron's real asking price.

But humor within an incident otherwise not humorous is quite different from a funny episode. A very ancient and rollicking story, and a coarse one, is contained in Judges III. The second of the twelve Judges was Ehud, in whose time the Lord had allowed the Israelites, through their sinfulness, to come under the dominion of Eglon, the King of Moab:

> The children of Israel cried to the Lord, and He raised up a redeemer, Ehud, the son of Gera, a Benjaminite, a left-handed man. The children of Israel sent a present to Eglon by him. Ehud had made himself a double-edged sword, a cubit

long. He had girded it under his clothing, on the right side.
He brought the present to Eglon, the King of Moab. Eglon
was a very fat man.

After offering the present, Ehud dismissed the people with
him who had borne the gift . . . and he said, "I have a
private matter [to discuss] with you, O king." The king said,
"Silence." He then dismissed all those who were standing in
his presence. Ehud went with him to the cool upper chamber
and was alone with him. Ehud said, "I have a word of God
for you." He arose from his seat and stretched forth his left
hand and took the sword from his right hip, and he stuck it
into Eglon's belly. The hilt followed the blade, and Eglon's
fat encased the hilt too, and the fluids oozed out. Ehud went
out onto the porch, closing the doors of the chamber behind
him. The servants went into the chamber, and noticed that the
doors were all closed. They said, 'Eglon is in the cool room,
defecating.' They waited until they were ashamed [of waiting so long], and still the doors were not opened. They took a
key and opened the door, and behold! their lord was fallen to
the floor, a corpse. While they lingered, Ehud fled. . . ."

This is, of course, a man's story, told in the marketplace between moments of business transactions, and told to elicit rough
and uncouth laughter. As soon as we meet Ehud, we learn the one
significant fact, that he is left-handed; the girding of the sword
on the right side, instead of the left, alerts us to expect something
unusual. We need know no more about Eglon of Moab than his
fatness. It helps, however, to know that the Moabites were traditional foes of the Hebrews, who ascribed their origin to an in-
cestuous union, that of the drunken Lot and a daughter (Gen.
XIX:30-38). The story of Ehud, then, is vindictive and mean-
spirited—especially in contrast with the tale of another Moabite
we shall soon encounter—but its purpose and its successful effect,
if we can get over our squeamishness, is that of low comedy. And
however much our sensibilities are wounded by the explanation
given by the servants about the emptiness of the room, men enjoyed laughing at the obligation, even of royalty, to the digestive
system.

There is also coarse humor in the story of Samson, another of the Judges. The Samson of ancient folkstories (XIV-XVI) was a country bumpkin, strong of body and weak of mind, a fit subject to laugh with and at.

Powerful Samson was betrothed to an unnamed Philistine woman (this prior to his meeting the better-known Delilah). So strong was he that he slew a lion with his bare hands; in the carcass of the lion a swarm of bees settled and planted their honey there. On his way to take his wife, Samson found the honey and ate of it. His father arranged the nuptials with the woman, and then Samson provided the customary feast, to which thirty young men came. Samson put a riddle to these men, offering to provide them with thirty linen suits and thirty festal garments if they would solve the riddle in seven days. Here is the riddle:

> "Out of the eater came what was to be eaten;
> Out of the strong there came forth the sweet."

Unable to solve the riddle, the young men turned to Samson's woman, demanding that she get the answer from Samson for them, for, if not, they would burn her and her father's house. The woman, weepingly, entreated Samson for the solution; at first he refused to tell her, but then he gave in. (He always gave in to women!) She promptly told the young men, and they in turn gave Samson their acquired answer. His comment was:

> "Had you not plowed with my heifer
> You would not have solved my riddle."

Samson promptly went to another Philistine town; there he slew thirty men, and he gave their possessions and garments to the riddle-solvers. He then returned to his father's house, to learn that his wife had been given to his best man. (He was most unlucky with women.)

Later, Samson went to visit this wife, but her father barred him from her chamber. He offered Samson a younger daughter in place of the wife. Thereupon Samson caught three hundred foxes, arranged them side by side, bound them, and put a torch between each pair of tails, and sent the foxes into the grain farms and the olive orchards of his wife's people. These Philistines, learning that Samson had taken vengeance on them because of the treatment accorded him by his wife's father, set a fire in retaliation, and burnt the wife and her father. In further retaliation, Samson slew these Philistines.

Is that funny? Not by our standards. But in folktales exaggeration is characteristic, life is far from precious, and the dignity of the individual absent from all consideration. To Bedouins around a camp fire, or to men idling away an hour in men's company in the broad place of a tiny city, these were exploits to gloat over, especially if the victims in the story were traditional foes, as were the Philistines. When we read the story with these considerations in mind, we can almost hear one of the auditors say, "That Samson —he was really something!"

In another episode, Samson agreed with the men of Judah to become a decoy to the Philistines. He was bound with new ropes, and he was exposed for the Philistines to see and to suppose that now they could do away with him. The Philistines did see him, and they came near him, but Samson broke the ropes, and, finding the jaw-bone of an ass, used it as a weapon with which to slay a thousand men. Later Samson went to another Philistine city, Gaza, to enjoy a harlot there. The Gazaites surrounded the house, and they lay in wait for Samson, intending to seize him in the morning light and to slay him. But Samson lay with the harlot only until midnight. At that hour he arose, and he escaped the ambush by taking hold of the doors of the gate to the city, and the two doorposts, then pulling them up, bar and all, and carrying them away to Hebron!

The combination of Samson's unequaled strength and his inability to resist a woman's blandishments comes to a climax in the account of Samson and Delilah. She, a Philistine, entered into a plot to discover the source of Samson's strength; for this betrayal she was to receive money. Samson put her off again and again, but succumbed to her persistence and told her that his strength lay in his long hair. Delilah, collecting her money from the Philistines summoned a man to shave him while he was asleep. The Philistines seized Samson, gouged out his eyes, and brought him to Gaza, bound in bronze fetters.

But his hair had begun to grow again.

At a festival to the god Dagon, his captors brought Samson from the prison to the temple, to taunt him there. Samson was put between two pillars; he leaned his strength on them and the building collapsed. The eulogy over him is this: "He slew more Philistines at his death than in his life."

If we see the earthy, violent humor in the stories about Samson, then we must notice also that the narrator feels no compunction at telling of Samson's whoring, nor at portraying him as putty in Delilah's hands. Violence—cruel, harsh, physical violence—is not a stranger to the pages of Scripture. The Samson folktales are preserved in a setting which a later author wrote, glorifying Samson by making him a sacred Nazirite, dedicated to God (Judges XIII: 2-21; XVI: 17).

What we have looked at so far is largely to be classified as ancient folk narration, natural, authentic, and unselfconscious. Yet this material, as we have suggested, has here been placed in the larger scriptural context of a carefully planned framework, supplied at a much later time than the early period in which the old folktale circulated by itself, indeed, often orally, prior to commitment in writing. We shall address ourselves later to the question of this scriptural framework, and to the style and manner of it. But we need first to look at a level of writing beyond the folktale, at writing which gives every evidence of deliberate, creative plan. The three narratives we shall look at are each self-contained and complete; they are not portions of longer works.

The story of Ruth is as subdued as the accounts of Samson are raucous. I have wondered if its unknown author were perhaps a woman, for it has a delicacy that seems to me feminine. We should notice, first of all, against a persistent modern theory that no fiction can exist unless it depicts a conflict, that Ruth is devoid of it.

Those who speak of the story as a series of vignettes are on the right track, for what takes place in Ruth is the unfolding narration of *subsequent* incidents, rather than *consequent* ones. The story begins with a statement of the time when the events took place, that is, in the long, long ago "when the judges were judging."[3] In that ancient time, so runs the story, a famine prevailed in the Holy land, and a man moved with his family from Bethlehem in Judah to sojourn in Moab—here described, as often, "in the fields of Moab." This promised the ancient listener or reader something out of the routine, for the mere mention of hated Moab would bring to mind ancient and bitter hostilities; a person of Moabite extraction, even though he was ten generations removed from his Moabite ancestor, was barred from entering the assembly of Israel (Deut. XXIII:3). The opening sentence, then, deliberately sets in juxtaposition the Judean family and the Moabite land. Only after this striking opening does the narrator give us the names of the characters. To the ancient auditor, the juxtaposition promptly created suspense, somewhat as if we were to begin a story this way: "In 1946 a certain Jewish family went to Germany."

Swiftly we are told that the father, Elimelech, died, and that his widow, Naomi, and their two sons, Mahlon and Chilion, survived him. With their father dead, the sons married Moabite women; is the text suggesting that had the father not perished, they would not have done that abominable thing? But so laconic is the narration that though we are given the names of the sons, Mahlon and Chilion (do these names mean, respectively, "tuberculous" or "enervating sickness," and "illness" or "consumption"?) and of the Moabite girls, Orpah and Ruth, we are not told at this point which man married which girl. But the narrative moves on. In time the sons also died, and then Naomi was totally bereft of her Judean family and had left only her Moabite daughters-in-law.

Word came to Naomi that the famine at home had ended, so she determined to return. She set out from the unnamed Moabite site where she had sojourned, and her two daughters-in-law accompanied her on the way. At the border Naomi advised them to return, each to her mother's home. She prayed that God would deal as reliably with them as they had with her and with the men who had died; moreover, she prayed that God would enable each of the Moabite women to find *repose* (note the word *repose*) in the home of some new husband. This is a noble and high-minded, yet stereotyped, farewell, but in its own way moving, so the three women "lifted up their voices and wept." The two Moabite women then proposed, again in stereotyped form, that they go on to Judea with Naomi, and settle there with her. Naomi replied:

> "Turn back, my daughters.
> To what end would you go with me?
> Have I still sons in my womb
> Who could be your husbands?
>
> "Turn back, my daughters;
> Go back!
> I have become too old to be some man's;
> [Or], if I said I had the hope
> To be some man's, even this night,
> And even if I bore sons,
> Could you wait for them until they grew up?
> Would you, for them, abstain from belonging to other men?
> No, my daughters!
>
> "It is far more bitter for me than it is for you,
> That God's hand went forth against me."
>   (Ruth I:11-13)

Again there were tears. Then Orpah (does her name mean "back of the neck," a word which in a Hebrew idiom meant to turn about-face?) kissed her farewell, and went back to her Moabite residence.

But Ruth (does it mean "friend"?) cleaved to Naomi. The elder woman said, "Your sister-in-law has returned, to her people and to her god; go back after her too." (Notice the words "and to her god.")

Ruth said,

> "Do not urge me to abandon you,
> To go back, away from you.
> Wherever you go, I will go;

> Wherever you lodge, I will lodge.
> Your people are my people,
> And your God is my God.
> Wherever you die, let me die,
> And there be buried. . . ."
>   (Ruth I: 16-17)

To the ancient hearer, the force of these immensely moving words transcended the elevated, loving sentiment, for the hearer was always aware that the woman speaking was a Moabite, and presumably loathsome. The issue for him, deliberately created by the author, was the earnestness of the Moabite Ruth; were these noble words idle, or were they meant in unremitting sincerity? The text tells us laconically that Naomi discerned that Ruth was persistent in her wish to go along, so that Naomi ceased trying to persuade her.

The author depicts their arrival at Bethlehem, and the sadness of Naomi's return. The whole city was astir, and the people wondered, "Can this be Naomi?" She said to them,

> "Do not call me *Naomi* ("pleasantness"),
> Call me *Marah* ("bitterness"),
> For God has treated me bitterly.
> I left here full,
> But God has brought me back empty.
> Why call me Naomi?
> God has attested against me,
> The Almighty has afflicted me!"
>   (Ruth I: 20-21)

We see Naomi's sorrow; she has called herself empty—though Ruth is with her! We wonder all the more about Ruth and her sincerity.

The two women were impoverished, and Ruth proposed to go to some field where she might find the favor of being allowed to glean corn. By chance she came to the field of a relative of Naomi's husband, a man named Boaz. When Boaz arrived at the field and saw an unknown woman gleaning, he asked who she was. His servant replied, "She is the Moabite girl who returned from the fields of Moab with Naomi," and he went on to say that she had asked to be allowed to glean, "and she has been doing this since morning, until now, when she must soon go home." The ancient hearer understood these words as praise, in that Ruth had labored, despite fatigue, the entire day. In reading these words, our doubts begin to dissolve about the sincerity of Ruth's devotion to Naomi. Boaz, too, so understood the words. He volunteered a welcome to Ruth, not only to glean, but to refresh herself, when thirsty, from the water drawn by his servants. In gratitude, Ruth fell to the ground, prostrating herself to the man.

> "In what way have I found favor in your eyes
> That you take notice of me who am a foreigner!"

He said,

> "The full account has been told me . . .
> May God recompense your deed. . . .
> Under Whose wings you have come for refuge."

She thanked him, most courteously, for accepting her, who was not one of his handmaids, as if she were indeed one.

At mealtime, he invited her to eat side by side with the reapers. Then he instructed his men to allow her to glean even where the corn was still ungathered, and, indeed, he bade them pull out bundles of corn for her. At evening she beat out the grain which she had gleaned, and brought the flour to Naomi. When Naomi learned from Ruth where she had gleaned, she said that Boaz was a kinsman, "one of our *gō'alīm*." The word, a plural of *go'el*, implies a closeness of relationship, for its literal meaning, in the singular, is "redeemer," a near relative obligated to come to the aid of a person in need. The ancient hearer was alert to the cue: in what way would the kinsman Boaz be a redeemer? Naomi bade Ruth to confine her gleaning to Boaz's fields.

At the intended parting in Moab, Naomi had advised the two daughters-in-law to return home where they would find *repose* in the home of some husband, Naomi now said that she must assume the task of finding some *repose*, that is, a husband, for Ruth.

And who other than Boaz, who that night was to winnow barley at the threshing floor? We bear in mind Ruth's having said, "Your people are my people": a wedding with a Judean would consummate that portion of Ruth's avowal.

At Naomi's behest, Ruth anointed herself, and dressed herself in her best clothing, and went to the threshing floor. Noami had enjoined her not to make herself known until Boaz had eaten and drunk. She waited until he lay down near a heap of grain, and then she came quietly, uncovered his feet, and lay beside him. At midnight he awakened, and, aware that some one lay at his feet, asked who it was. "I am Ruth, your maid-servant; spread your skirt over your maid-servant, for you are the next of kin." (The matter of uncovering his feet and of spreading his skirt over her was, in effect, her proposal to him that they be betrothed.) Boaz was delighted that Ruth had selected him, rather than one of the young men of the neighborhood; he told her that the whole city knew her to be a woman of valor. Though Boaz was prepared to marry her, he mentioned that there was a man who was an even nearer kinsman and who could claim a priority. If he refused, Boaz would meet the obligation. In the morning, while it was still dark, Boaz filled her scarf with six measures of barley, so that she would not return empty-handed to Naomi. When Ruth gave the barley to Naomi, the latter assured her that Boaz would not *rest* until he had finished the matter.

Boaz went to the gate of the city to await the arrival of this other, nearer kinsman. When the man came, Boaz, in the presence of ten elders of the city, put before him a double proposal. The first part of it was that the man purchase from Naomi the parcel of land she had inherited from her husband; this purchase was an act of "redeeming." The man assented. Then Boaz went on, "In acquiring Naomi's land, you also acquire Ruth the Moabitess, to perpetuate through her the seed of the dead whose land you are acquiring." The kinsman replied that he could not, for he already had a legacy to bequeath and he did not want to dilute that legacy; hence, he would forego his privilege to Boaz.

A strange ceremony now took place: "This used to be the

procedure, respecting redemption and exchange, and to confirm the matters, that a man would take off his shoe and hand it to his neighbor." Accordingly, the man drew off his shoe and handed it to Boaz, saying, "Acquire [the field and Ruth] for yourself."

Then Boaz said to the elders, and, indeed, to all the people, "You are witnesses this day that I have acquired from Naomi what belonged to Elimelech and Chilion and Mahlon. Moreover, I acquire Ruth the Moabitess, wife of Mahlon, to be my wife, to perpetuate the name of the dead on his portion of land, so that his name may not disappear from his city; you are witnesses."

The entire people and the elders said, "May God make the woman who is coming to your house like Rachel and Leah, both of whom built the household of Israel."

So they were married, and Ruth bore a son, Obed.

The book concludes with a brief genealogical table, picking up from earlier times, and ending in later ones: "Perez begot Hezron, and Hezron Ram, and Ram Amminadab, and Amminadab Nahshon, and Nahshon Salmon, and Salmon Boaz, and Boaz Obed, and Obed Jesse, and Jesse David." The David is King David, the great hero of Hebrew lore.

The theme of the book is the noble character of the girl, Ruth, who was of alien, disreputably alien, stock. That this should be the theme of a Hebrew book, and the book make its way into Scripture, surely more than overbalances the passages elsewhere which express scorn for and hostility to the Moabites.

The author stumbled a little in his antiquarianism in the matter of taking off the shoe, though all this really makes little difference. Even in being incorrect (in that he extends the usual obligation of a man to his brother's widow, Deut. XXV:5-10, into an unusual one binding on a quite distant relative), his recourse to ancient custom gives his account a special lift, as if thereby to say that long ago, in those by-gone peaceful times, this beautiful story took place. The charm of the agricultural setting cannot be lost on us. As to the character study, the girl Ruth is examined with some thoroughness, for we move from the point at which we might suspect her earnestness through to our being shown the full convincing measure of it. What must impress us most of all is the restraint in the narration, in that this quiet little story deals with the potentially explosive matter of the background of the heroine. The story would have lacked all its force had it been about an equally worthy Hebrew girl. The account, then, is of a "convert," whose background rendered her sincerity suspect but whose character emerged as completely beyond reproach, and whose name became linked in tradition with Rachel and Leah, the wives of the Patriarch Jacob.

The story is a simple one in the sense that it is not plotted, nor does it have any ups and downs, nor any dramatic climax. Its appeal lies in the attractiveness of the people, Naomi, Ruth, and Boaz, and of the residents of Bethlehem. Indeed, we are shown an ideal, almost unrealistic, picture of a happy community, peopled by worthy persons, benignly guided by the Deity.

A frequently expressed opinion of the Book of Ruth is that it was a protest against an exclusiveness which flourished in late times, as in Nehemiah XIII:23-27. I am uncertain about this, for I find it a little too pat an explanation. But surely the book is permeated by a gentle spirit of humanness. I never grow weary of rereading it.

Nothing in the Ruth story strains our credulity. In the Book of Jonah, on the other hand, our credulity goes through a number of strains. Jonah is a remarkable didactic tale, a story with a deliberate theme, and, as is the case with Ruth, that theme ran athwart popular opinion. Its author was a man of robust wit and of insight. The theme is the question: "Does our God, the God of us Hebrews, have any concern for a people who live endless miles away from us, and who long ago assaulted and conquered our kinsmen, and took them into an exile where they disappeared?" The Book of Jonah gives a surprising answer to the question. It is found in the section of the Prophets, but the book is a narrative, a story *about* Jonah, and is completely different in manner from the usual form of the prophetic books. Exaggerated details give the book an air of unreality, yet they drive home the "message" with even greater force than a less exotic story would.

Jonah himself is a kind of anti-hero, for the author so manipulates matters that we, who read the book, form our convictions against Jonah, not with or through him.

The book of Jonah is very short, and few stories are as terse. The word of God came to Jonah the son of Amittai, saying, "Arise, go to Nineveh the metropolis and proclaim against it that its wickedness has come before me." From other biblical materials we know that Nineveh was the great capitol of the Assyrian empire, which in 721 B.C. totally destroyed the northern kingdom of Israel. Immediately we encounter the unexpected: Nineveh lay far across the desert, to the east, and it could be reached by land alone; but Jonah instead went west, to Tarshish, traveling, as was necessary with Tarshish his destination, by ship. And indeed, Jonah did not *go*; rather he fled from before God! Thereupon God sent a great windstorm onto the Mediterranean, so that the ship came to the verge of breaking up. The sailors in their fright cried each to his god, and they cast the cargo overboard to lighten the ship and avert its breaking up. Jonah, meanwhile, had calmly descended into the innermost part of the ship, lain down, and fallen asleep. (The incongruity here is quite deliberate, and it is meant to be comical.[4]) The captain came to him, rebuked him for sleeping, and demanded that Jonah pray to his God, who might perchance save them all from perishing. We are not told that Jonah prayed; instead, the sailors cast lots to determine who was responsible for their danger, and the lot fell, of course, on Jonah. They demanded of Jonah a statement of his occupation, his place of origin, and his people. Jonah said, "I am a Hebrew, a worshiper of Yahve the God of heaven, who created the sea and the land." Immediately the sailors became all the more frightened, especially when Jonah told them that he was fleeing from God. They asked, "What can we do to still the sea?" He replied, "Throw me overboard; this terrible storm is on my account." They threw Jonah overboard, and the sea ceased from its raging. Thereafter the men in great awe offered sacrifices, and made appropriate vows—to Yahve!

God had prepared a great fish to swallow up Jonah, and Jonah was in the belly of the fish three days and three nights. God then spoke to the fish, and it vomited Jonah onto dry land.[5] (Pedestrian literalists, who miss the entire point of the book, have wondered whether or not Jonah was able to resist the flow of digestive juices in the fish! Since only a whale is big enough to swallow a man, the fish becomes a whale in most translations.)

By means of the fish, we are now back again where we were at the beginning of the story. For a second time God's word came to Jonah to proceed to Nineveh and there to make the requisite proclamation. This time Jonah went. He entered Nineveh, a city so immense that it required three days to traverse it. Jonah made his proclamation: "In forty days, Nineveh will be turned upside down." And the people of Nineveh believed God. They began to fast and to mourn in penitence so that God might possibly turn away from His anger, and they not perish. Indeed, God observed their repentance, and He changed His intention and did not punish the people of Nineveh.

This outcome angered Jonah. He complained to God—notice the author's irony—and said, "This is why I fled to Tarshish, for I knew then that You are compassionate, long-suffering, and abundant in mercy, and capable of altering Your intention to punish. Therefore kill me, for I would rather be dead than alive!"

God said, "How angry you are, Jonah!"

Then Jonah went outside the eastern part of the city and built a lean-to, and sat in the shade, waiting to see what would happen to the city. God caused a cactus-gourd to spring up overnight, to provide some shade for Jonah, and Jonah was pleased to have the gourd. The next day, however, God sent a worm at dawn to smite the gourd, and it withered. When the sun arose, God prepared a powerful east wind which added its heat to the sunshine, and Jonah fainted, and again he asked to die. God said, "Are you angry about the gourd?" Jonah said, "Angry to the point of death."

God said, "You take pity on a mere gourd, for which you did not labor, and you had nothing to do with its growth. It came up in a night and perished in a night. Should I not take pity on Nineveh, a metropolis with countless people—unlettered, simple people—and with many living beasts?"

The remarkable ending of Jonah—Jonah's wrath at the repentance by the Ninevehites, and the somewhat preachy matter of the gourd—would scarcely have been possible had they been joined to a story of perfectly ordinary and credible details. The story can make its point only by portraying Jonah as a kind of foil to God, and by the farfetched events of his flight by ship, his nap during the storm, and his sojourn in the fish's belly. Profound and serious as is the theme of Jonah, the narrator is never out of touch with humor, in a broad form at the beginning, and in a revealingly ironic vein at the end. And what a wondrous turn it is that Jonah, succeeding in his mission, is angry at his success! How nimbly the author lays bare, even in this improbable story, a facet of the nature of man. How dull the Book of Jonah would have been, how anticlimactic, had it ended with the repentance of Nineveh, and a satisfied, even smug Jonah. The narrator was too great a literary genius to turn to such a bathos.

The Book of Esther recounts an episode in the history of Jews in Persia, whereby the community, threatened by foes, was saved through the circumstance that the king's consort—queen, we might say—was the Jewish lass for whom the book came to be named. Information about Persia is in our time quite plenteous, and it fails to confirm the account, or the persons, in the book, apart from the king mentioned. It is right to speak of the Book of Esther as nonhistorical. But the central tensions in it are known in part from the experience of Jewish communities in the Grecian lands, into which Jews spread after Alexander the Great conquered Judea about 325; the author of Esther appears to have used the setting of Persia and its court as a disguise by which to describe some local fearsome threat to Jews, and their release from it, and in this sense Esther lies somewhere between fiction and history. On the affirmative side, the book offers encouragement to a beleaguered community; on the negative side it has a vindictive, even ferociously vengeful spirit in which retaliation becomes possible and then lamentably indiscriminate. I have no fondness for the close of the book, which describes the slaughter of foes.

That an author should write a narrative thinly disguising actual events is a somewhat natural development of that form of didactic instruction, normally very brief, which we call the parable. For example, the prophet Isaiah in a parable likens the people of Israel to a carefully tended vineyard which should have reproduced luxuriant fruit, but produced instead sour grapes, and Isaiah goes on to say that the vineyard was the people of Israel, the vineyard keeper God, and the sour grapes the sins of the people. In a sense, then, Esther is a very extended parable.

Its author was a man of tremendous literary skill, imagination, and psychological insight. His touch was sure, his perceptions acute, his intuitions truly remarkable. He created out of his fertile imagination a setting, characters, and responses to crises, all with a sure literary touch. The Book of Esther, indeed, in a sense anticipates Shakespeare in that farce and potential tragedy march along side by side, for the author veers from one to the other with astounding deftness. He provides two story lines which ultimately come together, these in a "plot" in which events cause subsequent events, so that there is always a causal literary connection between incident and its sequel. A normal pitfall in such parabolic writing is that the characters tend to lose their individuality and become mere types, puppets who must conform to the author's wishes or needs; not so in Esther, for each character maintains his individuality as the incidents rise steadily to a climax. What I have spoken of as farce is at times spoken of in the scholarly interpretation as satire, an unfortunate term and conception, for the humor in Esther is much broader than satire. There is some satire in Esther, but it is present as a broad travesty of the workings of royal protocol, and it is much more comical than satire usually is. Page after page discloses unmistakable evidence that the unknown author richly relished what he was writing, and was unwilling to allow his message to over-ride and destroy his pleasure in writing.

The book begins, in a vein of high good spirits, with a description of a most lavish royal party given by the mighty Persian monarch Ahasuerus, who reigned over a hundred and twenty-seven provinces, stretching from India to Ethiopia. The guests included all the high military officials and nobles and princes of all his provinces—everybody who was anybody was there—and the king exhibited his rich royal possessions to his guests. The feast lasted for six months! At its end, the king gave another feast for the people still present in Susa, the capital, this one of seven days' duration. The drinks were served in golden vessels, all of different design; drinking was the order of the day, and no one had to be compelled to drink! (This description is wondrously extravagant, calculated to whet the appetite of the ancient reader, much as today people read avidly the accounts of our gossip columnists about the social life of the highly placed.)

The queen, Vashti, also gave a party in the royal palace, this for the women. On the seventh day, when the king was a little tipsy—"when the heart of the king was jolly with wine"—he sent his seven eunuchs, whose names, still in humorous exaggeration, are all dutifully given by the narrator, to bring Vashti to the king, so that he could exhibit her beauty to the assembled dignitaries. The narrator, having clearly established the unparalleled and absolute power of the mighty king, proceeds to a startling item: Queen Vashti simply declined to come.

The king thereupon became furious, and "his anger burned in him." Faced by this profound challenge of the queen's disobedience, the king turned to his sage councillors, as he always did. Again the narrator gives us the precise names of the seven wise men who were to advise the monarch what to do about Vashti's disobedience. One of the councillors, Memuchan, sagaciously analyzed the issue (as we read his speech we should envisage him as swaying on his feet, and emitting a hiccough or two): "Not alone against the king has Vashti the queen trespassed, but against all the princes and all the peoples in all the king's provinces. When this matter of Vashti becomes known to all the women, how she treated the king contemptuously, then all women will do the same to their husbands!" To save the dignity of all males, Memuchan proposed that Vashti be deposed and a new queen desig-

nated. The king accepted the wise suggestion. He then sent letters to each province, and to every people in their own scripts and
languages, ordering that every man should rule in his own household! (Just how every man could carry out the injunction is not
told.)

This is an immensely masterful beginning, with its contrast between the unlimited royal power and the queen's impudent disobedience, and its satire on the ponderous manner of imperial
councillors. We are at this stage in the realm of farce, and it is
good farce because the characters involved all take themselves
with utmost seriousness.

The same mood of farce continues. Once Vashti has been deposed, she must be replaced. The king, by now recovered from
his fury, is ready to listen to the further advice of his councillors.
(He seems to have little mind of his own.) They propose a kind
of beauty contest; royal deputies should be designated in all the
provinces to collect beautiful virgins and bring them to the royal
palace to be placed in the charge of one Hegai, "keeper of the
women." These girls were first to be provided with an appropriate series of beauty treatments and cosmetics. Whichever one
of the girls would please the king would then take the place of
Vashti.

The account is now ready for the introduction of the heroine.
In Susa there dwelled a Jew named Mordecai, who had been exiled from Judea at the time of the Babylonian conquest. He had
raised a girl, Hadassah—"she is Esther"—who had become Mordecai's ward. When attractive young ladies were being assembled, Esther too was brought to the palace. She pleased Hegai to
the point that he gave her the best rooms in the harem, and the
appropriate cosmetics, and seven servants. Esther had not disclosed her people or her origin, for Mordecai had instructed her
not to reveal these matters. (This device is necessary for the author to work out his plot.) Mordecai strolled in front of the
harem every day, to learn what was happening to Esther.

The girls went through an elaborate course of beautification,
as did Esther. Thereafter a girl was brought to the king at eve-

ning and returned to the house of the concubines in the morning; she did not go back to the king unless the king wanted her specifically and had her summoned by name. (Our author, in the interest of his narrative, abstains from comment on or inquiry into the matter of a Jewish girl's becoming the concubine of a Gentile king.) On going to the king, a girl had the privilege of taking whatever cosmetics or ointments she wanted. When it came to be Esther's turn, she took none of these appurtenances with her. Nevertheless, "the king loved Esther above all the women, and she gained more favor than all the virgins, so that he put the royal crown on her head and made her queen in place of Vashti. He gave a party in Esther's honor and sent gifts and amnesties to the provinces."

Mordecai sat at the palace gate every day, and he learned that two of the king's servants, the gate-keepers Bigthan and Teresh, had become disgruntled and threatened some violence to the king. Mordecai informed Esther, and she in turn informed the king in Mordecai's name. An investigation was made, the two gate-keepers were hanged, and the matter of Mordecai's good turn was recorded in royal archives. (Here is a bit of foreshadowing.)

At this juncture we abandon farce. A certain Haman was elevated to the position of chief of state, and by the king's command the royal servants were to bow down and prostrate themselves before Haman. The ancient reader knew that such bowing and prostration to a man would appear blasphemous to a Jew, who would bow and prostrate himself only before God. Naturally, Mordecai abstained from bowing and prostrating himself. The slaves at the palace gate repeatedly chided him for disobeying the royal decree, and then deliberately reported the matter to Haman, so as to observe whether or not Mordecai would persist in his refusal.

When Haman experienced directly Mordecai's refusal to bow to him, he became very angry. He scorned laying hands on Mordecai alone; he determined instead to destroy all the Jews throughout the realm of Ahasuerus. There began the casting of Purim, "lots," to determine when that destruction should take

place; it was set ahead to the month called Adar. But first Haman
wanted royal authority for this plan. He said to the king, "There
is a certain people, scattered and dispersed among the peoples in
all the provinces of your kingdoms, whose laws are different from
those of any other people. They do not obey the royal laws."
(Jews in Grecian lands were exempted from some laws, and
indeed, were allowed in good measure to govern themselves under
Jewish law.) "It is not in the interest of the king to tolerate
them. Let a decree be issued to destroy them, and I will contribute ten thousand talents of silver to be conveyed to the royal
treasury." The gullible king assented to Haman's proposal: as
to the bribe, with a broad hint, "The money is yours"; that is, his
to do with as he pleased, even to hand to the king. Haman handed
it over.

Immediately royal decrees went out: all the Jews, young and
old, women and children, were to be destroyed, and their possessions confiscated, eleven months later, on the thirteenth of Adar.

The tone of the narration has now changed. No longer are we
dealing with humorous satire on the royal court; we are confronted instead with a crisis of life and death.

The response of the Jews of Susa in our story was to begin to
lament and to undergo the rites of mourning. Mordecai rent his
clothes, put on sackcloth and ashes, and sat at the king's gate.
Esther was informed about Mordecai's actions but not the reason
for them. She promptly sent him some garments in place of the
sackcloth and ashes, but he declined them. Then Esther sent a
eunuch to learn the reasons for Mordecai's conduct. Mordecai related the matters to him, including a mention of Haman's bribe
to the king, and he gave the eunuch a copy of the royal decree
respecting the destruction of the Jews, so that Esther, on receiving it, should go to the king and make supplication to him on behalf of her people. Esther sent her reply to Mordecai: it was universally known that the penalty for entering the king's inner
court without being summoned was death—unless the king
chanced to extend his golden scepter to the intruder. She had not
been summoned by the king for thirty days.

Thereupon Mordecai sent back a message to Esther: "Do not think that in the king's palace you will escape any more than the other Jews. If you do nothing, then in some way and from some other quarter deliverance will come. But you yourself, the last remnant of your father's house, will perish. Yet perhaps you have come to your royal station precisely for this occasion."

Esther sent her reply to Mordecai: "Assemble all the Jews in Susa, and fast for three days, just as I and my maidens will fast. I will then violate the law and go to the king. If I perish, then I perish." When Esther went to the king, and he saw her, he was pleased, and he extended the golden scepter. "What is your request, Queen Esther? It will be given you, even to half of the kingdom."

In what ensues we see the unusual skill of the author. He might well have brought the story to its climax at this point by having Esther make her intercession with Ahasuerus right there and then. More artistically, he chose to defer the intercession so as to have it take place in a setting in which Esther and Haman would confront each other alone and face to face. Esther said to the king that she had come to invite him to a dinner she had prepared. The king came, and he brought Haman along, but the narrator felt the need to extend the suspense and also to provide an interval of time for a humorous, though vindictive, episode. At this first dinner the king asked Esther if she had some request to make. Esther responded by inviting the king and Haman to return a second time for dinner, presumably the next day.

The relationship with the king being so affirmative, the narrator now feels free to proceed to the humorous episode, and he focuses his attention on the villain. Haman had left the queen's presence in joy at the royal attention, but as soon as he saw Mordecai at the king's gate, neither rising nor trembling before him, his anger returned, and even increased. He restrained himself, however, and did nothing to Mordecai. Returning to his home, he summoned his wife Zeresh and his friends, and to them he tabulated his achievements: the wealth he had amassed, the ten sons he had begotten, his elevation to his high position in the palace.

And he added, "Even Queen Esther had no one for her dinner except the king and me. And I am invited again tomorrow, along with the king! Yet all this does not satisfy me, so long as I observe Mordecai still sitting at the king's gate!" To this Zeresh and his friends replied, "Have a gallows built fifty cubits high, and persuade the king to hang Mordecai on it tomorrow morning. Then go merrily to the dinner with the king." The advice suited Haman, and he had the gallows built.

But that night the king suffered from insomnia. What better soporific than to have someone read to him from the royal archives! When the royal record was read, the king, not yet asleep, recalled the matter of Mordecai and the two gatesmen. The king asked, "What honor has been bestowed on Mordecai?" The answer was, "None." At that moment Haman entered the outer court of the king's palace, intending to mention to the king the gallows he had prepared for Mordecai. The king summoned Haman before him, and asked him, "What should be done to a man whom the king takes pleasure in honoring?"

Haman said to himself, "Whom would the king enjoy honoring more than me?" Aloud he said, "Let royal robes which the king himself has worn be provided for the man. Let him ride on a horse which the king has ridden, and let a royal crown be set on the horse. Let the man be mounted and led on horseback through the open square of the city, and let a herald proclaim, 'This is the way the king is pleased to honor a man.' "

Haman's suggestion was accepted, and when Mordecai was led through the city square, Haman himself served as the herald to make the repeated proclamation. Disheartened, he returned home and told his wife and his friends what had happened. They said to him, "Since Mordecai is a Jew, and you have begun to topple, you will not defeat him, but you will surely fall before him."

While this conversation was going on, the king's servants arrived to bring Haman to the feast which Esther had prepared for the king and for him. Then again the king invited Esther to make some request: "It will be given to you, up to half of the kingdom."

Queen Esther said, "Let my life be spared at my request, and my people at my petition. For I and my people have been victims of a bribe, to be destroyed, slain, and annihilated. Were it that we were merely sold as slaves, I would be silent, for then our distress would scarcely be worth the money which the king would lose."

Angrily, the king—as if this were all totally new to him—demanded to know who it was who would presume to do these things. (By this touch, the character of the king is revealed in its fullest dimensions; his vanity, his folly, his stupidity—an incompetent though perhaps likable person.)

Then Esther made her revelation: "An enemy, and a foe, this wicked Haman."

We are, it might seem, at the turning point in the dramatic confrontation. The author, though, has in reserve a crowning incident. Instead of the king's reacting promptly, he rose, because he had drunk wine, and he went out to the palace garden. We are not told explicitly why; it was to relieve himself, as the ancient reader clearly understood. Crucial to the author was the need to get the king, as it were, off the stage, so as to leave protagonist and antagonist alone to confront each other. The locale, we recall, is Esther's chamber—indeed, her boudoir. (The writers of French farce never did better!)

Haman rose to plead to Esther for his life, for he knew that the end had come for him. She retreated; he advanced. The king returned from the garden. The scene which he beheld was Haman fallen onto the bed where Esther was. The king said, "Are you even trying to rape the queen, with me here in this house!"

A eunuch, Harbonah, immediately invited the attention of the king to the gallows which Haman had prepared for Mordecai. "Hang *him* on it," said the king. One more sentence winds up the story of Esther and Mordecai: The king gave Esther Haman's dwelling, and Mordecai was put in charge of it.

What is left in the book is the rescinding of the letters which Haman had sent out to destroy the Jews. The Jews were allowed to assemble to defend their lives and to "destroy, slay, and annihilate" their enemies. Many Gentiles converted to Judaism in fear for their lives. On the day set for the slaughter of the Jews, the Jews smote all their enemies—and also Haman's ten sons (carefully mentioned by name). Yet the Jews took no plunder. Mordecai rose to the most eminent position in the court of the king.

For one today to be dissatisfied, or perhaps even offended, by the tone the last part of the Book of Esther is normal. That it is a response to hatred rather than the initiation of it seems to me to make the tone of the book intelligible, but this explanation scarcely condones it. I have elsewhere written that I should not be grieved if the book of Esther were somehow dropped out of Scripture. Even in ancient times, the Book raised dissatisfaction. This we know from a passage in rabbinic literature which discloses that some ancient rabbis opposed Esther's being incorporated into Scripture. We know of similar ancient questioning of the book, too, from its translation into Greek; the translators were troubled that the book does not mention God; they added to the book some prayers that a Jewish girl would have been well advised to have prayed in such dire circumstances.

If, however, the religion at the end of the Book of Esther leaves a great deal to be desired, as a piece of writing it reflects a high measure of artistry and literary control. Not only did the author plan his scenes so that the sequence of materials, now serious, now farcical, would benefit from contrast, but also he had a sure sense respecting humor, even of the humor which can arise from repetition, from the stuffy listing of meaningless names. The character of the bumbling king is well portrayed and well developed. We see growth in Esther, too; at first she is merely a pretty girl, but she develops into a mature and grand lady. Mordecai's fidelity to his principles and his sturdy directness cannot fail to strike us. The scenes of Haman at home with his wife and his friends ring true; he is, of course, a parvenu, and would be a pathetically comic character were he not a bloodthirsty and vengeful man.

For skill such as that found in the Book of Esther to be attached to a fictional piece attests to the Hebrew narrators' high literary attainment in craftsmanship. When once we recognize that this high skill existed, we are prepared to look at longer and much more involved works and, indeed, at works of infinitely greater importance and profundity. What we have noted—pathos, violence, tenderness, humor—all these are richly represented in longer works. These are so much more complex in their literary structure that they will require an introductory chapter.

But we must first deal with a prior consideration. These longer writings were motivated as much by religious considerations as by literary ones. Indeed, perhaps the religious motives outweighed the literary, though to my mind the two are inextricably blended. Much as the narrations deal with men and women, and do this so perceptively that even after the passing of thousands of years one can still peer comprehendingly into the hearts of people, the narrations essentially deal with God, directly or indirectly.

If we are to grasp the fullness of the literary flavor, we must have some sense of what God meant to the Hebrews. The question is not what you or I believe, but what they thought and believed.

II

God

We are so far removed from the ancient Hebrews that it is quite difficult for us to put ourselves in their place with respect to their thinking and feeling about God. Yet if we are to gain the fullest flavor for some of the most remarkable literature ever written, we must make some effort so to transport ourselves to their time. In beginning the effort, we must understand that our age does not take the existence of God for granted, but debates about it, toys with complex philosophical systems inherited from the Middle Ages which tried to prove His existence through analytical and systematic thinking, and has even recently given some imprudent attention to flamboyant people who have coined the nonsensical phrase that God is dead.

Again, our age is naturalistic; we are disinclined to believe in special miracles which interrupt the normal sequence of cause and effect. Even among those in our day who profess some kind of belief in God, such belief would scarcely extend to the point of holding that God today converses with men in clear and communicable language, in the way the Bible records. The skepticism of our age stems from many influences, among them modes of thinking, our historical inquiry, and our scientific studies. For the most part, though, our skepticism stems from the drastic reduction of the functions which our predecessors once attributed to

God. Thus we do not ordinarily believe, in a literal sense, that He causes storms and lightning, makes the wind blow, and occasionally induces the earth to quake. By implication we feel that to attribute such things to God is to trivialize Him, and, in effect, as we move away from this or that trivial item, or from some other unacceptable view, we tend severely to limit the area, if any, in which we concede that God does operate.

Curiously enough, the literature of the Bible itself reflects some aspects of this tendency to reduction, not so much with the purpose of diminishing the import of God, but rather of refining man's understanding of Him. Such refinement, in the Bible, is mostly indirect; Scripture tells us very little directly about the nature of God. We need not, however, be surprised at the existence of change and refinement in the understanding of God in the Bible, for, as we have said, the literature represents writings from a period at least a thousand years long. We must not expect that men of different ages all thought about God in exactly the same way.

The understanding of God in the Bible, and the refinement of that understanding, is complicated by some matters of history. It is worthwhile to review these, provided that we do not forget that the way in which biblical man *thought* about God is somewhat different from the way he *felt* about Him. Moreover, as the Hebrews through their gifted writers produced successions of new writings while preserving the old, they seem clearly to have reinterpreted the older ideas inherited from the past in the light of their new conceptions.

It is this double circumstance, of history on the one hand and new ideas on the other, which accounts for the fact that two principal words for God appear in Scripture. There are, indeed, more than two, but these are the most frequent ones. One term is Yahve; medieval monks so wrote this Hebrew word in Latin, yielding the well-known (and inaccurate) form Jehovah, but both forms, Yahve and Jehovah, are the same Hebrew word. The other word is Elohim. Both of these words mean god.

How shall we understand the difference in the impact of these two words, Yahve and Elohim? We begin, as we must, by noting that ultimately the two different terms came to mean exactly the same thing. At an early stage, however, the two had different nuances. "Yahve," so we may put it, was the proper name of the deity associated with Hebrews, and thus He was, as it were, a *particular* god. "Elohim," on the other hand, was a *general* word for a god, any god, without implicit identification with a particular people. We can put it this way: Yahve was the Elohim of the Hebrews, as Baal was the Elohim of the Canaanites.

In the course of centuries, it became the conviction of the Hebrews that Yahve was the one and only Elohim. They never entirely lost the sense that Yahve the god, or Yahve the God, was associated particularly with *them*. He had been associated with them for a very, very long time. It was Yahve Who had appeared to three successive patriarchs, Abraham, Isaac, and Jacob; it was Yahve Who had sent Moses on the mission to redeem Jacob's descendants, by then a full-fledged people, from slavery in Egypt. It was He Who at Sinai had entered into a corporate covenant with the people, thereby amplifying and confirming the individual covenants made with Abraham, Isaac, and Jacob. It was He Who had guided Moses' successor Joshua to a successful invasion of the land of Canaan, and had entrusted this land of His to the Hebrews. Again, it was this Yahve Who demanded full compliance on the part of the Hebrews to the obligation of the covenant, it was He Who punished the unfaithful tribes, or groups of tribes, through marauding foreigners, and it was He Who raised up great redeemers, Judges, to free the now chastened tribes from their oppressors. It was He Who had determined that kingship was necessary, and it was at His bidding that Saul had become Israel's first king. Because Saul was guilty of misdeeds, royalty was taken from him and, at Yahve's behest, given to David and his successors. It was He Who, in the age of the monarchy, had knowledge of the misdeeds of some of the kings and of the populace, and, through a succession of prophets, He had warned that the covenant was either in danger of being ruptured, or, indeed, was already ruptured. If ruptured, Israel was in effect cast off, and Yahve was no longer Israel's Elohim. Because Israel had been so cast off by Him, the northern kingdom was overrun in 722/21 B.C. by the Assyrians; indeed, Yahve, whose sway knew no boundaries, had deliberately brought Assyria from the East for the punishment of Israel. A century and a half later He brought in the Babylonians to overrun the southern kingdom of Judah.

History, then, was a succession of events, framed, fashioned, and executed by Yahve the Elohim with, or for, or even against His special people.

This sense of history was acute among the Hebrews, and further, they added some special aspects, that is to say, specific details, to amplify and deepen their view of historical processes. It was, so the Hebrews believed, an historical fact that there was a very early time, in the days before there were Hebrews, when Yahve was as yet not worshiped. The first man, Adam, had not worshiped Him, nor had Adam's son Seth; rather, the worship of Yahve began only with Adam's grandson, Enos. Yet even after this preliminary worship had been inaugurated, the full identity of Yahve had remained withheld from men.

Despite this absence of identification of Yahve, the great man Enoch had walked with Him; and later, in the age of Noah, Yahve had despaired about man's wickedness and had sent a flood which had destroyed all mankind save Noah and his family. From these few He had repopulated the world, yet Noah and his children had not known who He was. He had bidden Abraham to leave Ur of the Chaldees, and Abraham, unique in obedience, had obeyed unquestioningly; yet neither Abraham, Isaac, nor Jacob had fully known Him, and they worshiped Him without awareness that He was Yahve; they had worshiped Him as El Shaddai, the Mighty God. Only to Moses was the revelation made that Yahve was His proper name, and Moses had in turn made this identity known to the people. The relationship, then, between the Hebrews and Yahve was an ancient one, stretching from Abraham through Moses and down into the latest times of the Hebrews.

After Yahve had disclosed His name to Moses, He made the

covenant at Sinai with the corporate people. Sinai was in the Wilderness, and hence it was in the Wilderness that the encounter between the Hebrews and Yahve took place; one might even say, as some biblical writers do, that Yahve found Israel in the Wilderness. Sinai was His sacred mountain—though another tradition spoke of His mountain as Horeb. It was at Sinai/Horeb that He had appeared to all the people. Even though Sinai/Horeb was in some sense the place *par excellence* where He had appeared to the corporate people, He could not let His people traverse the Wilderness and proceed into Canaan without accompanying them and without periodically appearing to them. A Tent of Meeting, also called the Tabernacle, went along with the Hebrews, and Yahve and Moses met there periodically. Yahve's route from Sinai into Canaan traversed the land of Edom (south of the Dead Sea), for He had marched along with Israel when they had marched.

Yet even in that Wilderness period, the Hebrews encountered other peoples—Midianites, Moabites, Ammonites—for whom Yahve was not the Elohim. Each people had its own god whom the Hebrews considered not a true god. Moreover, once the Hebrews came into Canaan, they encountered a settled people who had an Elohim named Baal. Another people, on the southern coast, the Philistines, had an Elohim named Dagan; and, on the northern coast lived the Phoenicians, who had an Elohim named Melkart. There were Hebrews who went astray from Yahve to these false gods, not realizing, as they should have, that Yahve was the one and only true Elohim. The proof that Yahve was the Elohim, and such other gods were not, could be discerned in the first invasion of Canaan, when He led the Hebrews to victory over the people of Baal, and therefore over the Baal itself, at the important battle of Taanach in the days of the prophetess Deborah. If there had been previously any doubt as to the true Proprietor of the land flowing with milk and honey, the victory at Taanach showed clearly that Yahve and Yahve alone owned the land. People could not truly own it. It was Yahve's chosen land.

The Tent of Meeting was portable. It was to be expected that

a permanent shrine would come to replace it, and that happened
when Solomon built the Temple in Jerusalem. Yet Jerusalem
was only the center of His worship: His sway knew no geographical boundary, for He and He alone was the Elohim of the
whole world.

Thus, Elohim ceased to mean *a god* and came to mean *God*,
and since Yahve was an Elohim, He became in time *the* Elohim,
so that the words Yahve and Elohim came to be synonymous
and interchangeable names for God. In writings produced after
the early period, a writer might prefer to say simply Elohim, but
it was often customary to put the two together, Yahve Elohim.

The Bible begins by relating the acts of creation, telling us
that "In the beginning Elohim created heaven and earth." In the
next chapter, in dealing in greater detail with the account of
primitive man, we are told, "This is the account of the heaven
and earth, in the time when Yahve Elohim made them." It would
not conform entirely to biblical usage, but one can nevertheless
put matters in this way: early writings generally speak of Yahve
and later ones of Elohim. But when once we note that the identification of the two as the same was fully made, we are prepared
to encounter what we find in the latest writings, namely a kind
of indifference on the part of the writer as to which of the two
he uses, Yahve or Elohim.

But the conviction that Yahve, in addition to being the only
Elohim, had been Israel's particular God, brought about a notable
phenomenon. In stirring passages wherein an intimacy with God
is presupposed, as in the case of the poets who wrote the Psalms,
and of the prophets who spoke in His name, it was the word
Yahve rather than the word Elohim that was used, even though
the intention was the only God. If to our western minds this
appears to be an inconsistency, such was not the case with the
Hebrew mind. He could without awareness of any logical awk-
wardness, address himself to the Elohim as Yahve. Hence, one
reads in Psalm 23, "Yahve is my shepherd, I lack nothing"; the
intention here is not that one of many gods is the shepherd, but
that God Himself, the only Elohim, is the poet's shepherd.

There was a domain quite beyond that of history which thoroughly permeated the spiritual atmosphere of the Hebrew. For him Yahve was not a sporadic matter, not a matter of recollection only on sacred days; rather, He was an ongoing reality in the most vivid sense at all times. It was He Who had created the world which men inhabited and He Who governed the world, so that one could see daily that the sun and moon obeyed His bidding. He caused the wind to blow and the rain to fall. He caused the grass to grow, and the trees to bear fruit, and the flocks of sheep and the herds of cattle to increase. Every phenomenon of nature, whether benign, like the moderate rain which watered the crops, or maleficent, like the horrid drouth, directly reflected Him.

That which was benign was a gracious gift from Him, for He was a loving father to men. Yet just as a father might have occasion to punish a child who provoked him, so, too, God could and would punish men, either by withholding His benefits, or by sending some disaster.

One spoke of God as a father, not only because the figure of speech seemed so apt, but also because one could scarcely speak of God except in the same terms in which one spoke of man. God could become angry like a man, or change His mind like a man, or even speak like a man. Yet even while one used such human language, one needed constantly to remember, and to bear it keenly in his mind, that God and man were entirely different. Man was a creature, God the creator. Man was unreliable, selfish, prone to evil, ready to cheat, willing to kill. God, on the other hand, was reliable, good, selfless, free from any disposition to lie, eager to give man the boon of life.

He was near to man, ready to respond, and at hand to respond. On the other hand, He was the Creator of the world, and in a sense above it, and sometimes men thought that He was beyond it. Those who thought of Him as over and beyond the world tended to bridge the gap between themselves and the remote God by thinking of angels, "messengers" who could span the intervening space and come near to man. (The view that God is near at hand is called "immanence"; the view that He is beyond the world is called "transcendence.") The conception of angels in relation to transcendence exhibits its own peculiar development. In the latest biblical literature, some angels acquire names—for example, Gabriel, in Daniel VII:16 and IX:21, and Michael, in Daniel X:13 and 21. Still later, in rabbinic writings, they acquired specific responsibilities or functions. In the early biblical literature they are unnamed, and, indeed, seem to be little more than a way of speaking. In Genesis XXII, it is Elohim who tests Abraham, but it is an angel of Yahve who bids him desist from sacrificing Isaac. The point is that an author could use Elohim or Yahve in one sentence in a story, and in a later sentence in the same story shift to the term angel, without at all shifting his meaning consciously. There is at most a tendency, not a general practice, in some passages to express the gratifying nearness of the majestic and remote God by speaking of His angel. The earliest literature seems not to do this at all; the latest literature, as we have said, does so. The literature in between may by chance mention an angel, or may by chance not, but in either case nothing is affected by the mention or the lack of it. In general, then, an angel is simply a way of speaking of God as near to man, and in direct touch with him.[1] Hence we shall make very little of shifts within a narrative from Yahve or Elohim to an angel.

As a father can make demands on children, so Yahve made demands on man. The covenant—a contract of mutual responsibility—spelled out the reciprocal obligations. Yahve demanded fidelity from man. This meant that man must worship Yahve, and Him exclusively, on the simple premise that He was God and other deities were not God, and that to worship not-gods was an affront to God. Moreover, in the same way that a just father demands that his many children treat each other fairly, so Yahve demanded unswerving ethical conduct from men. He who cheated his neighbor, or stole, or robbed, or killed, was being unfaithful to Yahve Himself. The ethical demand is unique to the Hebrew religion. Hence, the phrase "ethical monotheism." This is not to imply that other ancient peoples lacked ethics or ethical concern, but that to the Hebrews ethics was an integral aspect of religion, while elsewhere ethics was not deemed an aspect of it, but only a mode of a natural, exclusively human, custom or practice or tradition.

On an individual basis, the Hebrew man who dealt falsely with his neighbor could and would forfeit God's beneficent providence. Yet on a corporate basis, the amassing of instances of individual corruption meant that the corporate body of the Hebrews was itself corrupt, and the implication was clear that the corruption of the community seemed to give a sanction to the individual to be corrupt. When the community—that is, society—reached a point of intolerable corruption, then the covenant was thereby ruptured and, in effect, annulled and canceled; Yahve was freed of His obligation to beneficence and could abandon the community, but He could also visit upon a community a wrathful punishment for its accumulated misdeeds.

Does a father punish a child only to do him damage? Or is it a father's intention and purpose to bring his child back to the right path? Surely Yahve, capable in His omnipotence to punish as He is, does so primarily to bring His people back to righteousness; and surely He is prepared, as a father is prepared, to receive back in joy the son who has been wayward.

It comes about, then, that man trespasses, and is punished. Men by their injustices do damage to their fellow men. From one's human neighbors, fickle and unreliable as they are, one can know calumny and hurt and acute damage, and in human affairs one can know external distress and internal loneliness and despair. All too seldom does relief come from one's fellow-man. Hence, the bruised and lonely person turns to Yahve, who is present in the brightness of the sun or the darkness of the cloud, in the gentleness of the dew or the bluster of the wind, in the ripening grain or in the infertility of a dessicated field. He is near to men; they can call on Him as one calls to a friend, and He answers the call in His own way of answering.

The progression of thought in the biblical period is best exemplified in the array of concerns we have reflected; perhaps, though, we should say in the level of those concerns. The early literature deals with the dilemmas and crises of history, such as the question of whether Israel, as God's people, should enter into an alliance with the Assyrians to the east, or with the Egyptians to the west—or whether both possible alliances are futile, and an affront to God as well. The Psalms, while frequently mentioning lightning and thunder, are oriented to the despair of a human heart caught in some need of God, or exultant in the joy of having found Him.

But whether in early or in late biblical literature, the existence of God was accepted as an axiom and was therefore in no need of proof. Since it was axiomatic that He existed and was free from the frailties of men, then the events of history, whether of the collective people or of the individual, often needed some explaining. If, for example, both Israel and other peoples were unjust, why then did Yahve visit punishment only upon Israel? If He was just, how could one explain His apparent injustice in singling out Israel for punishment? Or if a man was righteous, was it just that he could undergo suffering or even disaster? Was it just for an unrighteous man to prosper?

Realists as the Hebrews were, they necessarily observed, in both corporate and individual events, paradoxes such as these, and realized that there should be some correlation between the injustices they saw and the axiom that Yahve existed and that, unlike man, He was free of blemishes. Out of such observation, and its resultant perplexities and anxieties, the Hebrews fashioned their developing and deepening religious ideas, for they thought seriously about these things.

Because they wrote about their religious feeling, they left us an unsurpassed literature. They wrote little of what they thought about God, but a great deal of how they felt about Him—revering Him, yet loving Him; relying on Him, yet anxious when He seemed remote or absent. It is we who, analyzing what they felt, make modern summaries of what they thought. They felt deeply, keenly. In whatever they wrote, their writing was always as concerned as much with God as with men. They also probed into the meaning of existence in its profoundest sense. All this latter we have yet to see.

III

Compilers, Redactors, and Creators

Some of the materials which we have looked at, such as the story of Hannah and the exploits of Samson, have been excerpted (and here I am repeating myself) from much longer biblical books. In so excerpting, our procedure has in a sense been the reverse of an actual biblical process; the longer writings represent what can be called compilation, that is to say, the assembly of older material previously separate.

The readiest example of compilation is the Book of Psalms. The author of the book is traditionally King David, who in II Sam. XXIII:1 is called "the sweet singer of Israel." Yet within the book there are a good many psalms which declare in the first verse that they were composed by individuals other than David. For example, Psalms XLIV-XLIX are attributed to the "sons of Korah"; Psalm L is ascribed to "Asaph."

The Book of Psalms has come down to us arranged in five sections, with Psalm LXII ending the second section. Psalm LXXII is puzzling: its first verse attributes the Psalm to Solomon, but its last verse reads, "Here end the prayers of David." It would be easy (though premature) to conclude from this last verse that the Book of Psalms represents a compilation broader than simply the work of David, and that perhaps David's Psalms were restricted to the first two sections. Surprisingly, though, Psalm LXXXVI, in the third section, is identified in its first verse as a "Prayer of David," and Psalm CI, "To David, a Song," and Psalm CIII simply "To David." Hence the prayers of David do not end with Psalm LXXII.

That there are in the Book of Psalms 150 psalms written by various people means that the Book is a compilation. Perhaps prior to the time of their compilation, these 150 psalms were found recorded individually on small pieces of parchment, or possibly a few of them were already joined together. Perhaps, though, some of the psalms had as yet not been recorded in writing, but were still circulating orally, and were known among the people through their use in the worship at the Temple in Jerusalem. By "compiler," then, we would here mean in the most limited sense the person or persons who assembled the 150 psalms into the collection as we have had it for over two thousand years.

The Bible tells us absolutely nothing about the process of preservation of the separate psalms, or about the compilation of the totality. Conceivably the compilation took place in stages, and if some single stage required a period of many years, we would possibly need to think of a succession of compilers, though there well may have been a single person who ultimately completed the process of assembling the psalms as we know them now. If we knew more, we could wonder if the 150 poems comprised the total number available at the time, or whether they represent a subjective selection from a larger number in circulation. There are psalm-like poems in the Bible outside the Book of Psalms, and Psalm XVIII appears also in II Samuel XXII. Some psalms occur twice: Psalms XIV and LIII, and XXXI: 1-3 and LXXI: 1-3. But by and large we have no real basis for a judgment on the question of whether the compiler (or compilers) did the best possible job of compiling, or whether they simply settled on what was near at hand.

The sentence quoted above from the end of Psalm LXXII, "Here end the prayers of David," is not a part of Psalm LXXII in the strictest sense, but is, rather, a note or addendum attached to it. We do not know who wrote this note, or when it was written; we only know that it is there. On observing this sentence we become aware of the fact that something beyond mere mechanical compilation took place.

This additional activity we may describe as "editing," or "redacting." Either of these words would serve. Possibly because "editing" so strongly suggests modern literary processes, it is preferable to use the term "redacting" so as to escape the snare of excessive modernity.

In those psalms which begin with a note naming the reputed author, as Psalm XXIII begins with "A song of David," the note is not by the author, but by a "redactor." In this sense, redaction is no more than adding a few words about the authorship. Since we do not know when such redactorial notes were added, we do not know whether the compiler and the redactor were one and the same person.

There is, however, a considerable difference between the addition of the simple statement, "A song of David," and another type of redactor's introduction, found at the beginning of many a psalm. We will here notice three such introductions, each of which seeks to identify the occasion in David's lifetime when the particular psalm was supposedly written. Psalm LIV:2 reads: "When the Ziphites came and told Saul, 'David has hidden himself among us.'" Psalm LVI:1 reads: "When the Philistines seized him in Gath." Psalm LVII:1 reads: "When he fled into the cave from Saul."

If compilation was merely a mechanical process, redaction was clearly not. To some ancient person the conviction arose that the psalms, or at least some of them, needed to be allocated to occasions in David's career. Modern study raises a number of difficulties about these introductory identifications, for the content of particular psalms completely fails to suit the introductory identification, and the suspicion has arisen that the redactor was at least a little capricious or insufficiently careful. Also, we may wonder why some psalms contain an identifying introduction, but most do not; indeed, we may go on to wonder why some psalms state explicitly who the author was reputed to be, but a very large number totally lack even the words "A Song of David," or "of David." Why this inconsistency? We do not know.

If by redaction we mean the addition of introductory formulas, or notes such as "here end the prayers of David," it is clear that the redactor of the Psalms did only a limited amount of work. The truth is that there was very little he needed to do, for the chief chore in connection with the Book of Psalms was that of compilation, not that of redaction. This is mostly the case, also, with that compilation which is called the Book of Proverbs.

The prophetic books, too, are basically compilations, each book being a collection of the utterances of a given prophet. Redaction, however, is a discernible fact in the prophetic books. For example, virtually every prophetic book begins with a brief statement which, by the mention of the kings during whose reign the prophet spoke, situates the prophet in a particular historical period. Amos is the first of the literary prophets—that is, the first of the prophets from whom writings were preserved. From many prophets mentioned in Kings no writing has come down to us. The Book of Amos begins: "The words of Amos who was among the shepherds from Tekoa, who prophesied against [the kingdom of] Israel in the days of Uzziah the king of Judah and the days of Jeroboam the son of Joash, the king of Israel, two years before the earthquake." This sentence is not by Amos; it is by some redactor through whose work the Book of Amos took its shape. Within the Book of Amos, besides the introductory words, we can discern at least three types of contents: first, the quoted words of Amos; second, a brief narration of a series of visions which Amos had; and third, a short incident about Amos, told in the third person (VII:10-17). If we had only the three types of material and no more, we might want to speak only of the compiler of the Book of Amos. But the introductory sentence about the kings then reigning and, indeed, other material in the book, move us well into the realm of a redactor.

Let us admit freely that at times, in a given context, it is difficult for us today to see the precise difference between the compiler and the redactor. For example, there is a half verse which follows the mention of the kings and the earthquake (Amos I:2a): "The Lord roars from Zion and from Jerusalem sends forth his voice." This same half verse is also found in Joel III:16. Joel is to be found immediately before Amos in virtually all biblical manuscripts, and therefore in modern printed editions too. In Amos, an introductory word precedes the half verse: "*He* [Amos] *said*, 'The Lord roars.'" The phrase, "he said," does not appear in Joel, but the remaining half verse is exactly the same in both prophets. Did Amos and Joel both speak this same sentence? Did one speak it first, and the other hear of it and repeat it? Or did a redactor interpolate it from one prophetic book into another, moving it perhaps six inches on the scroll from a point near the end of Joel to the beginning of Amos?

Enough such instances occur in prophetic books to enable us to speak of "redactional interpolations." Such interpolation can be no more than some clarifying phrase, as is probably the case in Judges V:5: "The mountains quaked before the Lord; *this is Sinai*, before the Lord, the God of Israel." "This is Sinai" has no connection in syntax with the rest of the sentence; it appears to be a note, identifying which mountain. Scholars believe that at one stage it was written in the margin of the manuscript, and that it was later copied into the text itself. We speak of such interpolations as "glosses," marginal explanations which, as it were, "creep" into the text during hand-copying.

But interpolations can be more extended and much more significant. Two examples may be cited from the Book of Amos. The words of Amos are a relentless excoriation of the people for their injustice and social trespasses. Amos IX:8 reads: "Behold the eyes of the Lord God are against this sinful kingdom [saying]: 'I will destroy it off the face of the earth, *except I will not utterly destroy the house of Jacob.*'" The word in italics contradict both the previous words in the sentence and the denunciatory substance of the Book of Amos; they seem to be a deliberate qualification. Many scholars believe that the italicized words are a redactional interpolation (of which many examples could be cited) inserted to dilute the thorough-going denunciation in the preceding words and in the thrust of the whole book. Indeed, the last three verses (IX:13-15) of the Book of Amos announce a glowing future, thus thoroughly contradicting the dire tone of all that has come before. If these verses were added, then when? Perhaps it was when the Book was read in the precursor of the institution which later became the synagogue, and perhaps the purpose of the new verses was to give people some assurance of hope.

Redactional interpolations, then, are miscellaneous types of additions, of words, half-sentences, sentences, or even paragraphs. They came *after* compilation, or, at least, after compilation had begun to take place.

I have deliberately chosen to illustrate compilation and redaction in the case of the Book of Psalms and the Book of Amos because in these books no great effort was made by redactors to create a consecutive, tightly knit, and smoothly flowing entity.

The Book of Judges, on the other hand, presents us with both a compilation and a skillful redaction, for the redactor fashioned his compilation into a well-unified totality. This redactor supposes that there were twelve judges, "Great Redeemers." He mentions seven by name, giving us ample accounts of only five. Two matters contribute to the total unity. First, and recurrently, the people, or a tribe, of some region had been guilty of infidelity to Yahve, and as a consequence a foreign nation had conquered them, so that a Great Redeemer was needed in order to break the conqueror's yoke; thus, a similar setting introduces each of the judges. Second, a sentence occurs three times in the Book of Judges (XVII:6, XVIII:1, and XXI:25) as if it is a refrain: "In those days there was no king in Israel"; and in XVII:6 and XXI: 25 there is added another clause: "Each person did what was right in his own eyes." Put in another way, the redactor of Judges was committed to a proposition; namely, that religious anarchy prevailed in those early days of the Settlement of Canaan, and that monarchy necessarily arose to solve the acute problems of religious chaos.

The five accounts of Great Redeemers (plus two added narratives), can in a sense be regarded as kindred to individual psalms. Just as the individual psalms were compiled into one collection, so too these individual tales were compiled into a collection. But the difference must be clearly noted; the 150 psalms remain each a separate poem; the accounts in Judges have been incorporated into a consecutive, unified narration, illustrating a specific thesis. We must term the man who fashioned Judges more than a mere compiler and more than a redactor; he is, in his own right, an author.

The long narrations (the Pentateuch; the sequence of writings including Joshua-Judges-Samuel-Kings; and Chronicles-Ezra-Nehemiah), show evidence of compilation and redaction, but they are the end products of authors who understood literary unity and literary purpose and who had individual styles of writing which were reflective of their perceptive minds.

When we read these long narrations attentively, we can often, even usually, separate the older material from the later encasing framework.

The growth of a long work as a result of compilation of sources, of redaction, and of creative writing, is called "literary history," that is, the story of how a certain piece of writing went through stages and then achieved its surviving form.

Biblical compilers, redactors, and authors were men who believed in God, and their literary creativity and their religion went hand in hand. Their inherited accounts about men made sense to them only in the light of what they believed about God; they made the ancient contemporaneous by retouching as they copied, and the gifted among them expanded such retouching into genuinely creative rewriting.

IV

The Pentateuch

1. *Introduction*

The Pentateuch is a remarkable piece of writing; it reflects gifted minds and superb literary skills. It, more than any other writing in Scripture, is marked by an abundance of nuances and subtleties, and profundities that can readily escape the modern person who reads too fast. A very long writing, it contains, naturally, older sources, some quoted and some adapted and reworked, and, in the latest stage, there was added an encompassing framework. Here and there are loose ends, worth passing attention, but they are not disruptive of the inherent unity; an overstress on the sources and loose ends can lead one to miss the discerning minds which contributed to the totality. By the very nature of its purpose the work shows an interest in the origin of customs, practices, and standards, and because of this interest in origins, ancient folk legends or folktales appear. The folk materials are, superficially, relatively naïve, but the use to which they are put contributes a dimension of insight of some consequence. Moreover, these primitive tales retain their amusing or striking literary flavor.

For almost two centuries, scholars have inquired into the "literary history" of the Pentateuch, and they have reached a rather broad agreement. Four stages have been discerned; these are sometimes called "strata" or, more often, "codes." The oldest is called the J code. It is believed to have been recorded in the southern kingdom, Judah, and is marked by a preference for Yahve as the term for the Deity; in German Yahve is spelled Jahweh, so that Judah and Jahweh have provided the initial J. The code has a relatively secular tone and an acute interest in origins. The nineteenth-century scholarship assigned the J code to the period between 950 and 850 B.C., but more recent scholarship supposes that the J literary chain extended into a time much later than the period to which the stratum was initially assigned.

The second code has been called E, for it prefers Elohim as the divine name, and shows a geographical interest in Ephraim, the northern kingdom. The date given has been 850–750 to 650. The E code is regarded as a saga quite similar to J, though preserved in less extensive form, and marked by an advance beyond the relatively primitive character of J. In a good many passages, one finds what seems to be a blend of both J and E; for example, Genesis XXII, which relates that Abraham was commanded to sacrifice his son Isaac, begins with the Deity named as Elohim, but concludes with Him named as Yahve. From such phenomena the older scholarship inferred that around 650 some redactor blended together the J and E sagas into a single document.

The third stratum is called D, from Deuteronomy, the fifth book of the Pentateuch. Whereas in preceding books the career of Moses is presented as a third-person account, Deuteronomy presents Moses as speaking in the first person. Well over a century and a half ago the attractive theory was presented that D should be associated with a significant religious reformation occurring in the reign of King Josiah, about the year 621. The association of the D code with the Reformation of Josiah persists in scholarship, but in considerably modified form, for scholars detect materials in D that are both much earlier and much later than 621.

The Pentateuch reached its final form through a school of priestly writers, though it shows enough individuality to suggest

a single writer rather than a school; I shall not differentiate between the putative school and the individual, but speak rather
of the priestly author as P. He was a compiler; he was the gifted
author who completed the Pentateuch. He flourished around 450–
400 B.C. What he usually did was write his own connected account, and thereafter insert the older materials into it. Deuteronomy was once the beginning of a very long chain of writings, encompassing also Joshua, Judges, I and II Samuel, and I and II
Kings; the P author detached Deuteronomy from this chain of
writings, and incorporated it as part of the Pentateuch.

Such, in extremely brief terms, is a summary of the growth of
the Pentateuch.

In the nineteenth century, when the scholars came to a relative
agreement about this growth, they were led by a veritable giant
in learning, Julius Wellhausen (1844–1918), to a use of these
results for a description of the growth and development of the
religion of Israel. Today, while there are those, myself included,
who challenge some aspects of the earlier source analysis, the
primary accumulated dissent is from Wellhausen's brilliant rewriting of the growth of the Hebrew religion. Wellhausen assumed that a stratum, such as J or E, reflected the precise stage
of the Hebrew religion at the date assigned to the code; today
each stratum is regarded as reflecting older traditions of varying
antiquity, and that a code is an uncertain clue to the religion at
the particular date the code was recorded. Indeed, recent Scandinavian scholars have so stressed the oral nature of the Hebrew
manner as to regard the specific codes as of minor import, and
some of them reject the nineteenth-century source analysis in
toto. I am personally somewhere midway between the persisting
adherents to source analysis and the Scandinavian deniers. I dissent from the usual view of the analysts that J was an ancient
saga, a connected document, for I regard it rather as a series of
separate aggregates of older material; I belong to a small minority
who hold that E was never a single, separate document, but a
series of notes commenting on J, or even revising his account. I
ascribe much more significance to the writing down of materials

than the Scandinavians do. For the most part, I agree with the viewpoint expressed above, that Deuteronomy was once the first part of a very long chain of writings, that it was detached from them by P, and that it was incorporated by P into the Pentateuch. (One can read about the history of the Pentateuchal scholarship in a somewhat antiquated but fluent book, Ernest R. Trattner, *Unraveling the Book of Books*, New York City, 1929; Bible dictionaries and encyclopedias also provide these details for those who find fascination in the account of the work of scholars.)

For our purposes, terse summary can be enough: in the Pentateuch, early materials appear within a rather late framework which was both a compilation and also an original composition. Let it be stated frankly that there are passages in the Pentateuch which are strangely repetitious, such as two, or even three, accounts of the same incident, and that there are two lists of the generations of men from Adam to Noah, though they are discordant. Let it be acknowledged that there are the curious loose ends, as for example, chronological information shows that Abraham was still alive when his grandson Jacob was born, yet the author does not present them as knowing each other. There are also anomalies: we are told that Adam and Eve had two children, Cain and Abel, and that Cain killed Abel, and that thereafter Cain married and begot children. Where did Cain get his wife, if the total population of the world was only Adam, Eve, and Cain? Three generations ago, a celebrated American agnostic, Robert Ingersoll, traveled about the country delivering an address, still available at most large public libraries, called "The Mistakes of Moses." Such "mistakes" are not infrequent. They are not very important, except to literal-minded people, whether religious or irreligious, and they are of very little consequence in an inquiry into the literary grandeur of the Pentateuch; they are, as it were, the equivalent of typographical errors which the age of printing has made us acutely aware of. Shall we read a book for its inadvertent errors, or for the intent, and the laudable achievement, of the author?

Because the Pentateuch is the most significant of the biblical prose compositions, I present it with much more detail than is feasible for the chain of Deuteronomic writings. Moreover, the nuances and subtleties of the work seem to me to need some special attention.

The P writer, who was the final compiler-redactor-author of the Pentateuch, flourished in the fifth or fourth century B.C. Events such as the deeds of Abraham, remote and ancient, happened as much as twelve or thirteen centuries before P's time; indeed, the "date" of creation would be fixed, according to statements in the Pentateuch, as well over a thousand years earlier than Abraham. That is to say, there lay in the consciousness of the P author an awareness of the flow of much time: the period before the age of the patriarchs, then the patriarchs, Moses, the Judges, David, and Solomon, the divided monarchy, the destruction of the northern kingdom in 722 and the exile of the southern kingdom to Babylonia in 586, and the end of the exile about 520. Moreover, we should suppose that he knew the prophetic writings and the Psalms. He also knew an abundance of law and legal matters. He was, then, not an ignorant or naïve person, but a learned man. He chose to write only a restricted segment of the ancient history. He appears to have felt free to reproduce ancient naïve material, as if he regarded it to be understood in the light of his own sophistication. He did little "erasing" in what he reproduced; instead, he corrected by adding new material or inserting new versions of the old. Such addition for correction naturally increased the quantity of the inconsistencies and the contradictions discernible in the Pentateuch.

Since the author gives contradictory versions of the same incident or event, he presents what seems to some modern men a historical problem. If two versions of an incident contradict each other, then presumably only one is historically accurate. There exists a pre-possession among both religious traditionalists and uninformed non-religious people that the Bible provides accurate history. Curiously, non-religious people take the Bible literally in order to scorn it! Such undue emphasis on accurate history succeeds in obscuring the literary grandeur of the Bible (much as if one reads Macbeth under the illusion that it is an impeccable source for accurate Scottish history). To repeat, historical writing among the Hebrews, including the Pentateuch, never had the purpose of setting forth bare and unchallengeable facts; rather, the Hebrew bent was to blend fact and legend and theology and sentimental piety into a single amalgam. They lacked our acute sense of the distinction between history and non-history. It is *story*, not history, that we should look for. Once one makes his peace with the fact that the Bible has never pretended to be a modern work of accurate, footnoted history, he can be ready to absorb its literary greatness. The history in the Bible often is reliable, but that is a far cry from complete accuracy; after all, accuracy was not a purpose of a biblical writer. In Scripture we encounter a view *about* history, not researched history.

2.   *The Mood of the Modern Reader*

Whether or not a person can read the Pentateuch with enjoyment depends greatly on his attitude on picking up the book. Surely the gusto with which the Pentateuch was written makes it an inappropriate book for the person whose mood is cold and clammy. It is even less an appropriate book for one who tells himself that he is under an obligation to be inordinately edified and extravagantly inspired, for this kind of obligation destroys any reasonable possibility of edification and inspiration. Moreover, the person who believes that profundity is a matter of polysyllabic words and orotund expressions, or thinks in the technical phrases borrowed from the various branches of western philosophy, will seldom succeed in penetrating Scripture and absorbing its wisdom. Similarly, the person of religious bent who subscribes to metaphysical doctrines as formulated by the medieval Scholastics, and who reads the Pentateuch only so as to confirm this theology, will be disappointed.

The Pentateuch ought to speak to the reasonable reader in

Scripture's way of speaking: with verve, with dash, with sly or coarse humor, with perceptive understanding of the minds and hearts of human beings, and, recurrently, with startling perceptions. Its raw materials are often violence, horror, and sweet sentiment, and one ought not be surprised at their presence. Let the reader, then, forget grotesque solemnity and historical accuracy, and open himself to the joy that can come out of the skillfully written word.

From time to time I reread the narration in the Pentateuch as a single book, not as five. I skip most of the legal material, and some of the poetry, in order that the unity of the narration be heightened. Such a reading I can heartily commend,[1] especially to a person who has only a vague familiarity with the contents.

There is an important caution which I must repeat: One should not read too fast!

3. *The Scope of the Pentateuch*

The Pentateuch is an elaborate piece of writing. Its form and purpose were consciously planned by its author. We can distinguish a threefold intention on his part. First, the Pentateuch narrates its understanding of God, and especially the relationship of man—all men, and also Hebrew men—to Him. Second, it instructs its readers in tenets of exalted religion, and in their religious obligations. Third, it sets the Hebrew people into the context of a larger world peopled by many nations.

The Pentateuchal story covers a particular ancient epoch: it begins with the primeval creation of the physical world; it goes through the emergence of men, and, among men, the Hebrews, who grew from a succession of three single individuals into a people; and it concludes with the Wilderness experience of the Hebrew people after their release from enslavement in Egypt.

The narration is not only a review of that ancient epoch, it is also thoroughly saturated with the author's view that something special inheres in history. This is the case even when he uses old folktales, old "myths"—for his folktales have a meaning below the surface. To the author, history, as he relates it, is more than an account of events; history is the clue to truth itself, for the Pentateuch regards the flow of events as the clue to the meaning of life itself. Man is the legatee of the past, and his inheritance from the past is a rich one. Because of the spiritual dimension contained in what has already happened, this spiritual dimension must necessarily abide into the future, in order that a man may transcend his restricted span of life. Every man, inheriting the past, knows that he will not survive into the future, but nevertheless, his present is conditioned by both the past and the future.

The biblical author was concerned with God's relation to men, but he was also concerned with man's relation to God. He believed implicitly that not only are there divine laws which man must obey, but also that there are modes of worshiping God to which man must conform. Indeed, out of the past there have come down both laws of conduct and laws of worship. The author believed that these laws of conduct should be set out in a clear, orderly statement; moreover, being a priest, he believed that the laws would seem incomplete unless they were associated in some way with a functioning priesthood. For the final author of the Pentateuch, priesthood could not possibly be haphazard or sporadic, but needed itself to be quite as regular as the divine laws were regular. He had a deep interest in priesthood, and, indeed, in the origin of many institutions found among men.

Though the division of the Pentateuch into five books is an old convention, and an old convenience, the author himself made no such division. He gave no name to the book, nor any names to the five books. It was much later generations that did this. The Jews in Palestine called The Five Books The *Torah*, "the divine instruction"; Greek Jews called it "The Law." In the Hebrew Bible the names of individual books derive merely from the first significant word in each: *Berēshít*, "Beginning," from "In the beginning"; *Sh'mōt*, "Names," from "These are the *names* of the Children of Israel." The names of the books in the English Bible derive from the ancient Greek translation, made about 250 B.C.: "Beginning" became *Genesis*, "origin"; "Names" became *Exodus*, from the principal event, the exodus ("journey out") from Egypt; *Va-yiqrā*, "He called," became Leviticus, "concerning the Levites"; *Ba-midbár*, "In the Wilderness," became Numbers, from the tabulation of the tribes; *Devārím*, "words became Deuteronomy, "repetition of the Law."

4. *Creation and Primeval Man*

The author precedes his account of the emergence of the Hebrews by relating how the world, and then man, and then men and nations, came about (Gen. I-XI).

Creation resulted from the command of God; He spoke, and things came into being. At the beginning there existed nothing but darkness, chaos, and formlessness. Primeval matter was at hand, and also shapeless liquid and powerful wind. (Medieval Jews and Christians, however, held that creation took place *ex nihilo*, "out of nothing.")

God said, "Let there be light. There was light. There was evening and morning, one day." (If one asks, as countless generations have, how there could be evening and morning, and day and night, prior to the creation of the sun, then one has put a finger on a bit of illogic of which we can convict the author. But crucial to his conception is his view of an orderly progression in God's creation: hence out of chaos there first came time, and time was immediately measurable.)

After time there comes space, both earthly and heavenly. Rain comes from the sky above. Must there not be an ocean above, as there is one below? Were not these two oceans once a single body of water? Their separation into two bodies, at God's word, brought the sky into being, this on the second day of creation. God saw that all was good. On the third day, the lower waters were gathered together, with the result that dryness appeared; the gathered waters were called seas, and the dryness, land. Again at the divine command, vegetation and trees, in an abundance of varieties, came from the land. Thus, the acts of creation on that third day were two, the sea and land, and the growing vegetation. God saw that all was good.

The Deity then created the great luminaries of the sky, the sun and the moon. All was good, on the fourth day. On the fifth day, He created the living things of the sea and the birds of the air, and He enjoined them to multiply—and all was good. On the sixth day He created the living beings of the land, tame and wild animals and crawling things. His next step was His creation of man, who was also a being of earth. Man, however, was given authority to rule over all other living creations, and thus was to have to them the relation that God Himself had to the totality of creation over which man was not to rule, such as sun and moon. Hence, in man's broad rule over such creatures, he is a reflection of the image of God. Accordingly, God created man in His own likeness *with respect to ruling*. (One could see that men owned flocks and herds, and defended themselves from wild animals, and drew food from the fish in the waters of the earth.) Man, a living being, needed to increase; hence, God created man both male and female, and He blessed them and enjoined them to multiply and to fill the earth.

Significant in this priestly account of creation is its orderliness, and, inherent in the style, which is precise, noble, and direct, is a notable majesty. The acts of creation each result from God's speaking the creative word, in Hebrew *yehí*, "let there be"; creation by the spoken word is far removed from the alternate possibility, a god acting like a craftsman. Instead, God simply spoke, and the acts of creation resulted.

But the author has not yet finished. He had a bent, as we shall see again and again, for institutions and their origin. By his time the seven-day week had long been established and was widespread; hence it was a very old institution. It came into being, we are told, because God Himself rested on the seventh day, and He blessed it and made it holy. If to our minds it appears incongruous with the grandeur of God to envisage Him as resting, as if labor fatigued Him as it does us, then we should begin to glimpse a facet of the biblical mind: God was quite unlike man, but plain men could speak of God only in terms of man.

After this majestic priestly account of creation there ensues another account (Gen. II:4–24), which, by contrast, is quite folksy in manner. It has a zest which the ancient narrator and ancient audience unquestionably enjoyed, for the account is piquant and at points tinged with sly humor. The first account had told majestically what took place at creation and how man fitted in it; the second relates how the creation of man took place: There was an early time when the land was barren, for as yet Yahve the God had not caused rain to fall; moreover, there was as yet no man. At that early time an '*ēd* ("spring," or "mist" or "vapor") rose out of the ground to water the land. God Yahve fashioned '*ādấm*, "man" —and necessarily, of course, out of something!—out of dust of the earth. He transformed man into something alive by breathing a living breath into him. (Surely, so the ancients reckoned, a corpse which had lost its living breath decayed; life was breath, and how could life have come into an inanimate body unless God had put the life there?) Having created man, God planted a garden— somewhere in the east—and made grow there every kind of tree, whether a pleasure to look at or apt for its fruit to be eaten.[1] The garden at Eden was watered by a river which in turn split into four well-known rivers, which flowed, respectively, to the four corners of the earth.

God Yahve set man into the garden of Eden to work and guard it (just as, in much later times, gardens were worked and guarded against trespassers). But He commanded men not to eat of a certain tree in the garden, the tree of knowledge, for if man would eat from it he would perish on that very day.

Creation was manifestly incomplete: "It is not good for man to be alone; I will make him a helpmate." But first God created from the soil all the living beasts and the birds and brought them to man to give names to. (Now we know how one animal came to be called a lion, another a bear, and so on.) While man was no longer strictly alone, these animals were surely not helpmates to him, so God Yahve put man to sleep, extracted a rib, and then closed up the skin. The author shifts to another word for man, 'ish. The rib He built into an 'ishāh, "woman," and He brought her to the man. It was thereafter to become normal for a man to leave father and mother, and cleave to his woman, so that the two would become again (in sexual union) a single entity, a single flesh.

Both the man and the woman were 'arumím ("naked"—the prelude to a pun) but they were not ashamed. Of all the beasts which God Yahve had made, the serpent was the most 'arúm, "sly"—note the pun in 'aróm, and its plural form 'arumím, "naked," and 'arúm, "sly." At this time the serpent was, except for his slyness, a normal animal, with four legs and a tail. He said to the woman, "Did God say you should not eat of any tree in the garden?" She said, "We may eat of the trees, except the tree in the middle of the Garden. God said, 'Do not eat of it,' and"—here the woman adds something—"'do not touch it, lest you die.'" The serpent said, "You will not die! God knows that when you eat from it, you will become omniscient like Him." When the woman looked at the tree, its fruit appeared "pleasant to eat, an attraction to the eyes, a delight to gaze on." So she took of its fruit, and ate it, and she even gave some to her husband, and he too ate.

The motif of man's disobedience of God is present in this story, but can be overstressed to the point of missing the satirical strand. The great omniscience which came to man from eating the forbidden fruit turns out to be no more than the recognition that he and the woman were naked! (One does not become wise by eating fruit!) They sewed fig-leaves into girdles—surely a most primitive form of clothing for creatures who presumably now know everything; we shall soon see a sequel to this.

Wise as they were—the satire on their "wisdom" continues— they heard God Yahve's voice "strolling" about in the garden in the cool of the day, so they hid. God Yahve called out, "Man, where are you!" The man replied, "I heard your voice; I hid because I am naked." (How stupid can the supposedly wise be to think he can hide from God?) "Who told you that you are naked? Did you eat from the tree I told you not to eat from?"

The man, heroically, replied, "The woman you put with me gave me the fruit and I ate it." God Yahve said to the woman, "What was it you did?" She said (also excusing herself), "The serpent enticed me, and I ate." (Do not people tend to shift blame from themselves?)

There were consequences to this disobedience. The serpent was thereafter to walk on its belly, and mutual fear was to exist between its offspring and the woman's. Her offspring would *shā'af* the serpent on his head, and the serpent would *shūf* hers on the ankle; the Hebrew reader caught the pun in the Hebrew words *sha'af*, "to crush," and *shuf*, "to snap at." (We know now why a snake slithers instead of walks, and why dogs or cats become house pets, but snakes never.) The curse on the woman would be her pain in childbirth and her subservience to her husband. The greater consequences were on the man, for his life of ease and comfort was permanently lost. He would have to toil for his livelihood all his life: "By the sweat of your brow will you eat bread." (All men, Hebrew and Gentile, experience these burdens.)

The woman acquired a name, *Eve*, "she who begets living things"; from her all men are descended. Man, *'ādắm*, now became Adam, a name. The age of fig leaves was past; God Yahve made leather garments for the pair, and He dressed them in these (we know now how real clothing began).

But man, who in a silly way had reached out for the fruit of omniscience, might reach out for the fruit of immortality, which also grew on a tree in the garden. So God Yahve drove man out of the garden,[2] and He blocked the road to the tree of immortality by putting on the way to the garden both "cherubim and a revolving sword" (now we know why man cannot escape death).

Adam and Eve settled east of the garden, and there they begot two children, Cain and Abel. (A pun explains Cain's name: "I have gotten (*cānīti*) a male child from Yahve"; no such explanation accompanies the name of the other, Abel.) Even at that ancient time, men pursued diverse callings; Abel became a shepherd and Cain a farmer. The author conceived of the conflicts, known in his time, between sedentary farmers and desert marauders, as originating in the earliest history of man. Here the conflict took the form of a rivalry in the gifts brought to the Deity: Cain brought fruit as a gift to Yahve, while Abel's gift was of the first-born of his flock. Yahve was favorable to Abel's offering, but not to Cain's. (We are not told why; perhaps a preference for the nomadic life found in portions of Scripture accounts for the Divine partiality.) Thereupon Cain in jealousy killed Abel. The main thrust of the story is that *jealousy and murder began virtually with the origin of man.* The author then proceeds to a moral judgment: The Deity asked Cain, "Where is Abel?" Cain answered sarcastically: "Am I my brother's keeper?" The Deity replied: "The voice of your brother's blood calls out to me from the earth!" (Man *is* responsible for his fellowman's welfare; murder contradicts man's essential responsibility to his fellowman.)

So deeply did the author disapprove of Cain that, as the account proceeds, Cain was banished from his productive farm, to wander about the earth as a fugitive, in constant fear that whoever would find him would slay him—even though as yet there are no other people on earth! The extravagances of blood vengeance and blood feuds, of which the author knew and which he lamented, led him to a curious turn: A mark was put on Cain, lest someone should slay him and thereby inaugurate the abominable, first blood feud; the slayer would be avenged sevenfold. Cain wandered off, and he dwelled in *Nod* ("wandering").

Cain then fathered a son and he built the first city. That son, Enoch, in turn begot a son Irad, and Irad a son Mehujael, and Mehujael Methushael, and Methushael Lamech. Lamech had two wives; Adah bore for him Jabal, the father of those who dwell in tents, and Jubal, the father of those who play the lyre and pipe. Zillah bore for him Tubal-Cain, who was the first blacksmith.

In very brief compass, then, the author has accounted for the origin of diverse things: farming, herding, blood feuds, cities, cattleraisers, musicians, and smiths. Respecting Lamech, he cited an ancient, boastful poem:

Adah and Zillah, hear my voice,
My wives, listen to my words!
A man I have slain for [only] wounding me,
And a lad for striking me.
Cain is avenged sevenfold
But Lamech seventy-sevenfold.

(Among ancient men, too, there were braggarts.) Whatever may have been the full quantity of ancient traditions, such as Lamech's poem, known to the author is unknown to us; this brief poem suggests that our author might have included even more such material than he did, had he cared to.

The P author took from his old source a genealogy (IV:17-24), deriving from Cain, the murderer. He also introduced a somewhat different genealogy, however, as if he were reluctant to say that mankind was descended from a murderer. Eve bore another son to Adam; his name was Seth ("put"), "for Yahve has *put* another son with me in place of Abel." Seth in turn begot a son, Enos, (*'enósh*, "man," a third and least frequent term for the frequent *'ish* and the less frequent *'ādắm*).

The next milestone we come to is the age of Noah. Two genealogies from Adam to Noah are given, and they are not the same. P provides figures on the longevity of the men; in the good old days, before man's wickedness, the span of life was very long.

J	P
Adam	Adam, 930 years
Cain	*Seth*, 912 years
Enoch (*Ḥanoch*)	Enosh (*'Enosh*), 905 years
Irad	Kenan, 910 years
Mehujael	Mahalalel, 895 years
Methushael	Jared, 962 years
Lamech	Enoch (*Ḥanoch*), 365 years
Jabal-Jubal-Tubal-Cain	Methusaleh, 969 years
	Lamech, 777 years
	Noah, 500+ years

Details about the generations between Adam and Noah are mostly limited to the chronological, except in the case of Enoch.

We read of him, "Enoch walked with God, and he was not, for God took him." Exactly what is meant is elusive; a comparable tradition among the Babylonians speaks also of the seventh generation before the flood being "taken of God." In the time after the Bible, Enoch was naturally a figure about whom fanciful legends were told. Non-biblical books purporting to be by him, and revealing the future, have survived from the late biblical period.

In looking back now at what we have so far traversed, we need to understand that the tiny bits of narration, however serious their purpose, are usually tongue-in-cheek; the older materials are familiar items which ancient men relished telling and retelling, because they found them droll and pungent. If we can envisage a group of men sitting together while listening, for the tenth time, to the account of such events as the serpent in Eden, then we must envisage a man nudging his neighbor in pleasure as this or that recognizable item took its awaited turn. Yet withal the obvious folksiness, the fundamental seriousness is not lost, especially in the over-all structure. We are being told about the beginnings of man, and about the characteristics of all men, Hebrew and Gentile.

5. *Noah*

A universal flood came in the time of Noah. Men at that time had become thoroughly corrupt, for they had begotten daughters, and unhappily, these were pretty. Thereupon heavenly, divine beings ("sons of the gods"), succumbed to passion, and chose wives from among the human women. Yahve did not intend the offspring of these unions to be immortal, for man's span of life was to be at most 120 years.[1] A marginal gloss has come into the text here; it identifies the "sons of the gods"—a phrase that smacks of polytheism—with ancient, human heroes, the *Nefilim*,[2] "the fallen ones." (This vestige of mythology is virtually the only instance of it preserved in the Pentateuch; other instances, though, are found in Psalms and Job.)

The impropriety of these unions brought about great corruption among men (though we are not precisely told how or why; perhaps the beauty of the women inspired lust and lustful actions.) The author comments that every disposition of man's thought was toward evil. So thoroughly evil had collective man now become that Yahve regretted that He had created him; He decided to destroy all living things: man, beast, crawling things, and birds. But Noah had found favor in Yahve's eyes.

For his time, Noah was righteous. God told Noah of His intention to bring a destructive flood. Noah was to make an ark for himself and his family, and animals of every variety were to come in two by two. (Confusingly, another verse sets the number as seven of the pure animals and two of the impure ones, but the distinction between pure and impure is not given here!) After Noah and his family entered the ark, Yahve obligingly closed the portal. The flood came[3] and did its work of destruction.

The rains ceased. Soon Noah sent out a dove to learn how far the waters had receded; a vestige of a different account mentions a raven. The first dove returned, as did the second. The third time the dove[4] did not return.

At God's behest, Noah and all aboard the ark disembarked. Noah built an altar—the first mention of an altar—and he offered "pure" animals on it. Yahve decided never again to curse the earth on account of man, for He recognized man for what he is, frail of moral fibre and prone to sin. He would never again abruptly destroy all life, but, rather, nature would eternally proceed from planting to harvest, from cold to hot, from summer to winter, from day to night.

Scholarly attention usually focuses on certain parallel ancient narratives of a universal flood, especially that found in the Babylonian Gilgamish epic, where a universal flood resulted from the caprice of the gods. But the biblical flood is presented as a *moral* matter, a result of Yahve's judgment on men because of their evil actions. This contrast between the biblical and the Babylonian accounts provides a sure clue to the biblical view regarding history—that, as events unfold, man is constantly under the moral scrutiny of the Deity, Who is prepared to act in accord with moral judgment. We should not be misled by the manner of the narrative, in that Yahve is described in almost human terms, first regretting that He has made man, then destroying him, and finally concluding that He will never destroy mankind again. The author concludes his account by allusion to the rainbow. That heavenly portent, mysterious to him, was a sign Yahve had set in the sky as assurance that never again would He destroy all mankind. It is Yahve, not Noah, who is the true central character in the flood story.

There emerges from this account the Hebrew conception of man: lustful and prone to sin, man is nevertheless not capable of provoking the Deity to mechanical wrath. An individual man, indeed, might be destroyed; an individual man who has shed the blood of another man would in turn have his blood shed. Men should never eat blood, for blood is that part of a living thing wherein his being alive is found. (Ancient man must often have observed people bleeding to death.) Accordingly, a single man could indeed trespass, and be punished by death, but mankind as a totality would not be destroyed—especially when in a time of wickedness there existed a righteous man like Noah.

But Noah's righteousness was only relative. After the flood Noah became a tiller of the soil, planted a vineyard, and turned its fruit into wine, and he got drunk and wallowed in his tent. His second son, Ham, was not mindful of the natural respect due a parent. On discovering his father drunk, and unclothed (so that his sex organs were visible—to the Hebrews, a horrendous situation), Ham did nothing to protect his father from this shame. His brothers, Shem and Japheth, on being summoned, backed into the tent so as to abstain from the sight of their father's nakedness, and they covered him with a garment. In some way (the narrative does not tell us how), Noah knew about Ham's dereliction. He blessed his other two sons, but put on Ham the curse of being a slave[5] to the other two. (A father's blessing or his curse is regarded in Scripture as ensuring an unalterable fate.)

The curse on Ham rested on the historical observation that

among men there were slave peoples and slave-owning peoples. In general, the slave-owning peoples were either Semites, descendants of Shem, resident in the western portion of Asia, or the Japhethites, resident on the coast of the Mediterranean or in its eastern islands. The Hamites, by and large, were the residents of Africa. But the matter of Noah's second son turns out to contain a problem, as we presently see. In Genesis X the author gives us genealogical data.[6] He deliberately reserves Shem, the oldest son, for last. He begins with a list of the descendants of the youngest son, Japheth. Next, he lists the sons of Ham, including Cush[7] (Ethiopia), Egypt, and surprisingly, Canaan, for the land of Canaan is not in Africa. Moreover, Noah's curse on his second son here becomes confused; this son has now been called both Ham and Canaan, and Canaan, confusingly, seemed to be listed as Noah's son and also as his grandson. Whereas Ham seems clearly to be the forebear of Africans, Canaan is treated as the progenitor of those many peoples who dwelled in the land the Israelites were destined to occupy. This chapter on the descendants has apparently here been reshaped, to transfer the curse from the Africans to the nations resident in Canaan. The names of these nations are given; indeed, the precise boundaries of the land of Canaan are here provided. So much for Ham.

The author now turns to Shem, the oldest son, but defers for a bit the expected genealogy of Shem's descendants, in order to tell a story about origins. All peoples originally had spoken the same language. The descendants of Shem had journeyed eastward and settled in Shinar, and there they turned to making bricks and mortar, so that they might build a city and a sacred temple tower (a *ziggurat*), the top of which would reach into heaven. Yahve considered this an act of presumption (in that man was improperly attempting to reach into the divine domain). He "mixed up" (Hebrew, *bll*) the language of the people so that, no longer able to communicate with each other, they had to desist from building the tower. Through lacking a high landmark to keep them together, the descendants of Shem spread out over the whole earth. That place where the tower was to have been built was called

Babel (*bbl*), because Yahve had "mixed up" (*bll*) the languages.

At least four elements enter into this primitive but sophisticated story. First, the narrator could not resist the pun of *bbl* and *bll*. Second, the story is etiological, explaining the origin of the great diversity of peoples and of their languages. Third, man is arrogant and presumptuous. Yahve, after the disobedience in Eden and the corruption in the age of Noah, would not tolerate man's attempt to enter His domain, but the punishment now was the scattering of man, not his destruction. Last, the story is the introduction to the account of Abraham; that is, the Hebrew patriarch emerged in history at the point when impious man became divided into many nations and tongues, scattered over the earth. Out of the many nations, one was to arise to be Yahve's special people.

The story of the Tower of Babel completed, the author picks up the deferred genealogy of Shem's descendants, including Abraham.

6. *Abraham*

The Abraham stories reflect more than just the usual Hebrew narrative skill. The P author wrote on a double level—about the historic ancestor of long, long ago, and at the same time, about his own late age. He never abandoned his view of Abraham as a unique individual, who had clear and admirable personal characteristics, but at the same time he believed that Abraham's career foreshadowed the living situation of his own era. In that late age, there lived in proximity to the Hebrews—or, more precisely, the Judeans—people with languages and customs which were kindred to theirs; indeed, immediately to the north of Judea were the Samaritans, whose language and worship were quite similar to those of the Judeans. The author had to account for the manifest similarities, yet retain some sense of uniqueness for the Hebrews. He conceded to neighboring peoples a direct descent from the forefather Abraham, or an indirect one, from one of Abraham's two brothers or their children; however, he specified a special, preferred line of descent, by stressing that though Abraham had three wives, Sarah was the true one, while the other two, Hagar and Keturah, were lower in status. The preferred descent was through Sarah.

In portraying Abraham as the exemplar for his later descendants, the author faced the need for some restraint or limit, simply because the total of the inherited traditions ascribed some specific accomplishments to other ancient Hebrews. The author had to reserve some of his praise of Hebrew forebears for such men as Moses and Joshua, for example. In this dilemma he treated certain matters in Abraham's career in the form of broad clues, or else as exceedingly limited beginnings of matters, the ultimate full development of which the author would subsequently narrate in connection with these later men. Thus, for example, tradition held that the land of Canaan was not the original home of the Hebrews, and that their actual possession of Canaan came only at the time of Joshua. Again, the elaborate Hebrew worship of the Deity, through animal sacrifices presided over by priests, was inaugurated, according to tradition, only in the time of Moses and Aaron in the Wilderness. Hence, Abraham lived before the Hebrews came to possess Canaan, and before the inauguration of the formal Hebrew worship. Accordingly, the author does not portray Abraham as possessing the land of Canaan, but only as being a "sojourner" there; he portrays Abraham as building altars, but never as offering regular, scheduled, systematic sacrifices. Moreover, since the author believed that it was Yahve Who controls history, when Abraham went to Canaan, it was because Yahve had sent him there. Indeed, Yahve acted throughout Abraham's career. Yet—this is important!—it was not until the time of the great Moses, according to the tradition, that Yahve's name was disclosed to men. In his account of Abraham, the author mentions Yahve repeatedly, but he portrays Abraham, obedient, and even God-intoxicated, as quite unaware of Yahve's *name*.

Abraham was born in Ur of the Chaldees. Abraham was one of three brothers born to their father Terah; the other brothers were Haran and Nahor. In Ur, Abraham, then known as Abram, was married to Sarah, then known as Sarai; she was sterile. Haran died in Ur. The father Terah left Ur, intending to go to Canaan. He took with him Nahor, Abram, and Sarai, and Haran's son Lot. Terah, however, did not reach Canaan; he settled in Harran (not to be confused with Haran), which lay far to the northwest of Ur, but not far to the northeast of Canaan. The area where Harran lay is called elsewhere simply Aram, or else Aram of the Two Rivers (the Tigris and the Euphrates). Thus, while Ur was the place of Abraham's origin, Aram was the place where his family had come to dwell, and in that sense Aram was Abraham's real homeland.

The account of Abraham begins simply, and even tersely. Yahve said to Abraham, "Leave your country, your relatives, and your father's house, and go to a country I will show you. I will make you into a great nation." (In the fifth century, the Hebrews had descended into being a small nation; was it not good to believe in a divine promise of future greatness?) "I will bless you, and make your name so great that it will be used in blessings. Those who bless you, I will bless; those who curse you, I will curse. All the families on earth will wish to be blessed as you are blessed." (The contrast between that blessing and the reality of the shrunken post-exilic community could not be greater; Yahve, though, provided this tiny community with a fulfillment of the blessing bestowed on Abraham).

Obediently, Abraham departed, as God had commanded. He took with him his nephew Lot—a foreshadowing of indirect descendants—his wife Sarah, and some property he had acquired in Harran. (Abraham was no penniless immigrant.)

Once in Canaan, Abraham went as far as Shechem, where there was a sacred oak tree (it is mentioned a number of times in Scripture). Yahve appeared to him there, in that well-known place (that is, not in some by-way), and said, "To your offspring I will give this land." (The author then reminds us, in case we have forgotten, that at that time the land was inhabited by Canaanites.) Abraham built an altar—but we are not told that he offered a sacrifice. He then moved south and pitched his tent between Bethel and Ai, some twenty miles south of Shechem, again well-known places. Abraham built another altar (but he did not offer a sacrifice), and "he called on the name of Yahve." This is not in contradiction to the statement that Abraham did not know Yahve's name; "to call on the name" means to pray. Abraham then journeyed to the Negeb, the wilderness area in southern Judea. Abraham thus traversed the land from north to south, but he did not settle anywhere; it is as if he had made a preliminary survey of the land he had been promised, without making any contact with the native population.

Next we are told more definitely about Abraham's possessions. A famine in Canaan prompted him to go to Egypt. He knew that the Egyptians would have designs on Sarah because of her beauty. She was to forfend against the Egyptians slaying him and taking her, as they would do if they knew he was her husband, by passing herself off as his sister. The Egyptian courtiers praised Sarah's beauty to the Pharaoh, and the Pharaoh took Sarah into his household, and rewarded Abraham with an abundance of gifts of livestock and slaves. Yahve, however, inflicted diseases on Pharaoh and his household. Inferentially—the narration here is not only terse, it is telescoped—the Pharaoh soon learned the reason for the punishing diseases; he restored Sarah to Abraham, and then sent Abraham away with rich gifts. (The patriarch's conduct here is scarcely seemly. But why this narrative at all? Because the author insists that Abraham was no pauper when he came to settle in Canaan. How, then, did he acquire great wealth? Through his shrewdness! At whose expense? Within some fifty Hebrew pages, Abraham's descendants will be enslaved in Egypt; the author provides what we might call an advance retaliation.) The end of the story is so short as to suggest that some older story has been recast, but inadequately; moreover, the role of Abraham implies that he was a liar. The matter of the disease suggests that the author began to make some alteration or correction in the account, but did not finish it. Later, he tells a similar story but one free of the defects found here.

Abraham, now rich, returned to Canaan. The wealth of Abraham, and his nephew Lot, created a problem, for the land could not provide enough fodder for the abundant flocks and herds which the two owned. Abraham magnanimously allowed Lot to make a choice of the region in which he would settle, with Abraham to take what was left. Lot chose the plain along the Jordan river, and he crossed to the east side of the river, settling in the fertile area of Sodom. (Lot had no reluctance in settling in an area where the inhabitants were wicked.) After Lot's departure, Yahve said to Abraham: "Look out, from where you are, north and south, and east and west. All the land you can see I give to you and your offspring, for all time. I will make your offspring as innumerable as the grains of dust of the earth. Now, traverse the length and breadth of the land, for I shall give it to you." (This is not yet possession, but it is the divine promise of ultimate possession.)

The region of Sodom was subject to four eastern monarchs. Five of the kings in the area of Sodom rebelled against these monarchs, who marched westward, crushed the rebellion, and put the rebelling kings to flight. They captured Lot, and a fugitive brought this news to Abraham. Abraham thereupon assembled those of the household servants who were trained, and he set out to pursue the eastern monarchs who had now moved far to the north. Surrounding them at night, Abraham put them to flight, and he pursued them as far northeast as Hobah, north of Damascus. He freed Lot and recovered all the flocks and herds and the various human captives. The king of Sodom left his hiding place, and met the victorious Abraham.

We notice that some places have been mentioned, but that there has been no mention of Jerusalem: it is presumed that the city did not yet exist. A problem for the author is that the forefather of the Hebrews lived before there was a Jerusalem and before there was a Temple presided over by priests. Abraham has just won a military victory; did he not owe his triumph to the Deity? And should he not thank the Deity? The P author—we cannot know whether he is drawing on some ancient source or creating new material—relates that one Melchizedek, king of Salem, the priest to *El Elyon* ("the lofty god") brought out wine and bread for Abraham. (We recall that Yahve's name was still unknown and hence the Deity here is "the lofty god"; Jeru*salem* was still not founded and hence the city was *Salem*.) Abraham gave Melchizedek a tenth of all he had acquired. (In later times his descendants would be enjoined to give tithes to priests.) The narrative is rounded off by Abraham's magnanimous refusal to accept a reward from the king of Sodom (XIV).

Sarah, we recall, was barren; Yahve had promised that the land of Canaan was to belong to Abraham's descendants. How could that promise be reconciled with Sarah's barrenness? The author describes a vision Abraham had one night: Yahve assured Abraham that he would lack for nothing, but in reply, Abraham mentioned plainly that he was childless, and that his chief steward was his heir presumptive; how, then, could Abraham trust in Yahve? Yahve drew Abraham out of doors and asked him to count the uncountable stars, for his offspring would be that numerous. (Before, it was the grains of dust which were beyond counting.) Thereupon Abraham believed in Yahve, and He considered this belief as a deed of righteousness.

The Deity continued (still in the vision): "I am Yahve who brought you out of the Chaldees to give you the land to bequeath." Abraham replied, "O master Yahve, how am I to know that I shall bequeath it?" (Since this was a vision, the anomaly that the Deity's name was to remain unknown until the time of Moses fades from consideration.) The reassuring answer to Abraham came by means of a covenant, a mutual pact between Abraham and the Deity. Abraham, at a divine command, took a three-year-old heifer, a three-year-old ram, a three-year-old goat, and a dove. Slaughtering these, Abraham divided each into two segments and set the segments in two lines. A vulture descended, but Abraham, to retain the purity of the pieces, drove the bird away. It was now dusk; a deep sleep came over Abraham, and with it a great and dark terror. Yahve spoke these words to Abraham: "Your offspring will be strangers in a land not theirs, whose people will enslave and oppress them for four hundred years. But that people I will judge, and your offspring will depart with a great amount of property. Before that time, you will pass away peacefully, in fullness of years. But the actual possessions of the land [of Canaan] must wait until then, for the sin of the Amorites [a Canaanite people] is not yet fully accomplished." (These latter words explain to us the delay in possessing the land until the time of Joshua.) When dusk turned to dark, a burning flame passed between the segments of the animals.

By this mysterious act, Yahve made His covenant with Abraham about the land of Canaan. Before, when Lot had departed, Abraham had looked in all directions; now, however, the author specifies the precise future boundaries: the Nile on the west, and the Euphrates in the east.[1]

Abraham had believed and had made his covenant with the Deity, but still he had no son. Sarah proposed that Abraham mate with her Egyptian slave Hagar, and he would have offspring thereby. After Hagar became pregnant she began to treat Sarah disrespectfully. (Perhaps the author had witnessed comparable situations; Proverbs XXX:23 cites examples of an intolerable situation which occurs when "a fool becomes king . . . a maidservant succeeds her mistress.") Sarah demanded that Abraham discipline Hagar, but he replied that she herself should do it. Sarah thereupon so abused Hagar that she fled. (Do Sarah and Abraham seem uncharitable here? Does Abraham seem unduly unconcerned?)

Hagar wandered into the Wilderness of Shur. There an angel of Yahve found her, and he assured her that she would bear a son, who would be a marauder. She was, however, to return to Sarah and subject herself to her mistress, yet through her son she would have a multitude of descendants. In due course, the babe Ishmael was born in the household of Abraham. (The author here accounts for the centuries-long experience of the Hebrews, that the desert marauders, the Ishmaelites, were a plague, and yet were in language and other ways kindred to the Hebrews.)

The Deity again appeared to Abraham to assure him of preferred offspring. The new assurance took the form, first, of altering Abraham's name. A pun, amusing to the Hebrews, was involved. Inserting the Hebrew letter of "h" makes Abram Abraham, with a final syllable *ham*, sounding somewhat like the word *hmn*—"multitude." In becoming Abraham, the patriarch was assured of being the *ab* ("father") of *hmn* ("multitudes"). The covenant with Yahve, still valid, was to be expressed in male circumcision, obligatory on Abraham's lineal descendants, and even on his purchased slaves. Sarai's name, too, was changed, and it became Sarah; she was to have a son, the progenitor of kings. Abraham laughed (*yizhāq*), at the thought of offspring, for he was a hundred and Sarah was ninety. The Deity spoke: "Sarah will bear a child whom you shall call *yizhāq* ('Isaac')!" (This account explains the origin of Hebrew circumcision; it seems to be a new composition by the P author, not an adaptation of an older narrative.)

There ensues now a rather long section (XVIII-XIX) made up of parts which, although separable, are well united; there is evidence in the first portion of some incomplete effort at rewriting. Three angels, or else Yahve Himself, came to Abraham. (The three visitors are at times treated in the plural and at times in the singular.) Abraham exhibited warm hospitality to the three. After eating, they asked, "Where is Sarah?" He said, "In the tent." They (here the Hebrew has "He") said, "Precisely a year from now Sarah will have a son." Sarah listened in the tent; not only was she past her fertility, but also her husband was old, so she laughed! (In the preceding chapter, it had been Abraham who had laughed; perhaps the repetition appears now in order to transfer the unseemly, skeptical laughter to Sarah.) Yahve (not the three men!) said: "Why did Sarah laugh? Is anything too wondrous for Me?" Sarah, fearful, denied that she had laughed; "He" insisted that she had. So much for the first portion, with its confusion of the three visitors and Yahve, and of singulars and plurals.

After the angels departed on an errand immediately to be re-

lated, Yahve pondered, "Shall I conceal from Abraham what I
am about to do?" (Yahve, of course, if He wished, could reveal
His intention, as He did to His prophets.) Now comes the clarification of what is to happen. Yahve said, "The report of the violence in Sodom and Gomorrah[2] has come to Me. I shall descend
to see if their deeds are in proportion to the shouts of violence."
That is, Yahve was about to punish the wicked. It was to Sodom
that two of the three men had gone.

Abraham, meanwhile, was standing with Yahve, and he asked
Him, "Will you destroy the righteous with the wicked indiscrim-
inately? Perhaps there are fifty righteous people there. It would
be unthinkable to destroy them indifferently. Should not the
Judge of all the earth do justice?"

"I will not destroy Sodom if I find there fifty righteous men."

"Who am I, dust and ashes, to presume to speak to You? Perhaps the fifty may lack five." Then, as if this exchange is a routine barter between two men, Abraham succeeded in persuading
Yahve to reduce the required number of righteous people as low
as ten.

The author of the Pentateuch knows that five cities in the region of the Dead Sea were destroyed a long, long time ago
(probably by an earthquake). Must not this destruction have been
punishment for evil? Imaginatively, he brings Abraham into relationship with this ancient destruction; the prophetic allusions to
this destruction do not do so. The author touches here on two
facets of a theological issue: First, is guilt or innocence a collective matter, or can it be individual? The usual Hebrew answer
had been that it was always collective; but the passage here presumes the opposite, that innocence or guilt is individual. Second,
can the merit of some suffice to overbalance the iniquity of the
many? The answer in the incident is affirmative. (In this remarkable passage, one of my favorites, perceptive theology is presented concretely in the form of narration.)

The men—now they are actually called angels, and now they
number two, not three—went to Sodom, where Lot, in a reminiscence of the hospitality of his uncle Abraham, brought them

into his home and feasted them. Would there be as many as ten righteous men to save the city? And what was the specific form of the extreme evil in those cities which could occasion a destructive punishment? The author provides an episode reminiscent of another incident we saw above (pp. 17-18), of the outrage on a Levite's concubine.

How well our author tells the story, to the point of even momentarily forgetting about Abraham! The angels advised Lot and his family to depart from Sodom so as to escape the destruction to come. Lot had two sons-in-law; they did not believe him when he told them of the impending destruction, so they did not leave. The angels wished Lot and his family to flee to the mountains; he gained their consent to head instead for the town named Zoar. As they fled, Lot's wife—she is left unnamed—looked back at the destruction overtaking Sodom, and she became a pillar of salt.[3]

Our author now reverts to Abraham. He arose in the morning and, from the place where he had spoken with Yahve, he looked toward Sodom and Gomorrah and he saw the smoking ruins, for Yahve had rained fire and brimstone on those places. Lot's escape was due to the Deity's remembering Abraham.

The author proceeds now to an addendum: Lot, fearing to dwell in Zoar, moved with his daughters to a mountain cave. The daughters thought that the whole world had been destroyed. They plied their father with wine; on successive nights, Lot, drunk and unaware, had intercourse with them. The elder daughter proceeded to bear a son Moab, and the younger a son Ammon. (These hated peoples were indeed cousins to the Hebrews, but they were the offspring of incest!)

The author, as we saw above (p. 85), had had difficulty with the incident of Sarah and Pharaoh in Egypt. He now relates a similar incident, which took place in Gerar, in Philistia (which was on the southern coast of Palestine). The stories are similar: Sarah, again passed off as Abraham's sister, was again taken to the royal residence, this time of King Abimelech. Here, though, the Deity appeared in a dream to Abimelech, to inform him that Sarah was a married woman, and Abraham, questioned by Abimelech, denied there was any deception about Sarah: "She is actually my sister; we have a common father, but different mothers." In Egypt, the matriarch's chastity seemed tarnished, but here it is clearly preserved; in Egypt the patriarch seemed to be careless of the truth, but here he is fully truthful. Our author, instead of expunging the earlier story, has now told us this version, probably with the intention that we understand the earlier one in the light of this new one.

Yahve remembered Sarah, as He had said He would (in the incident of the three visitors.) She conceived and bore the son, Isaac; he was, of course, circumcised on the eighth day.

When Hagar had become impudent to Sarah, and Abraham had given Sarah free rein to do as she would, one could feel that Sarah was arbitrary and Abraham too quickly and too lightly compliant. We are now given another similar incident. The two lads, Ishmael the elder, and Isaac the younger, were growing up together. Sarah observed that Ishmael was doing something objectionable. (The Hebrew word used here is *metzāḥéq*, but the text is deficient, lacking a direct object of the verb. The root meaning of *metzāḥéq* is to laugh; some translations render it "to make sport"; the connotation of the word can be sexual.)

Sarah here had specific grounds for complaint, beyond that of mere impudence. She demanded that Abraham cast out both Ishmael and Hagar. Because Abraham was grieved, the Deity spoke to him: "Do as Sarah asks, for your offspring are to be through Isaac. As for the son of the slave, I will make him into a mighty people, because he is your seed." (Here, then, Abraham is not as quickly compliant as he was in the earlier version, and the author provides a divine sanction for his deed of expulsion.) In the Wilderness, the Deity (or His angel) enabled Hagar to find a well after the water gave out. Ishmael, an archer, dwelt in the wilderness of Paran, in the Sinai peninsula; he married an Egyptian whom his mother found for him (Gen. XXI: 1-21).

The best known incident in the Abraham stories is the account of the Deity's "testing" him, to discover whether or not he was as truly faithful to Him as was implicitly required in the covenant in Gen. XV. The Deity bade Abraham to take Isaac to a distant mountain named Moriah and to sacrifice him there on an altar.

A good many biblical passages disclose that it was scarcely unusual in those days and in that environment for a man to sacrifice his son. (In II Kings III:26, the king of Moab, when a battle was going against him, offered his oldest son as a burnt sacrifice. The Deity of the Moabites was named Molech. Lev. XVIII:21 prohibits giving children "by fire" to Molech. Deut. XVIII:6 provides the same prohibition, though it does not mention Molech.)[4] This unseemly rite once existed among the Hebrews, but became outlawed. Accordingly, the incident of the intended sacrifice of Isaac is often interpreted as a didactic prohibition, that is, a prohibition taught through a story about Abraham, rather than one made by a legal statement. I believe this explanation is correct.

In progressive retelling, however, the original didactic element gave way to a fuller exposition of Abraham's character, his unreserved obedience to the Deity. The incident is related with fine sensitivity; the suspense is excellent, and the dialogue touching. The words of the Deity were these: "Take your son (he had two), your only son (both Ishmael and Isaac were only sons to their mothers), whom you love (he loved them both), Isaac, and offer him as a holocaust on a certain mountain which I will show you."

Abraham rose in the morning, saddled his ass, and cut wood for kindling. He took two slaves along, and headed for the place which the Deity had mentioned. Three days later Abraham saw the place from the distance. He left the servants and the ass where they were, while he and Isaac went on. Abraham laid the kindling wood, which had to be carried, on Isaac; he himself carried the pan of fire and the knife, and the two went on together. Isaac said, "Father!" "Yes, my son." "Here are the wood and the fire, but where is the lamb for the offering?" Abraham said, "God will provide the lamb, my son." The latter sentence reveals the full masterly skill of the writer, for it has clear overtones quite beyond its words, in that Abraham is answering Isaac, and at the same time speaking to himself of his confidence in the Deity.

Abraham built an altar, and, in a most orderly way, he laid the kindling wood on it. He tied Isaac, and he laid him on the altar, on top of the wood. He then stretched forth his hand and took hold of the knife.

How quickly, and surely, all has moved toward the climax! And how moving is the dialogue! And we, remembering from the earlier narration Abraham's eagerness for a son, need not be told explicitly of the emotions within him. When an angel calls to him to desist, we should share in Abraham's gratification. We can nod our heads at the words, "Now I know that you truly revere God, for you have not held back your son, your only son, from Me."

In place of Isaac, Abraham saw a ram (which the Deity had indeed provided), and it was the ram which Abraham sacrificed.

Perhaps to a modern reader the episode dissipates in anticlimax; I have heard such judgments, and certainly diverse tastes can respond to the material in different ways. It does not seem to me, however, that such a response conforms with the author's intention, for to him the climax simply could not be the sacrifice of the child, but had to be the supernatural intervention which obstructed and canceled the human sacrifice. Indeed, the pathos in the dialogue of father and son, as they walk along together, would have been lugubrious and therefore repellent were it not for the happy ending. The dialogue is marked by its simplicity, especially in portraying the moving dignity of the patriarch and his son. The "binding" of Isaac, as the ancient rabbis named the account, is properly a high point in biblical narration.

Abraham dwelt in Beersheba, the southernmost city of Canaan. Isaac progressed toward manhood, so that his marriage was in the offing. To prepare us for the bride whom Isaac will have, there comes now a description of Abraham's family in Aram of the Two Rivers. Eight sons had been born to Abraham's brother Nahor. The last to be listed was Bethuel, who, we are told, was the father of Rebekah; this bare mention of Rebekah was sufficient for the ancient reader to recall the story which he already knew. At this point we are told that the matriarch Sarah died; her death, however, is not the focus of the narrative that follows. Rather, it is a causative factor: since Abraham has not taken possession of the land of Canaan, he now has to acquire a plot of ground for her burial. The author gives us a humorous scene. Ephron, a Hittite, possessed a cave, Machpelah by name, probably meaning "double." Abraham, describing himself as an alien and a sojourner, asked the Hittites for a burial plot. The Hittites replied that a man as eminent as Abraham, a mighty prince, could select the best of the burial plots available. Abraham acknowledged the courtesy of this reply by rising up and then bowing down. He said that he wanted to acquire Ephron's cave of Machpelah, paying the full price for it. The cave was at the end of a field. Ephron replied, "I give you the field; I give you the cave; in the presence of my kindred I give these to you. What are four hundred *shekels* between you and me?" (This is a travesty on the way in which merchants did their bartering.) Ephron was saying, "If you are prepared to buy the field as well as the cave and to pay four hundred *shekels*, I will sell." Abraham paid the four hundred *shekels*. This plot of land in Canaan which Abraham came to possess, he bought without murmuring at the price or at the need to buy the field as well as the cave. (He had bargained with Yahve about Sodom; he did not bargain with Ephron.)

But the marriage of Isaac remained the author's chief concern. Abraham was by then an old man, so he did not himself do the actual choosing of the girl. Instead, he designated the chief servant of his house—unnamed here, but earlier called Eliezer. Abraham laid on Eliezer the restriction that the servant would not select a girl for Isaac from among the Canaanites where they were dwelling; indeed, Abraham extracted from him an oath[5] to that effect. (Why this restriction? We need to remind ourselves again of the perspective of our writer; he does not wish to portray Isaac as marrying outside the fold, as it were, but in the age of Abraham there was as yet no fold within which to marry. Our narrator handles the problem by having the bride selected from among Abraham's kinsmen.)

Abraham assured his servant that an angel would lead him in his quest for Isaac's bride. The narrative proceeds, blending together divine guidance with charming romance. That girl in Aram would be suitable as Isaac's bride who, at a well, would respond to the servant's request for a drink by giving him one and then volunteering to draw water for the accompanying ten camels. The servant came to Aram, to the well there. Rebekah—beautiful and a virgin—was at the well to give the servant his drink, and she drew water for the camels. The servant gave her some expensive ornaments. She told him that she was the daughter of Bethuel,[6] and that there was room at her father's home for him and the camels.

So Rebekah ran to her home. Her brother, Laban, on seeing the generous gifts given to Rebekah, ran to the well to welcome the servant, addressing him as "Blessed of Yahve"—our author has again ignored the assertion that Yahve's name was still unknown. (It is prudent to be hospitable to the emissary of a rich relative.) As in the usual folktale, the servant gave Laban a full recital of Abraham's injunction to him. He and Laban agreed that Rebekah could be Isaac's bride.

The servant wanted to return to Canaan with Rebekah the very next morning. His hosts wanted him to delay some ten days, but he did not wish to linger. Rebekah was willing to go immediately.

The author tells us how the bride and groom met. While the servant was away, Isaac had moved to the Negeb. One evening, he went into the open country, hoping to glimpse the returning servant; he saw some camels approaching. From the caravan Rebekah spied Isaac, and she asked, "Who is that man?" The servant answered "He is my master." Modestly she covered her face. Arriving, the servant related to Isaac all that had happened. Isaac brought Rebekah into his tent[7] and took her as his wife.

The narration promptly reverts to Abraham. He married another wife, Keturah; nothing at all is told of her. From this union with this otherwise unknown woman were descended some peoples kindred to the Hebrews. These did not share in Abraham's primary legacy, which went to Isaac. Abraham thereafter died, and his two sons Ishmael and Isaac buried him in the cave of Machpelah beside Sarah.

We can note, in passing, some anomalies: for example, Abraham's death is narrated after the return of the servant with Rebekah, but the narration does not bring Rebekah and Abraham together at all. The ancient rabbis, noticing such anomalies, devised a dictum to the effect that Scripture is not to be scrutinized for a strict ordering of events.[8] If the compilation and redaction have not been altogether smooth here, there is nevertheless a very large measure of unity in the Abraham stories. Certainly our author has contrived to make Abraham's character emerge clearly and consistently. Wherever Abraham went, it was always at Yahve's command and under Yahve's guidance. He was no pauper, but a man of wealth. Magnanimous to his nephew, he even rescued him from his captors. He interceded with the Deity on behalf of the wicked people of Sodom. He was faithful to the Deity, and he demonstrated his obedience to Him in his willingness to sacrifice Isaac. That tiny part of the Promised Land which he took possession of to bury Sarah, he paid for in full. He provided for the proper marriage of his son, Isaac. He died in ripe old age, after a long and praiseworthy career. Rather than concentrating on incident, the author has given us a perceptive character study. As is the case in the Book of Ruth, we are given vignettes, episodes, and they are only loosely connected. Three pairs of these, those of the matriarch and the king, the expulsions of Hagar, and the ascriptions of laughter (the basis for Isaac's name) first to Abraham and then to Sarah, appear to represent stages in the growth of the material; we see an additional stage in the recurrent notes of the P writer about Abraham's age at various times, and by the P chapter on circumcision. The unity, then, is not total, but it is quite enough for the character of Abraham, in his own right and as the exemplar for his descendants, to stand out in full clarity.

That this is the case is borne out in the legends which arose about Abraham in the age immediately after the completion of the Bible, in which the clarity of the biblical characterization is underscored by the nature of the expansions, for these add details, but scarcely affect the biblical characterization. Curiously, Abraham goes unmentioned in the writings of the earliest prophets, though Isaac and Jacob are often spoken of. It is quite possible that the author has drawn not on sources, but on a fertile imagination; if so, he succeeded in giving an unmistakable sense of reality to what he created. Moreover, he never loses the sense of historic continuity so important to his total view, for Abraham is clearly that hinge in history at which attention turns from men in general to the Hebrews in particular.

7. *Isaac*

The author, in turning to Isaac, does not do as well as he did with Abraham. Isaac appears as the central character in only a single chapter, Genesis XXVI. To escape a famine, he went to the Philistine city of Gerar, for Yahve had instructed him not to go to Egypt. Like Abraham, Isaac passed his wife off as his sister, but this in fear of the people rather than of the king. The king was named Abimelech, as in the account of Abraham (also in Gerar). From his window, Abimelech observed Isaac and Rebekah "making sport," so that he knew Rebekah was Isaac's wife, not his sister. Abimelech thereupon warned his people against touching Isaac or Rebekah, on penalty of death. Thereafter Isaac grew wealthy in flocks, herds, and slaves. Conflict arose with the Philistines over the wells; we encounter a repetition of an item told earlier about Abraham, the naming of the city of "seven wells," as *Beersheba*.

It is puzzling that this material duplicates the Abraham material. Did the author have no independent incidents about Isaac? Some have guessed that since ancient tradition, recorded in the prophets, spoke repeatedly about a patriarch named Isaac, the author was obliged either to tell something about him, or else to omit him completely. He is not creative here. The incident here of the patriarch's wife is held by some to be the oldest version, with the other two (Gen. XII:10-20 and Gen. XX:1-18; see pp. 85 and 91) derived from it. To my mind it is this version that is the latest, for here the matriarch is not brought to a harem at all.

Historic continuity, however, is safeguarded: Isaac, as the son of Abraham, is presented as the second of three individuals from whom the Hebrews are regarded as descended.

8. *Jacob*

Whereas Abraham is presented as an ideal man of rectitude and probity, the essential core of the fascinating Jacob material is almost exactly the reverse. Our author has inherited and preserved very, very ancient traditions, apparently much older than the Abraham material, and has blended them into the historic continuity from which the Hebrews have sprung. Two matters seem to be of concern to him. The first is that he must account for the transition from solitary individual forebears into a people; this he does through the circumstance that this third forebear, Jacob, had many children, indeed, thirteen. Whereas in the case of Abraham and Isaac there was a preferred line through one of two children, in the case of Jacob all of the children are within the preferred line. The second matter is that he must explain the origin of the collective name Israel, a name infinitely more frequent than the name Hebrew, as we shall see.

In the ancient core material, Jacob is something of a lovable scoundrel. A verse, Hosea XII:3, reads:

> In the womb, he cheated his brother,
> And in his strength, he contended with a deity.

This old material depicts Jacob as a picaresque character, whose exploits brought laughter to early generations in somewhat the same way that Americans of Scottish extraction are amused about their horse-stealing ancestors in the Scottish highlands. Our redactor-compiler enjoys the stories of Jacob's somewhat improper conduct, but at the same time he progressively worries about having such a person as one's ancestor. In his recasting, he adds a few touches here and there to suggest that Jacob was in reality a respectable ancestor, and when we are at the end, Jacob has emerged as a man of sterling dignity and integrity, as should be the case in the ancestor whose name was borne by the nation sprung from him. Since much of the core material is so ancient, we encounter passages which are of the primitive substance of folktales, almost as if we were not in a religious atmosphere at all. We shall veer often between folktale and religious narration.

After Isaac married Rebekah, she was childless for a time, so that Isaac prayed to Yahve on her behalf, and she conceived. In her womb twin sons pressed against her (and caused her discomfort). She went to inquire of Yahve, presumably to some sanctuary. Yahve told her that she bore two nations in her womb, and it was destined that the older would become enslaved to the younger. Our narrator interprets the still-unborn individuals as symbols of collective peoples, but he does not let the individuals lose their personal characteristics.

Rebekah gave birth to the twins. The first was ruddy (*'admōnî*) and he was hairy, as if he were wearing a mantle of hair (*sēʿār*); since children are normally born with hairless bodies, this hairy child looked mature, so that he was named Esau (*'esáu*, "fully done"). Puns inhere in the words for *'admōnî*, ruddy, and *sēʿār*, hairy; the first pun yields a second name for Esau, namely *Edŏm*, and the second the region where Esau settled, *Sēʿîr*.

The younger child, on emerging from the mother's womb, was holding on to the ankle (*'aqéb*) of the elder, so that he was named Jacob (*yaʿaqŏb*, "ankle-holder"). Perhaps the intention in the ankle-holding incident is to foreshadow the even fuller rivalry of the brothers, to which the ankle-holding was meant only as a prelude. Or perhaps this pun was meant to divert us from another meaning of the word *yaʿaqŏb*, "sharpy," in the sense of "cheater."

Esau became an expert hunter, an out-of-doors man; Jacob became a quiet man, preferring the tent. (The contrast intended is that between the unsophisticated man and the sophisticated.) Isaac preferred Esau to Jacob, for Esau kept him supplied with the delicacies of the hunt; Rebekah, however, preferred Jacob.

One day Jacob prepared a thick lentil soup, the color of which has significance. Esau returned from the out-of-doors, fatigued. He said to Jacob, "Let me gulp down some of that *'adōm* ("red") soup, for I am fatigued." Hence, they called him *Edom* (the usual biblical term for Esau's descendants). Jacob replied to him, "Sell me your right of the first-born." (In Hebrew law, the bulk of an estate went to the first-born.) Esau said, "I am at the point of death; what do I care about a birthright?" Thereupon Jacob gave him some bread and the soup, and Esau ate and drank. He then went his way, having despised his birthright. (Older translations render the lentil soup as "a mass of pottage," a phrase which has come to mean something of virtually no value that is bartered for something of high value.) The Hebrew word for birthright is *bekōrāh*.

Next, Esau married two wives, both Hittites, that is, *local* girls. These caused distress to Rebekah and Isaac.

When Isaac grew old, he became blind. He summoned his favorite son, Esau, and bade him to go out to hunt, so as to provide some delicacy for him, and thereafter Isaac would bless him (and a father's blessing, we remember, could not be retracted). Rebekah overheard this, and recounted it to Jacob. She bade him to go to the flocks to fetch two fine kids which she would prepare in Isaac's favorite way, so that Isaac would give his blessing to Jacob in place of Esau. Jacob reminded his mother of Esau's hairiness, and of the smoothness of his own skin. "If my father should feel me, I will be a deceiver in his [blind] eyes, and bring a curse upon me instead of a blessing." She said, "That curse be upon me! Do as I say."

There were favorite clothes of Esau's in the house; these Rebekah put on her younger son Jacob. The skins of the kids, which she had asked Jacob to fetch to her, were put on his arms and on the smooth part of his neck. She put the food into his hands. He came into his father's presence, saying, "I am your first-born, Esau. I have done what you have asked me to do. Now, eat of what I have hunted, so that you may bless me." Isaac said, "Come here and let me feel, are you or are you not my own Esau?" The father felt him. He said, "The voice is that of Jacob, but the hands are Esau's. Are you indeed Esau?"

Jacob said yes, and Isaac ate the food and said, "Draw near and kiss me." Isaac smelled the odor of Esau's garments; he proceeded to bless Jacob.

Jacob had scarcely left his father's presence when Esau entered with his delicacies. Isaac asked, "Who are you?" "I am your first-born son, Esau." Isaac began to tremble, horribly. "Then who was it who went hunting, and brought food to me? I blessed him —blessed must he be!"

Esau cried out loudly in great bitterness, "Bless me too." Isaac said, "Your brother"—one remembers *the voice of Jacob*—"came in deception, and took your blessing."

Esau said, "Is his name *Ya'aqōb*, cheater, because he has twice cheated me? He took my birthright, *bekōrāh*; now he has taken my blessing, *berākāh*." Esau hated Jacob because of the *berakāh*. He intended to slay Jacob. Rebekah urged Jacob to flee, until Esau's wrath would abate. He should go to her brother Laban, whom we have already met.

The actions of Jacob and Rebekah can disturb us, especially if, understandably, we read with stern moral judgment in our hearts. In that case, though, we will be forming a somewhat premature opinion, for the author differs from us not in moral standards, which are like ours, but only in that he relished this folktale. Yet while the author was amused, he was distressed, as illustrated by two additions he makes. He goes on to ascribe to Rebekah a fear that the two brothers might well kill each other: "Why should I become bereft of the two of you in one day?" That is to say, Rebekah is portrayed as quite concerned for Esau. Next, the author ascribes a new reason, rather than fearful flight, for Jacob's leaving home. He portrays Rebekah as telling Isaac that she is sick to death of the Hittite girls whom Esau had married. Were Jacob to marry a local girl, she might as well die. Isaac thereupon summoned Jacob, enjoined him not to marry a Canaanite woman, but go to Aram and there marry a daughter of his uncle Laban, that is, to marry in the clan.

The first incident in Jacob's journey, or flight, a most colorful one, concludes with a statement that Jacob gave to a place which was originally known as Luz, the name of Bethel (this despite our having already encountered the place named Bethel, above, page 84). Bethel is a compound word, *bēth-ēl*, "house of God." Why this name? When Jacob set out from Beersheba, darkness overtook him, so that he had to pause for the night. He took one of the stones of the place and put it at his head and fell asleep. In a dream he saw a ladder, its bottom resting on the earth and its top stretching into heaven, with angels going up and down on it. Then Yahve stood by and said, "I am Yahve the God of your father Abraham and Isaac. I shall give the land on which you lie to you and your seed, which will be numerous as the sand of the earth. You will spread west and east, north and south. In you will all the families of the earth be blessed." (This passage repeats the promises made earlier to Abraham and to Isaac; what continues, however, is peculiar to the Jacob story.) "I will be with you, and watch over you wherever you go, and I will bring you back to this land, for I will not abandon you, but will fulfill what I have said to you." The journey of Jacob is now no longer the same fearful flight it has been in the ancient, secular folktale, for Yahve's guidance has now entered into it.

Jacob awoke from his sleep, thinking, "How awesome is this place! It is no other than the *house of God*, and here is the gate of heaven!" Arising early in the morning, he took the stone which he had put near his head, set it up as a holy pillar, and [to ensure its holiness] poured oil on it. He called the place Bethel. (Inconsistently, in this episode Jacob seems to know the as-yet unrevealed name of Yahve!)

Though this story is brief, and has some motifs we have already seen, it also has some overtones which are new. By now we have already met variation between divine angels and Yahve himself. Hitherto, however, the account of Jacob has been predominantly secular; from here on it becomes increasingly theological, though folk materials are still used. Nothing in this episode suggests any direct bond with the earlier episodes of the sly acquisition of the birthright and the blessing. Some interpreters discern here a profound spiritual crisis in Jacob's maturation, moving him to foresake his earlier bent as a deceiver and to become a worthy person; if such an intention was in the author's mind, he is certainly not explicit about it. Yet we are well on the way to a praiseworthy Jacob.

The author now reverts to the old folktale material. Jacob moved on to Aram, and came to a well. A rock so huge covered it that shepherds would need the combined strength of many to move the rock. Rachel, a shepherdess, and the daughter of Laban, came to the well. Jacob single-handedly moved the rock. Jacob and Rachel thus became acquainted. She ran to inform Laban, her father, and Laban came to the well to embrace Jacob, and to bring him home. Because Laban hospitably welcomed him as "bone and flesh" (we would say, "flesh and blood"), Jacob stayed there a month. Then Laban, offering him employment, said, "Should you, because you are my kinsman, serve me for nothing? Tell me what your salary should be."

To the ancient reader the question about salary was calculated to elicit a smile, for the reader knew already the character of Laban, and enjoyed the hypocritical question.

Laban had two daughters. The elder, Leah, had some eye blemish; Rachel, though, was fair of form and pretty to see. Jacob had fallen in love with Rachel. He replied, "I will serve you for seven years, for your daughter Rachel." Laban said, piously, "It is better for me to give her to you than to someone else."

The seven years passed like a few days. Laban assembled the people and he arranged a banquet. In the dark of night, Laban brought Leah to Jacob's nuptial tent. In the morning light, Jacob saw it was Leah he had spent the night with. He complained to Laban: "Why did you cheat me?"

"It is not the way here to marry off a younger girl before her older sister. Finish up the week of feasting, and then start another seven years for Rachel."

So, Jacob labored another seven years. To Leah, Laban gave a maid-servant named Zilpah, and to the bride Rachel, he gave Bilhah. Jacob continued to prefer Rachel to Leah.

Yahve noticed that Leah was unloved; He provided that she bore children ("He opened her womb"), but Rachel was childless. In succession Leah bore Reuben, Simeon, Levi, and Judah. She then "paused in her child-bearing."

Rachel, jealous of her sister, demanded of Jacob, "Provide me children, or I shall perish!" She said, "Lie with my maid Bilhah, and let her bear children to belong to me (literally, "to be put on my knees") so that I may have descendants through her." So Bilhah bore one child whom Rachel named Dan, and then another, Naphtali. Leah, for the moment not pregnant, then gave her maid-servant Zilpah to Jacob. The first son whom Zilpah bore, Leah named Gad, and the second Leah named Asher.

A curious episode ensues. Leah's son Reuben, at the harvesttime of the wheat, found in the field some mandrake roots—they were regarded as a sure cure for sterility—and he gave them to Leah, who wished to become pregnant again. Rachel wanted them. Leah refused: "Is it not enough that you have taken my man? Will you also take my mandrake roots?"

Rachel replied, "In return for giving me the mandrake roots, let Jacob sleep with you tonight." When Jacob returned from the field at evening, Leah went out to meet him and said, "You sleep with me tonight, for I have hired you with my son's mandrake roots." A gloss, insisting that children come through divine intervention, not mandrake roots, tells that God heard Leah, so that she became pregnant, and bore a son, Issachar, a name which puns on *sāchār*, "hire." She also bore a daughter, Dinah.

God then remembered Rachel; the mandrake roots somehow disappear from the account. She bore a son, Joseph. But she wanted still another son.

At this juncture, Jacob wished to return home. Courteously he asked Laban to let him go, and to let him take his wives and sons with him. Laban said, "Tell me what pay I owe you, and I will give it to you." Jacob proposed that he receive no money, but a selection from the flocks of sheep of any striped and spotted sheep, or any black lamb.[1] (Since striped or spotted sheep and black lambs were rare, Jacob was offering what Laban would surely consider a fine bargain.) Agreeing, sly Laban promptly requestered from his flock all such animals and sent his sons off with them a distance of three days' journey away. Jacob had charge of the remainder of the flock. Taking fresh rods of several trees (poplar, almond, and plane), he peeled them in such a way that he left them striped. He set the striped role in the watering troughs, where the female animals, when in heat, could see them. After the animals mated, the females bore offspring which were striped and spotted. Jacob allowed his rams to run only with ewes that were black! He put his rods in the troughs only when strong goats came near, thereby amassing flocks of only strong animals! (also, according to a gloss, he acquired male and female slaves, and camels and asses; that is, he was in no way done in by Laban!)

Jacob thereafter learned of the resentment felt by Laban's children at his accrued wealth; moreover, Laban ceased to be overtly pleasant as previously he had been. Hence, while Laban was away to shear his sheep, Jacob put his wives and his sons on camels, mustered the flocks he had amassed, and set out for Canaan. Rachel stole her father's teraphim,[2] and Jacob, so our narrator tells us, "stole" the heart of Laban in not informing him that he was secretly leaving. Jacob and his retinue proceeded to ford the river [Euphrates].

Three days later, when Laban learned of Jacob's departure, he set out in pursuit, overtaking Jacob in the hill country of Gilead, east of the Jordan river. (An intrusive gloss tells us that the Deity appeared to Laban in a dream and warned him against doing any harm to Jacob.) Laban said to Jacob, "Why did you run away secretly, and cheat me, and not tell me? I would have sent you away with mirth and songs, with tambourine and lyre!" He added, "Why did you steal my gods?" Jacob did not know that Rachel had taken the gods. Laban searched the tents, Jacob's, Leah's, and Bilhah's and Zilpah's. Then he went into Rachel's tent. She had put the teraphim in the camel-bag, on which she was sitting, and said that she was unable courteously to rise in his presence, for it was her period. Laban did not find the teraphim, and Jacob thereupon lost his temper with him. Laban proposed, placatingly, that they make a covenant of friendship. They did so, agreeing that neither would cross the border, of which a mound and the pillar were to be the boundary markers. (This covenant is more a *national* treaty than an agreement between individuals.) Laban then kissed his daughters and returned home.

Theological elements have intruded as glosses into the above account; possibly they somewhat obscure the amusing by-play between Jacob and Laban, especially in the speeches, which are full of deliberate hypocrisy. The theft of the teraphim, and Laban's futile search, is coarse but funny. The recurrent intrusive theological notes have not succeeded in totally obliterating the amiable folk-character Jacob, able to outsmart even his sly uncle Laban, whose name means "the smooth one." But from here on in the account of Jacob is never again of the picaresque folk-character; he is henceforth the respected, dignified ancestor, no longer a youth, but a responsible mature man.

He had fled to Aram out of fear of Esau. Now, eager to appease Esau, Jacob sent messengers to him in Seir, with respectful greetings. The messengers returned to report that Esau was approaching, accompanied by four hundred men. Frightened, Jacob divided his people and his possessions into two encampments, in the hope that, should Esau attack one encampment, the other could serve as a refuge. Then he prayed: "O God of my father Abraham and my father Isaac, you, Yahve, who have told me to return to my native land for You would look out for me, I am unworthy of all the true reliability You have shown me. I crossed the Jordan, having only my staff with me, but now I have grown into two encampments. Save me, I pray, from my brother Esau. . . ."

The next morning Jacob set apart a series of flocks, each flock in turn to be offered as a gift, so that the succession of presents might allay Esau's wrath. He took one further step. He led his wives and children across the river Jabbok for their safety, and then sent them on ahead. He remained alone.

The effort on the part of Jacob to allay Esau's wrath could appear to be in keeping with Jacob's earlier character, and insincere. A careful reading, however, shows no trace in the episode of any unworthy motive. We deal now with a new and different Jacob; this becomes even more unmistakable in the very next incident, in which Jacob wrestles with some divine being.

This story is simplicity itself, but its overtones are complex. Like old folk-stories, it begins in a pun, indeed, a triple one. Our scene is the river Jabbok (*yabbōq*); there a man "wrestled" (*ye'ābēq*) with Jacob (*ya'aqōb*) until daybreak. The man could not throw Jacob, but he injured Jacob's thigh. The man said, "Send me away, for dawn has come." Jacob said, "Not until you bless me." He said, "What is your name?" "Jacob." The man said, "It will no longer be Jacob, but *Israel* ['God strives,' or 'He strives with God'], for you have striven with God and men, and have prevailed." Jacob said, "Tell me your name." "You need not know my name." But he blessed Jacob. Jacob called the place Peniel ("face of God"), for "I have seen God *face to face*, yet my soul has survived." When the sun shone, Jacob passed on from Peniel, limping because of his thigh, so that thereafter the *children of Israel* do not eat the sinew of the joint of the thigh, "until this day."

The curious words, "until this day," occur a number of times in Scriptural accounts, and indicate the difference in time between the late age of the narrator and the early setting of the events he is narrating. The abstention from eating the thigh sinew is not mentioned anywhere else in Scripture, and this has led scholars to the view that it was a dietary practice that disappeared. Here for the first time Scripture mentions the "children of Israel";[3] it will become the usual designation for the people hitherto called the Hebrews.

The central incident, that of a human wrestling with a divine being, is very ancient and has parallels in other folklores. Some have suggested that this ancient story was originally not told about Jacob, but was brought into the story here to account for the phenomenon observed often in the Prophets and the Psalms, that Jacob and Israel are names of the same person, and to explain the origin of the collective name Israel.

When Esau reached Jacob, he responded most affirmatively to Jacob's overtures, to the point of needing persuasion to accept the gifts which Jacob had offered. He proposed to leave some of his men with Jacob, presumably as guards, but Jacob saw no need, and Esau promptly returned to Seir. (Is this an anticlimax? Or does the author mean to imply that Jacob's changed character won over Esau?)

The remainder of the Jacob material lacks color; it seems to come from the pen of a very late author. Laban's teraphim, which Rachel had stolen, were buried near Shechem.[4] (This city was the Samaritan center in late times, and possibly the passage is anti-Samaritan.) Jacob and his family resumed their journey southward. Rachel, now pregnant, went into a most painful and perilous labor, and she was dying. A son was born to her, and Jacob named him Benjamin. Then Rachel died. At Ephratha[5] (which was also known as Bethlehem), Jacob set up a pillar to mark Rachel's tomb.[6]

As already noted, the Jacob material veers between the ancient folktale of the clever deceiver and the recastings by which he is re-interpreted first as the ancestor of the people who bore his acquired name, Israel, and then as a most respected ancestor. Why did the author who recast the matter retain the somewhat dubious folk material; why did he not expunge it? Possibly because, though he might have expunged it from a written piece of parchment, he could not expunge it from the oral traditions of the people. Unable, or probably unwilling, to expunge, he made his additions and recastings, doing so more noticeably and abundantly in the Jacob material than anywhere else in the Pentateuch.

Jacob is the third of the three individuals from whom the Hebrews believed they were sprung. When did the Hebrews grow into a people? Moreover, how did it chance that they, a people who, through Abraham, had originated in the east, became enslaved, as their traditions told, in Egypt, to the west? These answers, so essential to our author's convictions about historic continuity, arise from the story of Jacob's son, Joseph.

9. *Joseph*

In the Joseph materials we should be struck by two qualities unlike what we have seen in the writing in Genesis hitherto. First, the Deity is not an active participant, as He is in the Abraham and Jacob material, but is, as it were, only behind the scenes, though there significantly. Second, the unity in the Abraham and Jacob cycles was a result of the compilation and redaction of diverse and separate materials; the Joseph material, on the other hand, is highly unified, as if it was a completely new literary creation. To the limited extent that unity[1] is at times ruptured in the Joseph story, it is primarily a result of later, minor recasting here and there, and not a result of using earlier, divergent sources. The unity in the Joseph story is not merely the absence of divergent sources; it is quite affirmative, in that each incident in the story leads to a consequent incident. Because of this skillful plot line, interpreters often prefer to speak of the Joseph material as a novel, or, because it is not as long as the usual novel, as a novelette.

The story, most briefly outlined, runs as follows. In Jacob's old age, his preference for Joseph evoked the hatred of his other sons for the favored brother. Not only was Joseph a tale-bearer, he also regaled his brothers with dreams of his future greatness, when they would bow down to him. The occasion arose for them to vent their spite. Joseph was sent to visit them while they were pasturing their sheep. They fell upon him, stripped him of a fine garment, a cloak of many colors, which had been given him by their father, and they threw him into a pit. Passing Ishmaelites carried Joseph into slavery in Egypt. The brothers dipped Joseph's cloak in the blood of an animal and sent it to Jacob so that he would believe that a wild animal had slain his favorite son.

Guided by Yahve, Joseph in Egypt rose to become the overseer to Potiphar, the Egyptian official who had bought him from the Ishmaelites. But Potiphar's wife conceived a lust for Joseph, and when he scorned her, she accused him to her husband of attempted rape, showing her husband Joseph's robe, which she had tried to take off him; the truth was that he fled from her, leaving the robe in her hand. Potiphar had Joseph jailed. With him in prison were two minor officials of Pharaoh. Each of these dreamed a dream, and Joseph was able to interpret them. One, a baker, was hanged. The other, a wine steward, was restored to his post. He had promised to intercede with Pharaoh on Joseph's behalf, but he forgot. When Pharaoh dreamed two strange, successive dreams which none of his court could interpret, the wine steward then remembered Joseph. Summoned to the court, Joseph interpreted Pharaoh's dreams to mean that seven years of abundant crops would be followed by seven years of crop failure and famine, and that during the first seven years the produce should be preserved against the famine to come. The Pharaoh expressed his gratitude to Joseph by putting him in charge of the food program; he gave Joseph an Egyptian name and an Egyptian wife who bore him two sons.

When the years of famine arrived, Jacob, in Canaan, learned there was food available in Egypt, and he sent all his sons but Benjamin to buy food. They were brought before Joseph. He recognized them, but they did not recognize him. Joseph toyed with them; he charged them with being spies, and he threatened to keep them all in prison unless they could prove their authentic identity by summoning Benjamin to Egypt. Then he settled for keeping only Simeon in Egypt, letting the others return to Canaan, and he demanded as a price for further food that they bring Benjamin to Egypt. He had the money they paid for the food returned to their bags, a matter that caused them anxiety.

Back in Canaan, Jacob was dismayed when he heard that Benjamin was required to return to Egypt, and he refused to send the boy, but at last the hunger of his people compelled him to assent. In Egypt Joseph again toyed with his brothers, deepening their anxiety and mystification. When finally he sent them off, he ordered his steward to put the goblet with which he did his magic into Benjamin's bag of food. Then he sent an officer after them, to accuse them of stealing the goblet. The brothers denied the theft, but the goblet was found in Benjamin's bag. Benjamin was eligible for execution.

Thoroughly shaken, the brothers, bowing down to Joseph, listened to his scolding and threat. Then Judah pleaded with Joseph, offering himself in place of Benjamin. Moved by Judah's words, Joseph disclosed himself to his brothers. The Pharaoh, hearing of the joyful reunion, invited Jacob to come to Egypt, and in warm welcome he gave the family the permission to settle in the area called Goshen. Joseph used the stored grain as a means for the Pharaoh to acquire the possessions and the land of his subjects, becoming exceedingly wealthy thereby.

Jacob, grown old,[2] died and was buried in Canaan.[3] The brothers were fearful that now Joseph would avenge himself on them, and they offered themselves as his slaves. He declined; they had intended evil against him, but God had converted that evil into good, in order to preserve the people.

This bare outline cannot do justice to the richness of the detail, the perceptiveness of the characterizations, and the deftness of the story line. The dreams are wondrous inventions; the one garment which he wore symbolizes his brothers' jealousy and hatred, while the other garment symbolizes the fierce anger of Potiphar's wife. Above all, the story progresses because action causes subsequent action: the father's partiality caused Joseph's youthful arrogance, the arrogance evoked the brothers' hatred of him, the hatred led to their resentful act, the act led to Joseph's enslavement in Egypt, the enslavement led to his being purchased by Potiphar, and that in turn led to the wife's lust for him, and that led to his imprisonment. And so on. Curiously, the Deity is never portrayed as appearing to Joseph. He is very active in guiding Joseph's destiny, but it is always behind the scene, never within it. Just enough such touches are to be found to justify the author's statement of his theme, found in Joseph's reply to his brothers after the death of Jacob, that what men devise as evil, God converts into good.

So unified is the story that traces of divergent older sources are absent; certain doublets are present, but these are the result of a late set of interpolations, not of earlier sources. In these interpolations, Judah supplants Reuben as the leader of the brothers, possibly because an account in Genesis XXXV:22 ascribes to Reuben an unseemly episode with his father's concubine Bilhah. Twice the author, or a later interpolator, slips. On the return of the brothers to Egypt, Jacob, entirely without preparation in the story, appears to be accusing the brothers of their attack on Joseph, as if he knows the truth. Another slip is a needless anticipation of the specific theme, for Joseph is twice portrayed as announcing the capacity of the Deity to convert men's evil intentions to good: first at the time when he discloses himself to his brothers, and again after Jacob dies. This would be stronger if it appeared only once, and only at the end.

The characterizations are no less than excellent. We can follow Joseph from his beginnings as a prig into his becoming the great wise man of Egypt. Jacob's change from the doting to the bereaved father is touching. The wine steward, when in jail, had promised to intercede with Pharaoh on Joseph's behalf; restored to the palace, he conveniently forgot. The warmth of the Pharaoh is, in the total structure, a subtle preparation for the story of a succeeding Pharaoh, whose attitude would be entirely the reverse.

At the end of the story Jacob, just before his death, blesses Joseph's two sons. Here our author has remembered keenly his prevailing interest in hisorical continuity, for the sons, like Joseph's brothers, are progenitors of tribes of Israel. Indeed, the Joseph story, beyond its fascinating narrative, serves several purposes. It accounts for the enlargement of the Hebrews from the succession of solitary individuals through to the establishment of the twelve tribes, laying the basis for the enlargement of the tribes into a numerous people, a nation. It explains that facet of the Hebrew tradition which spoke repeatedly of a period of enslavement in Egypt. Lastly, it provides a harmonization of two divergent and almost contradictory traditions: in The Prophets, the view is that the Hebrews originated in the Wilderness, but in Genesis their origin, through Abraham, is traced back to Ur, in the eastern area of Chaldea. The Joseph story sets the stage for a Wilderness period following the enslavement in Egypt. Thereby the eastern and the Wilderness origins were blended together.

This multiple use to which the Joseph novelette is put should surely elicit our admiration for the planning mind behind the construction of the total Pentateuch. Yet we should admire no less the narrative skill within the Joseph story itself. An occasional scholar attributes certain episodes to preceding folktales—for example, the effort at seduction by Potiphar's wife. Possibly this is so. But the Joseph story is not at all an aggregate of sources; it is a fresh composition, reflecting a single author (except for later interpolations), an author of alertness, insight, and the highest artistry. The P compiler seems to have been able to include the Joseph novelette with scarcely any changes. It is sad not to know who the original author was, or any facts about him; perhaps, though, he would have preferred the preservation of his art to the preservation of his name.

In turning from Genesis to Exodus, we should strive to counteract the natural supposition that we are moving out of one book and into another. Genesis ends where it does simply because its bulk exhausted the usual, manageable parchment scroll. One should turn the page from Genesis to Exodus without any sense of having ended one item and begun a second; continuity is the keynote.

10. *Moses*

The account of Moses transcends in its grand conception even its remarkable array of perceptive and dramatic details. There are three principal characters: Moses, the people, and, of course, the Deity. The author's conception has imposed on him a task of greatest difficulty. Moses, of course, is the protagonist. Yet, strangely, the people of Israel are the essential antagonists, and, even so, the author must avoid making them into direct villains. The tension between Moses and the people of Israel at times rises almost to the breaking point; nevertheless, the people never lose the basic partisanship of the author.

The narration is interrupted by sections of legal materials, some short and some very long, and it is these, rather than narration itself, which fill most of the pages of Exodus, Leviticus, and Numbers. The closing chapter of Deuteronomy, equivalent to half a page, belongs with this basic narration, and not with Deuteronomy.

Consistent with what we have glimpsed already of the Hebrew mind, the author does not indulge himself in abstractions: he expresses his ideas through people and incidents. Abstract conceptions, however, dominate his narration, and these are, fortunately, clear enough so that we can view them quite unmistakably. Whereas Abraham, Isaac, Jacob, and the twelve sons are from time to time conceived of as symbols for their collective descendants, Moses, on the other hand, remains invariably an individual: the teacher, the leader, the prophet, and the lawgiver.

The author, we recall, began in Genesis with the story of man, universal man, and then narrowed his focus to the Hebrews, to the succession of the three founding patriarchs, Abraham, Isaac, and Jacob. He proceeded then to speak of the progenitors of twelve tribes, and even stated for us that at the time Jacob settled in Egypt, the number of Hebrews had risen to seventy. At the beginning of the account of Moses, their number has increased so greatly that the Hebrews are to be alluded to as an *'am*. This word we can readily translate as "nation," provided that we abstain from reading into the ancient Hebrew word those overtones which have clustered about the term "nation" in the past one hundred years.

While twelve tribes constituted this nation, the concern of the author was almost entirely with the entire nation, and not with the individual tribes. Hence the author uses over and over again the phrase "*all* the children of Israel." The original seventy, in the author's view, had grown into a nation by natural increase in Egypt in the period between Joseph's time and Moses. How long was it? Stray chronological notices in Scripture raise unimportant problems. The period in Egypt is set forth in Genesis XV as destined to endure for four hundred years, but, according to Exodus XII:40, it lasted 430 years; on the other hand, the genealogy of Moses makes him the fifth generation descended from Jacob, suggesting a period much less than four hundred years, perhaps one hundred and fifty. Never mind; the major intention of the author is to let us know that, in the interval between Joseph and Moses, the Hebrews had grown from seventy souls to very, very many; he gives the figure as 600,000, with only the males included in this amazing—and extravagant—sum total.

Jacob had been welcomed into Egypt by a hospitable Pharaoh; now, though, a new Pharaoh arose whose hateful attitude is clearly depicted in the telling phrase that he "knew not Joseph." This new, ungrateful, and wicked Pharaoh, fearful that the numerous Israelites resident within his borders might in time of war be disloyal to Egypt, made all the Hebrews into slaves, and he mistreated them and oppressed them. Nevertheless, the Hebrews kept increasing in numbers.

Sources external to the Bible as recovered so far by archeology have not contained any confirmation of the enslavement of the Hebrews in Egypt. There are those who wonder if it is a historical fact. Yet if one observes the tendency among ancient peoples to trace their ancestry back to gods and to an ancient age of great triumphs, then one is struck by the sharp contrast, for the Hebrews alone among the ancient peoples described their corporate origin in slavery. Indeed, the allusions to this origin occurs very often in the prophetic literature and the Psalms. Would an ancient people have created a fiction of slave ancestors? The bare fact of an enslavement of some kind ought not be doubted.

It would be reasonable to suppose that the increasing Hebrew people developed some kind of inner life in Egypt in four hundred years. The author tells us nothing of it; to the contrary, he supposes that virtually all the inner life of the people—organization, religious beliefs, and religious observances—awaited the period of the sojourn of the Wilderness. Hence, the Hebrews whom Moses freed were a shapeless people. Moses was necessarily a creative innovator; when he first led the Hebrews they had little more antecedent than the sense of a remote common ancestry from Abraham, Isaac, and Jacob, and the bitter, present experience of enslavement. Indeed, the Hebrews had as yet no God in any vivid, possessive sense, for though God had revealed Himself to Abraham, Isaac, and Jacob, He had not revealed Himself since their days. Moses started from almost bare beginnings.

The enslavement in Egypt is the prelude to the introduction of Moses. The full extent and cruel rigor of the enslavement are described in a few short lines. The immediate background of Moses' early life was a pitiless decree by the Pharaoh, that all the Hebrew male babes were to be thrown into the Nile. Moses was the third child of Amram and Jochebed, of the tribe of Levi. There were two older children: Miriam, who plays a role in the early account of Moses, and Aaron, who at this stage is given only a bare mention. Since the enslavement was total, our author had to account for the surprising circumstance that Moses escaped it. That came about in a wondrous way: Jochebed was able for a while to conceal the birth of Moses and to prevent his being cast into the Nile, but she could not continue to conceal him. When he was three months old, she made a tiny ark, waterproofed it, put the baby into it, and set the ark to float in the river Nile. The daughter of Pharaoh came to the Nile to bathe; she heard the baby cry. She quickly inferred that it was a Hebrew child; nevertheless, she decided to save it. We are not told why. Miriam had been stationed to watch what would happen; she approached the princess and proposed that a Hebrew woman be engaged to care for the child. That woman, by a pleasant coincidence, was no other than Moses' mother, Jochebed. The princess, indeed, paid the mother for rearing her own child!

We are given no information about Moses' youth. Our imaginations are left free to speculate about the early influence on him. One thing is clear, he continued to be free from the enslavement under which his fellow Hebrews groaned.

Quickly, though, we are led to a decisive incident. Moses saw an Egyptian task-master beating a Hebrew slave. He intervened to slay the Egyptian and hid the body in the sand. (By this incident we see that Moses has made the choice of where he was to fit.) Yet the next day—here the author shows one of his touches of genius—Moses saw two Hebrews fighting; he intervened to scold the aggressor. This man was the Hebrew slave whom Moses had saved from the Egyptian. Scornfully this man said to Moses, "Who made you a prince and a judge over us? Do you mean to kill me as you killed the Egyptian?" Moses now had reason to fear that his slaying of the Egyptian was becoming public property and, high as his position in the court may have been, he was in such potential danger from the Pharaoh that he fled the scene, and, indeed, fled from Egypt and from his enslaved fellow Hebrews. We should understand that this incident is important: it is a foreshadowing of the experiences which Moses was later to go through repeatedly with the Israelites, for in the Wilderness they would constantly reject his efforts to benefit them. The entire account of Moses, though it is dedicated to past glories, is by no means a glorification of the past; to the contrary, it is the story of a paradox; it is about a people who were sacred to the Deity, but who constantly fell short of the requisite sanctity. They acted like ordinary people, but the assumption of the author is that they had the obligation to be extraordinary. They were destined to conquer the land of Canaan, but they were in no sense to be ordinary conquerors, or to fashion a world empire as other ancient peoples did. They were to be extraordinary only in their sanctity, and it was herein that they repeatedly fell short.

Moses' flight led him to the land of Midian, an area south of the Dead Sea. (The Midianites were descendants of Abraham and Keturah.) At a well—the servant of Abraham, and Jacob himself, had also had incidents at a well—Moses rescued the seven daughters of the priest of Midian from some wicked people, and even drew water for them and watered their flocks. The daughters described him to their father as an Egyptian. The priest then welcomed Moses to a meal. Moses then settled there, and he married Zipporah, one of the seven daughters of the priest. (The priest is given four different names in Scripture: Reuel, Jethro, Jether, and Hobab.) From the union with Zipporah there was born a son, and he was given a significant name, Gershom, "a stranger in that place," for Moses was a stranger in an alien land.

A short paragraph underscores the meaning of Moses' settling in Midian and marrying there; he was estranged from his people. It tells that the Israelites continued to groan under the continuing oppression, and they cried out to God, and He heard their cry, and He remembered His covenants with Abraham, Isaac, and Jacob.

Moses had become a shepherd for his father-in-law. He led his sheep toward the "mountain of God, toward Horeb." (This mountain is more frequently known as Sinai.) At the mountain Moses saw a miraculous sight, a bush which burned yet was not consumed by the fire. When he determined to approach the bush, Yahve called to him, "Moses! Moses! Do not come here. Remove your shoes, for you are standing on sacred soil." (Bush in Hebrew is *sne*; some scholars see a pun in *sne* and Sinai.)

The dialogue between the Deity and Moses is remarkable, not only for what it contains, but also for its overtones. Two elements especially are to be noted. One is Moses' reluctance to accept a divine commission enjoined on him; this may readily call to our minds a similar reluctance on the part of Isaiah in Isaiah VI. The second we have alluded to before, that Yahve, despite His appearances in the past to Abraham, Isaac, and Jacob, is virtually completely unknown to the Hebrews! The two themes are brought together: Moses was enjoined to undertake a task for the Deity whom both he and his people know nothing about.

The Deity began by identifying Himself. "I am the God of your father, God of Abraham, God of Isaac, God of Jacob." Moses hid his face, fearful of looking at God. Yahve went on: "I have seen clearly the affliction of my people in Egypt. I have heard their outcries at their oppressors, for I know their pain. I shall descend to save the people from Egypt and bring them to the good and open land which flows with milk and honey. . . . Now I send you to Pharaoh; you shall bring my people out of Egypt."

Moses said, "Were I to come to the Israelites and say to them, 'The God of your fathers sent me to you,' they would say to me, 'What is His Name?'" (That is, the people would reply in some bewilderment.)

The direct reply was: "*Ehyeh asher Ehyeh.* Tell the Israelites that *Ehyeh* has sent you to them." The literal translation of *'ehyéh 'ashér 'ehyéh* is "I am (*ehyeh*) what (*asher*) I am (*ehyeh*)." The words "I am what I am" have been meditated over by countless generations of Jews and Christians, and they have stimulated fertile imaginations, and imaginative interpretations. The basic element here is a pun, linking *ehyeh* with the divine name *yahve*; it is designed to convey the basic meaning of *yahve*, "He who causes things to be." The author's procedure is, first, to give us the denotation of Yahve by means of this pun, and then only after that, in the next sentence, to give us the name *yahve* itself. Hence, the reply to the question, What is His name? runs as follows: "*Ehyeh asher ehyeh.* Tell the Israelites that *ehyeh* has sent you to them. This is what you shall say to the children of Israel, '*Yahve*, the God of your fathers, the God of Abraham, the God of Isaac, and the God of Jacob, has sent me to you.' This [Yahve] is My eternal name, and this is how I am to be known in generation after generation."

Now, Moses has said that the Israelites would ask the name of the Deity. The author, more for his late readers than for the Israelites in Egypt, first provides an explanatory pun, and then, *supposedly for the very first time*, reveals the hitherto unknown divine name Yahve. (There is a second version of the revelation of the divine name, in a P passage (Ex. VI:3); "I appeared to Abraham, Isaac, and Jacob in the form of *El Shaddai*, but I did not make myself known to them by my name Yahve.")

In all that has come before in Genesis, the Deity has abstained from disclosing His name. The author, as we have noted, has used the name, but the biblical persons ostensibly do not know the divine name until it is here revealed to Moses (though we have seen some inconsistencies in this). In Genesis, the Deity has, of course, acted repeatedly, but all this activity has been in advance of the moment at which the corporate body of the Hebrews was to receive the climactic disclosure. Hence, all that occurred before the age of Moses was in a sense preparatory, for it is now through the career of Moses that the Hebrews as a corporate body are to come to a clear and specific relationship with the Deity.

Reverting now to our account, Moses was enjoined to go to Egypt and tell the Israelite elders that Yahve had come to him; that he and the elders were then to go to the Pharaoh and tell him that Yahve had appeared to them; and that the Pharaoh—a new ruler, even more cruel than the one who had instituted the enslavement—would not hearken until after Yahve had smitten the Egyptians with His mighty arm. Then, after His wondrous deeds, the Hebrews would be able to leave—and not with empty hands.

To this Moses replied, "But maybe the Hebrews will not believe me, or listen to me. They will say, 'Yahve has not appeared to you.' " In reply, Yahve had Moses cast his rod on the ground, and it became a snake; when Moses took hold of the tail, the snake reverted into a rod. The purpose of this sign was that the people should believe that Yahve had indeed appeared to Moses. If, perhaps, this miracle might be insufficient to induce belief, a second miracle was available: the hand of Moses would become leprous, and then free of leprosy. Indeed, even a third miracle, the turning of the Nile into blood, was to be available to Moses.

Moses' reluctance nevertheless persisted. He was not, he said, a fluent man. Yahve said, "Who gave the tongue to man? I will

teach you what to say." Moses said, "Send someone else!" Yahve
became angry at Moses. "Your brother Aaron is fluent. He will
come out to meet you. You will tell him what to say, and he will
be your mouth, and you will be his instructor." (The author has
blended together, in his usual laconic manner, the highly important matters of the revelation of the divine name, Moses' reluctance, the disbelief which the Hebrews might exhibit, and the future adamancy of the Pharaoh.)

Moses returned to his father-in-law to tell him he was returning
to Egypt, and heard the encouraging reply, "Go in peace." He set
out on his journey with his wife[1] and his *sons*—the author has
slipped here, for the birth of a second son is as yet untold.

A short section foreshadows the future events in Egypt, which
would come to a climax with the death of all Egyptian firstborn
males; Israel is now likened to God's firstborn, for Pharaoh was
to be told, "Send forth *My* firstborn to worship Me: If you refuse, I will slay *your* firstborn."

The events which ensued in Egypt are so narrated as to stress
the great adamancy of Pharaoh, and the consequent succession
of ten plagues. We shall not follow these in detail. We should
notice, however, that Aaron, at the divine word, went out to meet
Moses at the mountain of the Deity (though how he left the enslavement in Egypt is not told us). Moses told Aaron all that
had occurred. The two then went to Egypt and assembled the
elders (who seemed to be free to assemble!); Aaron informed
them of all that Yahve had spoken to Moses, and Moses performed
the miracles so that the people would believe. (Old tradition
associated Aaron with Moses' activities; in the Pentateuch, Aaron
is portrayed as the ancestor of the priests; it was priests who were
the final creators of the Pentateuch. Modern scholars believe that
the role of Aaron in many passages results from a late, literary
expansion of his role by the priestly writer; they believe that evidence for this is discernible in certain repeated insertions, exemplified by that in X: 1-3: "Yahve said to Moses, 'Go in to Pharaoh.'
. . . So Moses *and Aaron* went in to Pharaoh." That is, the name
of Aaron was inserted into some older materials; at the same
time, newer materials, either freshly created works or total re-

writings of older passages, tend to shift some of the focus from Moses to Aaron.)

Before the Pharaoh, Moses and Aaron said, "Yahve, the God of Israel, has said, 'Send out My people and let them observe a sacred day to Me in the Wilderness.'" Pharaoh said, "Who is Yahve that I should obey him? I do not know Yahve. I will not send Israel out." (If the Hebrews have not heard Yahve's name, naturally the Pharaoh too has not.) They replied, "The God of the Hebrews encountered us. We would make a three-day journey into the Wilderness and offer sacrifices to Yahve."

The Egyptian king said, "Why, Moses and Aaron, are you interrupting the work of the people? Go to your chores!" Then the Pharaoh instructed the officials to cease to supply the straw for the bricks; the Hebrews were to gather it, and, despite this additional burden, they were to produce just as many bricks as they had when the straw was supplied. If the burdens were severe enough on them, they would not turn to the falsehoods told them by Moses and Aaron. The officials complied, so that the Hebrews had to go out to gather straw. The Hebrew overseers, appointed by the Egyptians, were beaten because the quantity of bricks declined. They complained to Pharaoh in vain. Then they met Moses and Aaron. "Why have you damaged us with Pharaoh and his servants? May Yahve see and judge you for damaging us with Pharaoh and his officials!"

Moses said to Yahve, "Lord, why have You done harm to this people, and why have You sent me? Since I came to speak in Your name to the Pharaoh, he has done greater harm to the people, and You have not yet saved Your people." (Moses is recurrently discouraged by the responses of the Israelites.) Yahve said, "Now you will see what I shall do to Pharaoh." Yet when Moses conveyed this new promise of divine help to the Hebrews, the latter were so beset by "shortness of breath and hard work" that they would not listen. When Yahve next said to Moses, "Go tell Pharaoh to send the children of Israel away," Moses said, "The children of Israel do not listen to me; how then will Pharaoh listen?"

Now the plagues were about to begin. Aaron cast his rod before

Pharaoh and it became a crocodile; the Egyptian magicians cast their rods, and these also became crocodiles, but Aaron's rod swallowed the rods of the Egyptians. Nevertheless, the Pharaoh would not release the Hebrews.

Thereupon the succession of ten plagues came. When a particular plague was at its height, the Pharaoh was usually prepared to release the Hebrews; promptly, though, he changed his mind. A curiously repeated motif explains the change of mind: Yahve hardened the Pharaoh's heart. To modern readers it could thereby readily appear that Yahve, as it were, was working against His own interest, in that if the plagues were brought upon Egypt to coerce the Pharaoh, the hardening of his heart only stiffened his resistance. In explanation, we must remember something we have touched on before, that Yahve controls all the events of history; hence, if the Pharaoh changed his mind, it was Yahve who caused this change of mind.

The plagues culminated in a climactic tenth plague, the slaying of the firstborn, but there does not seem to be any direct ascent toward this climax, since the plagues, except for the last, seem all to be on the same plane. There are some incidental matters, however, which do contribute to the sense of rising action. The Egyptian magicians were able to duplicate the wonders wrought by Moses in the first three plagues—blood in the waters, frogs, and lice—but at the third plague they were moved to recognize in Moses' actions the "finger of God." After this, the magicians appear only in the sixth plague, there not to duplicate the acts of Moses, but only to admit their inability to withstand the divine punishment (IX:11). In the eighth plague, it is Pharaoh's servants, not the magicians, who express the growing Egyptian despair; by now the magicians seem to have been completely defeated. From another standpoint, the Hebrews, living in the province of Goshen, are unmentioned in the first three plagues, but we are told that the fourth was swarms of flies, and that the region of Goshen escaped that misfortune; the fifth plague, infections, we are told the Hebrews escaped. The ninth plague, darkness, was felt only by the Egyptians; the Hebrews experienced light. The seventh and eighth plagues, hail and locusts, are described (IX:24 and X:6) as unprecedented in all of Egyptian history.

The purpose of the plagues was not only to bring release to the Hebrews, but to force the Pharaoh to move from his contemptuous earlier words, "Who is Yahve?," to admitting that he has now learned who Yahve is. Thus, at the first plague the Pharaoh seems indifferent; at the second he seems prepared to release the Hebrews the next day. At the fourth, he gives permission for the Hebrews to go, but then reverses himself. At the seventh, he admits that "Yahve is righteous," but Moses comments that as yet the Egyptians do not fear Yahve; at the eighth the Pharaoh is prepared for the adult males among the Hebrews to go, and at the ninth, he is willing for all the Hebrews to go, provided they leave their flocks and herds behind.

What most clearly informs us that we are approaching the climax is the transition from the ninth to the tenth plague. The Hebrews, barely mentioned in the course of the earlier plagues, were now enjoined (Ex. XI) to prepare for the last of the plagues, for it would bring their release. All Egypt would suffer from the death of the firstborn children, but the Hebrews, and even their animals, would escape it. In anticipation of their release, the Hebrews were to "borrow" from their Egyptian neighbors vessels of silver and gold; in view of the eminence that Moses had achieved, the Egyptians would graciously provide these "loans."

The release was to be an event of such consequence that later generations would need to commemorate it. Toward that end, there are provided (in Ex. XII), *for the first time in the Pentateuch*, precise legal injunctions, which are depicted as coming from the Deity. On the tenth day of that month (identified as the *first* month of the calendar year), the male head of every household was to procure a lamb, though poorer people could share a lamb with neighbors. They would hold the lamb until the fourteenth day, and then slaughter it at twilight, and smear its blood on the two doorposts and on the lintel of the door. They would then roast the lamb and eat it, along with *matzo* ("unleavened bread") and bitter herbs, the latter in recollection of the bitterness of the enslavement. Moreover, when eating it, they were to have their girdles fastened, their shoes on their feet, and their staffs in their hands—as if prepared for a journey. They should eat this *Passover* meal in haste, for in the middle of the night Yahve would go through the land to bring the Egyptians to justice; the blood on the doorposts would identify Hebrew homes, so that Yahve would *pass over* these; the pun, Passover and pass over, is in the Hebrew. (We should notice that we encounter here the prescriptions for the annual celebration of an event which is soon to take place, but has not yet occurred.) The prescriptions are quite specific for the future annual week of observance. Indeed, they require that at some future time, when children would ask, "What is the meaning of this observance?" they were to be told, "This is the Passover sacrifice to Yahve, who passed over the houses of the children of Israel in Egypt when he smote the Egyptians, but spared our houses."

Modern research has established that the festival of Passover has a long history, stretching far back into antiquity. Indeed, the evidence suggests that two quite different festivals[2] were blended together, the first being the pastoral Passover of the sacrifice of the lamb, and the second the agricultural Matzoth festival, which celebrated the first growth of grain. The bond between the composite festival and the events in Egypt, though ancient, was a secondary development, a product of a marked tendency in the Pentateuch respecting *all* the festivals to set forth some connection with a significant ancient event; that is to say, the Hebrews first had their festivals, and only after having them did they attribute historical, commemorative bases to them. Such attribution of a commemorative purpose to the festivals was entirely consistent with their view of history as disclosing the activities of God.

Modern scholars usually view the chapter enjoining the observance of the Passover as a relatively late bit of writing, a P passage younger than the narration itself. If this is indeed the case, all the more does the skill of the final author emerge, in that the Passover legislation intensifies the mounting climax of the events in Egypt. If, as some scholars suggest, the entire narrative was designed to be either read or acted out at a sanctuary—I doubt the latter—then the brief passage relating to the question that children would ask suggests that the purpose of the celebration was not so much to hearken back to the past as to renew faith in God in every succeeding generation.

At midnight, Yahve slew all the firstborn of Egypt; from the royal palace to the humblest prison, no Egyptian house escaped. A great outcry arose, and the Pharaoh summoned Moses and Aaron at night. His capitulation was complete. The Hebrews were all to go, and they were even to take their flocks with them. He added to his words of surrender, "Bless me also."

Perhaps one should notice an interesting bit of variation. In some passages the Hebrews, through Moses, ask for permission to leave Egypt; in other passages, especially at the end of the account (and in later recollection), the assumption is that they were driven out. Indeed, the origin of the eating of the Matzo supposes that the haste of the departure—making it impossible to allow time for the dough to rise, so that the bread was eaten unleavened—is evidence that they were driven out.

The Hebrews journeyed quickly across the Egyptian desert toward the Sea of Reeds. Their number is given as 600,000, but these were men; there were, besides, women and children, and, also, some people called "a mixed multitude," but not further identified. These numbers can raise legitimate questions of the logistics both at the Exodus and in the subsequent Wilderness wandering, but when used by people who had no bent for abstractions they should be understood as only signifying a great abundance.

One last event closes the account of the sojourn in Egypt, the crossing of the Sea of Reeds (usually, and wrongly, called "the Red Sea" in English translations; the Sea of Reeds is a shallow body of water west of the Suez-Sinai peninsula; the Red Sea is east of Sinai). It is likely that some reliable historical reminiscence lies behind the account of the fording of the water; the biblical author, however, has imaginatively embroidered the account. The Israelites journeyed, we are told, across the Egyptian wilderness toward the water. They were led miraculously, by a pillar of cloud in the daytime and a pillar of fire at night, and also by an angel of God, who at times went ahead of them and at times protected their rear. The Egyptians were aware of their zig-zagging route, but they wrongly concluded that the Hebrews were astray and lost in the wilderness sands. The Pharaoh, now regretting that he had sent away his slaves, marshaled his six hundred chariots, and, indeed, all the chariots in Egypt, assigned them to the charge of his officers, and sent them in pursuit. The Egyptians began to overtake the Hebrews, who were encamped near the water. When the Hebrews saw the approaching Egyptians they became terrified. To Moses they complained—the first of many subsequent complaints: "Is it because of an insufficiency of graves in Egypt that you brought us into the wilderness to die? Did we not ask you in Egypt to desist? It would have been better to be enslaved in Egypt than to perish in the wilderness!"

Moses replied, "Rise up and see Yahve's rescue. The Egyptians you see now, you will never see again. Yahve will battle for you, and you need only keep silent." Yahve said to Moses, "Tell the children of Israel to move forward."

Perhaps the kernel of historical truth is contained in a verse (XIV:21) which tells that an east wind drove away the water, so that the Hebrews could cross on foot, while the Egyptian chariots would become mired in the mud. But the author tells us that it was Yahve who caused the opportune east wind to blow. Moreover, the angel of Yahve stationed himself between the Hebrews and the Egyptians, preventing the Egyptians from making an onslaught.

When the Hebrews began to cross, Moses stretched forth his hand, and the waters separated and formed walls on both sides of them. The Egyptian chariots moved forward, but Yahve impeded the wheels so that the chariots scarcely moved. The Egyptians then wanted to flee, for they knew that Yahve was fighting for the Israelites against them. At Yahve's word, Moses again stretched forth his hand over the sea; now the waters returned to their channel, and drowned the Egyptians. The Hebrews saw the great deliverance, and they revered Yahve.

And they believed in Yahve and in his servant Moses. (The plagues and the miraculous rescue had brought the Israelites from not knowing Yahve to having faith in Him.)

The author now cites two poems, one that is purported to have been sung by Moses and the children of Israel, and the other, a single couplet, sung by Miriam. She appears here unexpectedly, for the author has let us lose sight of her. The purpose of the poems, even beyond celebrating the deliverance, is to underscore the statement that the Israelites believed in Yehve *and* in his servant Moses. The author has presented primarily an account of the actions of God, yet Moses is at all times involved in the working out of what God does; indeed, when once Moses arrives in Egypt, he is at all times only God's agent, and he seems not to act at all on his own. Yet once the exodus has taken place, more and more responsibility seems to fall directly upon Moses.

Moses led the Hebrews away from the sea, into the desert, where they faced shortages of water and danger from foes. At every hardship they murmured against Moses. When they moved into the wilderness of Sin, they complained: "Would that we had died in Egypt where we sat by the fleshpots and ate our fill of bread!" They journeyed on to Rephidim, where there were two places, *Massah*, "testing," and *Meribah*, "quarreling," so called because the people had tested Yahve and had quarreled with Him.

The Amalekites, a desert people, attacked them. Moses designated Joshua—here mentioned for the first time—to choose men to fight the foe. Moses, Aaron, and a man named Hur, ascended a hill to watch the battle. When Moses raised his hand, Israel prevailed; when he lowered it, Amalek prevailed. Moses grew weary; he sat on a rock, and Aaron and Hur held up his hands. Joshua conquered the Amalekites. A war of extermination against the Amalekites[3] was thereupon enjoined. Now Jethro, the father-in-law of Moses, came to visit and to bring to Moses his wife Zip-

porah and his two sons, Gershom and Eliezer. Moses narrated to
Jethro all that Yahve had done in Egypt, and all the hardship of
their journey. Jethro exclaimed, "Blessed is Yahve who saved you
from Egypt and from Pharaoh. . . . Now I know that Yahve
is greater than all the gods!"

When, on the next day, Moses sat to judge disputes between
litigants from morning until night, Jethro chided him: "What
you are donig is not good. You will wear out yourself and the
people, for you cannot do this alone. You need to represent the
people to Yahve and to bring [undecided] cases to Him. You
should teach the people the statutes and laws and the way in
which they are to walk and the deeds they are to do. But you
must select worthy, pious people, who are trustworthy and impossible to bribe, and appoint them as officials for groups of
thousands, hundreds, fifties, and tens. Let them be the usual
judges, bringing to you the great matters, but settling the minor
ones themselves." (In this advice of Jethro lies the epitome of
Moses' significant achievement.) Through this narrative our author has told us about a specific body of laws.

The Hebrews arrived in the Wilderness of Sinai three months
after leaving Egypt, and they encamped near the sacred mountain. Moses then ascended Mount Sinai. Yahve spoke to him:
"Tell the Israelites that they have seen what I did to the Egyptians and that I brought you here, as on the wings of an eagle. If,
now, you obey Me and keep My covenant, you will be My special possession out of all the peoples of the earth. The whole
earth is mine, but you will be My kingdom of priests and My
holy people." Moses then returned and spoke to the leaders, putting Yahve's words before them. They all answered, "We shall do
all that Yahve has said!" Moses brought this word to Yahve.
(That is to say, the conditions of the covenant had been agreed
to; now the covenant itself was to come.)

Yahve said to Moses, "I will come to you in a thick cloud; the
people will hear me speak to you, and they will believe you forever." Moses reported this to the people. Yahve said to him further, "Today and tomorrow sanctify the people; have them wash

their clothes. The day after tomorrow, I, Yahve, will descend onto Mount Sinai, in the sight of all the people. Set boundaries so that no one will prematurely ascend even the edges of the mountain; anyone, man or beast, who does shall be put to death." Moses conveyed these instructions to the people, adding that no man should touch a woman.

On the third day, there was thunder and lightning, and a thick cloud descended on the mountain. The trumpet sounded, and the people, gathered in the camp, began to tremble. Moses then led them out of the camp, to the foot of the mountain. Mount Sinai was enveloped in smoke, for Yahve was descended on it in fire; the smoke ascended as if from a kiln, and the whole mountain trembled. Yahve summoned Moses, and Moses ascended.[4] Yahve said to him, "Go down and warn the people, lest they press forward to see, and many of them perish. Go down [for the present]; when you come up again, bring Aaron with you." Moses went down, and he spoke the words which God had spoken.

Those words were the Ten Commandments, the substance of the covenant between Yahve and Israel. The one party to the covenant was Yahve: "I am Yahve your God, Who brought you out of Egypt, out of the house of bondage." The other party was the people of Israel, upon whom were enjoined these requirements:

I. You shall have no god besides me.
II. You shall not make any carved image, or any representation of any kind, nor bow to them and worship them.
III. You shall not invoke the name of Yahve your God in any untrue oath.
IV. Remember the Sabbath to sanctify it.
V. Honor your father and mother.
VI. You shall not kill.
VII. You shall not be adulterous.
VIII. You shall not steal.
IX. You shall not testify falsely against your fellowman.
X. You shall not covet the possessions of your fellowmen.

Some of these commandments are stated laconically; others appear to have been expanded from statements that were originally laconic. (In a second version of the Ten Commandments, in Deuteronomy V, some, such as the fourth, are even more greatly expanded.)

The completion of the covenant, interrupted in the text by the presence of additional legislation,[5] appears presently (in XXIV: 3): "The people answered with one voice, saying, 'We shall carry out all the commandments of Yahve.' Moses then wrote down the commandments. The next morning, he built an altar at the foot of the mountain, setting up twelve pillars, one for each of the tribes. Burnt offerings and peace offerings were sacrificed. Moses collected the blood of the animals into basins, throwing half of the blood on the altar. He then read, in the hearing of the people, the *'book of the covenant,'* which he had written down. They said, 'All that Yahve has spoken we will carry out and will be obedient.' Moses then threw the remainder of the blood upon the people, saying 'This is the blood of the covenant which Yahve has made with you and these are the terms.' "

The unity of the totality is somewhat disturbed by the intrusion of the legislation, but we can nevertheless see the main sequence of the events: Moses brought the people to the sacred mountain,[6] prepared them for the covenant, then read it to them and received their assent; thereafter he wrote it down, and led them through a ceremony of ratification, during which he again read the specific terms, and again the people ratified it, and then he completed the ceremony.

What is the meaning of the Sinai episode? In answer, we can deal with three ingredients. One is an ancient Hebrew tradition that in the distant southern desert there was a sacred mountain at which it was the practice of the Deity to reveal Himself. This ancient tradition persisted even after another view arose, that Yahve dwelled in Heaven and was not limited to the mountain in the Wilderness. Second, there was an inherited tradition that the tie which bound Yahve to His people was expressed in a covenant. The writings of the prophets especially allude to the covenant, usually without specifying its contents, for these were presumed known. Third, there was the significant development in the history of the Hebrews that when the Babylonians conquered the land, in the sixth century B.C., the Hebrew monarchy ended. The Babylonians exiled the people, and when, under the Persians, the people returned from exile in Babylon, they were ruled by a high priest, not by a king. Though there was this shift of rulers, laws already well known abided, but, since they were now administered by priests, these inherited laws, whatever their origin, now came to be conceived of as divinely revealed to the priests. Sinai answers the questions, where and when and how did the Hebrews first receive their divinely revealed laws? The Sinai episode, then, is an account of origins. People, then as now, wished to know what authority was behind the laws; the Sinai episode supplied the answer.

If the question is asked, how historical is Sinai, then one must first assert that this is a modern question, not an ancient one. The sharp division between pure history and legend which the modern mind makes was foreign to the Hebrew mind. The Hebrews shaped the elaborated account of Moses at Sinai out of inherited ancient materials, and they accepted the account.

The vivid depiction of the act of revelation at Sinai, with the thunder and lightning and earthquake, is of a piece with the similar descriptions elsewhere in the Bible about the revealing act of Yahve. To the Hebrew mind these phenomena lent awe and majesty to the important event of God's self-disclosure.

However often minor inconsistencies or inserted materials intrude into the unity of the Sinai episode, the author's major conception still successfully dominates the account, that Moses led a formless and shapeless people to the sacred mountain and that there he inducted them into a covenant with the Deity, through whose commandments they became a sacred people. In the view of the author, however, Sinai was not in itself an end, or the final goal; rather, Sinai was what transformed a rabble into a unique people.

But how successfully, from the standpoint of the author, did Sinai transform the people? Few insights in any literature seem to me as perceptive as what this author now unfolds for us. After the covenant was concluded, Moses ascended the mountain again, and he stayed there for forty days and nights, to receive more divine regulations (XXV: 1–XXXI: 17), devoted primarily to the instruments of paraphernalia to be used in the cult worship. When Yahve finished speaking with Moses on the peak of Mount Sinai, He gave him "two tables of Testimony," which attested to the covenant, these written on stone (XXXI: 18). But, below, at the foot of the mountain, the people, perturbed that Moses was away so long and not knowing what might have happened to him, gathered about Aaron, demanding that he should make some god for them. Thereupon, in utter infidelity to Yahve, Aaron made a golden calf, and set it up as an idol. Thus, the direct sequel to the transforming covenant was the most extreme violation of it, abetted, and even led, by Moses' own brother, Aaron.

On the mountain, Yahve disclosed to Moses that this horrendous act of infidelity was taking place, and He told him that people were saying of the calf, "This is your god, O Israel, who brought you up out of the land of Egypt." Yahve then said to Moses, "Let me destroy them in my great wrath, and raise a new nation out of you!" To this Moses said, placatingly, "The Egyptians will scorn what You have done, contending that You brought forth the pepole to slay them in the mountains, and to consume them off the face of the earth. Turn away from your anger! Leave off this evil against your people! Remember Abraham, Isaac, and Israel, Your servants to whom You swore to multiply their descendants and to give them a land to inherit forever." Yahve thereupon abandoned His intention to do this evil. (Here we are being told not only of Moses' magnanimity, but of the baseness of the people.)

When Moses descended and came near the camp, he heard the sound of singing, and then he saw the calf and the people dancing around it. In anger, he threw down the two tablets and they broke into pieces. Punishment came; the traditions of it given here are diverse. According to one tradition, the Levites—mentioned here as a group for the first time—went among the people, who were out of control, and slew three thousand of them; by this action the tribe of Levi merited a special holy rank for the future. Another tradition supposes that Moses ground up the golden calf into powder, mixed it with water, and made the Israelites drink the mixture; those who thereafter became sick merited being put to death. Still another tradition, probably ironic, attempts to exculpate Aaron by having him give the naïve explanation that, on gathering from the people the golden ornaments with which to make the idol, he cast them into the fire, and the golden calf emerged as of itself.[7]

There next ensues a narrative remarkable in its naïveté and, at the same time, in its didactic skill. Yahve commanded Moses to lead the people on to the land of Canaan. Moses replied, "You tell me to lead this people on, but You have not told me whom You will send with me to lead the way."

Yahve said, "My face will go with you."

Moses said, "If your face does not come along, do not take us along from here. You must show that I and the people have merited Your favor by coming with us."

Yahve said, "This I will do." Moses said, "Show me your face."[8]

He said, "You cannot see my face, for no man can see my face and live. But here is a place by me; you may stand on the rock. I shall set you in a cleft of the rock; when my face[9] passes it, I shall put the palm of my hand over it. You will see my back, but not my face."

Some disorder in the narration intervenes. The sequel narrates that, as arranged, Moses was in the cleft of the rock, and Yahve passed by it, identifying Himself in these words: "Yahve, Yahve, a God merciful and gracious, slow to anger, but abundant in reliability and truth, who preserves His reliability for thousands, who forgives iniquity, trespass, and sin, yet without ignoring guilt, punishing sons, grandsons, and greatgrandsons for the sins of the forebears."

The naïveté in the story consists in Moses' request to see the divine face, and seeing, at the end, the back of Yahve. The didactic element is twofold. The first is the theological formulation which asserts that Yahve is forgiving and forbearing, but capable of sternness. The second is the clear assertion that Yahve is not visible as idols are, and it is this that was the point of the now-expanded narrative. The matured view in Scripture is that Yahve is totally without form and body, and hence not visible. Prophets such as Amos (IX:1) and Isaiah (VI:1) report having seen visions of Yahve. Exodus XXIV:9-11 states that Moses and those who ascended Sinai with him "saw the God of Israel." In Num. XII:8, Moses is described as one who sees the divine countenance, and in Deut. XXXIV:10, we are told that Yahve spoke to him "face to face." Our author is here denying, through this account, that such visions, whether told of Amos or Moses, are to be taken literally. Perhaps a less naïvely-told story would not have included a vision of the Deity's back. Nevertheless, the story makes the point quite clearly that, unlike the golden calf, the Deity is invisible. (An unresolved contradiction abides between this narrative and the two later assertions that Moses did see Yahve's face.)

The material just above, which has seemed out of order, narrates that, with the first tablets of stone broken, Yahve commanded Moses to prepare two new tablets and to ascend the mountain, so that a new covenant could replace the earlier one eradicated by the incident of the golden calf. Now a new element is introduced into the account, an injunction for the future: When the Hebrews will have come into Canaan, whose six nations would ultimately be driven out, it will be essential to make no covenant with them, for they could thereby become a snare to the Hebrews, diverting them from their loyalty solely to Yahve. The Canaanite altars should be torn down, and their *asherim* ("sacred poles") destroyed, lest the Hebrews succumb to their

idolatry; indeed, intermarriage with these natives was to be pro-
hibited, for it could surely lead to apostasy. Yahve's name is Jealous, for He is a jealous God, insisting on exclusive loyalty.[10]
(How easy it has been for usual readers, or even students, of
Scripture to be blind to the intolerance and cruelties here
sanctioned!)

Moses descended from the mountain, not knowing that his skin
had become radiant.[11] The Israelites were fearful of approaching
him. Moses conveyed to them what Yahve had said, and then he
put a veil over his face. It became the usual procedure that when
Moses came before Yahve, he removed the veil, and that when he
came before the people to speak to them, he restored it.

Narration up to this point has dominated the account, even
though we have encountered several instances of brief, or even
extended, legal sections. From Exodus XXXV, and throughout
Leviticus and through Numbers X, it is legislation which dominates; in this long portion the narration is both sporadic and brief.
Exodus XXV-XXXI consist of instructions to Moses for the cult
observances; Exodus XXXV-XL depict the carrying out of the
instructions. Leviticus and Numbers I-X extend the cult legislation.

Only two narratives are found in Leviticus. One (Lev. I-IX)
deals with the investiture of Aaron as the first high priest. By this
account the office of high priest is traced back to the Wilderness
period and to the eminent brother of Moses, as is also the institution of an array of repetitive animal sacrifices. The other narrative (Lev. X:1-4) is a curious one. Two sons of Aaron, Nadab
and Abihu, took each his fire-pan, put fire and incense on it, and
offered unholy fire to Yahve. From the Deity there came forth
sacred fire which killed them. This strange story is held by some
to account for the curious development that the line of high
priesthood went through Aaron's third son Eleazar, rather than
one of the two older sons. As to the unholy fire, students of folklore explain that among Semitic peoples there was a view that on
the spring and fall equinoxes, sacred fire descended from the
Deity and kindled the altar; Nadab and Abihu would appear to

have trespassed by offering man-made fire. Later legislation erased the supposition of the descent of sacred fire (an aspect of sun worship) through commanding that the fire on the altar needed to burn perpetually.

The narration resumes in Numbers XI. Eleven months have elapsed since the arrival at Sinai, and during that time the cult paraphernalia have been made. These included the movable shrine (called both the Tent of Meeting and, by P, the Tabernacle) wherein there was the Ark of the Covenant in which the two stone tablets were kept. The march from Sinai to Canaan was about to begin, with the Ark of the Covenant going before the people to ensure their military victory.

But when at last the journey resumed, immediately the complaints of the people arose again: "Who will give us meat? We remember the free fish we ate in Egypt, and the cucumbers, and melons, and leeks, and onions and garlic. We feel so flat, with nothing to look at but the manna." Yahve was very angry at this. Moses was greatly disturbed, and he said to Him, "Why have You put such a burden on me? Have I no favor in Your eyes? Did I give birth to this people, did I bear them? Why do You ask me to carry them in my bosom as a nurse carries a nursing child?"

Yahve replied, "Select seventy leaders and bring them to the Tent of Meeting. I will descend to speak to you there. Some of the spirit which I put on you, I will take away and put on them, so that they may share in your burden." The divine spirit fell on the seventy, so that they were able to prophesy. Two men, Eldad and Medan, were to have been among the seventy who assembled at the Tent of Meeting, but they had remained in the camp; even so, the divine spirit fell upon them, too. A young man came to Moses, telling him that Eldad and Medad were prophesying in the midst of the camp. Joshua advised Moses to stop them. Moses said, "Would that all the people of Yahve were prophets!"

This episode is important. One element is, of course, the renewed complaint of the people. The other element is the question of ongoing prophecy. Though we are not told so here specifically, we are approaching the end of the career of Moses. Joshua is to succeed him, but in turn Joshua's career was also to be limited in time. While the episode suggests no more than that the divine spirit *at that time* ceased to rest on Moses alone and came to rest on others, the implication is clearly that, subsequent to Moses and Joshua, the divine spirit would rest on certain prophets, so that in the future the people would not be bereft of divine guidance.[12]

Still in the same context of Moses' discomfitures, he went through a most bitter experience. Aaron, his brother, and Miriam, his sister, spoke against him because of his wife.[13] Moreover, they asked, "Is Moses the only one through whom Yahve has spoken? He has spoken through us too!" Yahve heard this. Abruptly, He summoned the three of them to the Tent of Meeting. Yahve called to Aaron and Miriam from the pillar of cloud:

> "Hear My words.
> If someone is a prophet,
> I make Myself known to him in a vision,
> In a dream I speak to him.
> Not so with my servant Moses.
> In all My house no one is as reliable as he.
> I speak to him mouth to mouth,
> Clearly, and never in riddles.
> He is allowed to see My form."[14]

(Prophets would indeed arise, but none would have the stature of Moses.) Miriam immediately became leprous, as white as snow, and was banished from the camp, as a matter of shame, for seven days.[15] On her being re-admitted, the people moved on, and they next encamped in the Wilderness of Paran.

Yahve instructed Moses to send men, one from each of the twelve tribes, to spy out the land of Canaan. All their names are given, but we need to notice only two, Joshua and Caleb, the latter of the tribe of Judah. After forty days, the spies returned with a report, and they also brought back some grapes, pomegranates, and figs. The land of Canaan, they reported, was indeed flowing in milk and honey. The residents, though, were strong, and their cities were fortified. Caleb spoke of his confidence in the Israelites' ability to conquer the land. The others, except for Joshua, disputed him, arguing that the Canaanites were too strong. The people were frightened, and they murmured against Moses. It would have been better, they said, to have died in Egypt or in the Wilderness; indeed, it would be better to go back to Egypt. The cry arose, "Let us choose a leader, and return to Egypt."

The assembly seemed about to stone Moses, Aaron, Joshua, and Caleb. Then the fiery radiance[16] of Yahve appeared to all the Israelites at the Tent of Meeting. Yahve said to Moses, "How long will this people scorn Me? How long will they persist in not believing in Me, despite the miraculous signs I have done in their midst? Let Me strike them with a pestilence; let Me disinherit them, and make you a greater and stronger nation."

Moses said: "If You now slay this people at one stroke, then the nations who have heard of Your fame will say, 'Yahve did not have the power to bring this people to the land He swore was theirs, so He slaughtered them in the Wilderness.' Forgive the trespass of this people according to the magnitude of Your constancy, just as You have forgiven this people from Egypt unto this place."

Yahve said, "I forgive, as you ask. Yet I swear that these people shall not see the land I swore to give their fathers. Only Caleb and Joshua shall see it. . . . All the others will perish in the Wilderness. Your children will come to know the land which you yourselves have despised." The spies who made the discouraging report died in a plague sent by Yahve. The next morning the people initiated a move to journey on to Canaan, but Moses informed them that they had lost Yahve's protection. Then the Amalekites and the Canaanites attacked the Israelites and defeated them, pursuing them to Hormah.[17]

Thereafter a full-fledged rebellion against the leadership of

Moses and Aaron took place. Indeed, two rebellions seem reflected in Numbers XVI; this account is not well unified, and it has a diversity of endings. The rebels were Korah, a cousin of Moses and hence a Levite, and some Reubenites.[18] The Levite rebellion would appear to have involved the privileged sacred role of the Levites, while the Reubenite rebellion was more secular. Earlier, in Exodus XXXII, the Levites had been set aside as a tribe of sacred workers. The Levite rebels, well-known leaders, assembled against Moses and Aaron, saying, "You take too much to yourselves. All the people are holy and Yahve is in their midst; why have you elevated yourselves over the people?" Moses said, "Tomorrow morning Yahve will disclose who are His, and who is holy, and whom He chooses to approach Him. You, Korah, and all your people, bring each of your fire-pans here before Yahve, with incense on them. In the morning Yahve will select the person sacred to Him. . . ." So much, for the moment, of the Levite rebellion; it appears to be directed against the special role of the priests, who were a single family within the tribe of Levi.

The account goes on to say that Moses summoned the Reubenites, Dathan and Abiram, to him, but they refused to obey him.

The story now seems to veer back to Korah the Levite. The next morning, when they all were gathered at the Tent of Meeting, the fiery radiance of Yahve appeared. Yahve said to Moses and Aaron, "Stand apart from the assembly, for I shall destroy them in a single instant."

The two accounts then become for the moment united. Yahve said to Moses, "Instruct the assembly to move away from near the dwellings of Korah, Dathan, and Abiram." Moses did so. Then the Reubenites, Dathan and Abiram, together with their wives and children and babes, came out of their dwellings. The ground opened up and swallowed them and their households alive. The Israelites fled from the vicinity.

We seem then to return to the Korah strand of the story again. Fire came from Yahve and consumed the Levites with their fire-pans. Aaron's son Eleazar gathered the fire-pans out of the blaze, and hammered them into a covering for the altar; the covering became a reminder for the Israelites that only one who was a descendant of Aaron,[19] and no other, should approach the altar to offer incense.

The next day, the Israelites complained that Moses and Aaron had caused the deaths of the adherents of Korah. Yahve sent a plague on the people; at Moses' request Aaron made expiation for this new trespass by the complainants, but not until fourteen thousand seven hundred perished in the plague. (The incident seems designed to emphasize the role of the priests in expiating the trespass of the people.) Yahve wished the complaints to cease. He therefore had a representative of every tribe deposit his staff, with his name written on it, in the Tent of Meeting; Aaron was to be the representative of the tribe of Levi. The following day Aaron's staff had sprouted, blossomed, and bore ripe almonds. The other staffs were returned to their owners, but Aaron's remained in the Tent of Meeting, before the Ark, as a sign of the eternal authority of Aaron's descendants. (Perhaps the rebellion of Dathan and Abiram is an old tradition, onto which was engrafted the Levite rebellion, this to emphasize the authority of the priests over the Levites.)

The narration now resumes (XX:1). Miriam died at Kadesh, and was buried there. Again there was no water, and again the Israelites complained. Yahve instructed Moses to assemble the people and Aaron; he was to take his rod with him, and speak to a rock, from which water would then flow. But instead of speaking to the rock, Moses struck it twice with the rod. Though water flowed from the rock, Yahve said to Moses and Aaron, "Because you did not trust Me in showing My holiness to the people, you will not bring them into the land I have given them."

This is surely a strange narrative, and the punishment on Moses seems completely out of proportion to the trespass. We have read about the death of Miriam, and a half-page further on we will read of the death of Aaron; the implication appears to be that the forty years of wandering in the Wilderness are now ending. The entire adult generation, as we recall, was to pass away. Possibly this story explains the tradition which ascribed leadership to Moses in the Wilderness, but named Joshua as the leader of the invasion of Canaan. This story seems to answer that implied question, what happened to Moses? The author, unhappily for us, ends the incident without describing Moses' reaction.[20]

Moses had sent emissaries to the king of Edom, asking for permission to pass through his territory. The Edomites refused, and they mustered an army to prevent the passage of the Israelites. At the border of Edom, Aaron died, and his robes as high priest were given to his son Eleazar. We read now of a defeat of Canaanite attackers at *Hormah* ("destruction") where earlier (p. 140) the Israelites were defeated (Num. XIV:39-45). The Hebrews, denied passage through Edom, had to go around it, by journeying far to the south and then to the east. On this journey there were yet again complaints about the lack of food and water. In punishment Yahve sent a plague of fiery serpents which bit the people. Moses prayed to Yahve. He said to Moses, "Make a bronze serpent, and put it on a pole. A man who has been bitten may cure himself by looking at the bronze serpent."[21] (This is a most primitive episode; it may have been preserved because it was too well known to have been expunged.)

They traveled on—the route is not precisely clear, though it is in general (Num. XXXIII:1-49 reviews the itinerary, and adds both clarity and additional problems). They seem to have journeyed east of the Dead Sea as far as the River Arnon, the northern boundary of Moab. Beyond Moab lay the land of the Amorites, ruled by their king, Sihon. They sent emissaries to him, as they had to the king of Edom, asking for the privilege of passing through his domain. Instead, Sihon attacked them, but he was defeated, and the Israelites took possession of his land, as far as the border of Ammon. Further north, Og, the king of Bashan, attacked them, and the Israelites defeated him too, and took possession of his land. That is to say, prior to the conquest of Canaan west of the Jordan, the Israelites conquered territories east of it.

There ensues now one of the strangest accounts in all Scripture, that of Balaam ben Beor. The episode of Balaam has no direct connection with any specific incident in the itinerary; it could be lifted out of the narrative without affecting the continuity. It is set at the time when the Israelites had come to the plains of Jericho, across the Jordan at Jericho, to the end of the journey under the leadership of Moses. Balaam ben Beor was a Mesopotamian wonder-worker who was hired by Balak ben Zippor, the king of Moab, to come and put a curse on Israel. Balaam seems to appear in two different roles: there is an early account which, though scorning him, treats him somewhat seriously, and a later account which makes him a comic bumbler. Balak sent some agents to Balaam, with money in their hands, to hire him to come and put a curse on Israel, so that Balak would be able to conquer them. That night Yahve appeared to Balaam, saying, "You are not to go with them. You are not to curse the people, for they are blessed." So, in the morning, Balaam turned down the offer of the money, and he sent the emissaries back to Balak. Balak thereupon sent a new set of emissaries, men of even higher status than the first emissaries. Yahve again appeared to Balaam in the night, saying, "You may go with these men, but you shall do only what I tell you."

Balaam arose in the morning and saddled his ass, and went with the noblemen of Moab. So far the account has been the early version. The later version narrates that God was angry, so that as the comic Balaam traveled with the emissaries, an angel of Yahve, invisible to Balaam, stationed himself on the way to impede him. Balaam was riding on the ass; two of his servants were with him. The ass saw the angel, standing with sword drawn, and turned out of the road and into the field. Angry, Balaam struck the ass and headed her back to the road. The angel then stood in a narrow place in the vineyards, with a wall on each side. When the ass pushed against a wall, pressing Balaam's leg against it, he struck her again. The angel then moved onto a place so narrow that there was no room to turn right or left; the ass thereupon simply lay down under Balaam. Angry, Balaam struck her with his staff. Yahve opened the ass' mouth, and she said to Balaam, "Why have you hit me three times?" Balaam said, "If I had a sword, I would kill you!" Then Yahve opened the Balaam's eyes, so that he too saw the angel, standing with sword in hand. Balaam bowed his head and fell on his face. The angel said, "If the ass had not turned aside, I would have killed you." Balaam said, "I have sinned. I will go back home." The angel said, "No. Go with the emissaries, but speak only what I tell you to."

The next morning, Balak brought Balaam to a hilltop, from where he could see the Israelites. Balaam then spoke the first of four "oracles." Four successive times he tried to curse the Israelites, but each time he was impelled to bless them.

> "God is not human that He should tell lies,
> Nor a mortal, that He should change His mind. . . .
> Behold, I received [the command] to bless;
> I shall bless, and not repudiate:
>> One can discern no blemish in Jacob,
>> Or iniquity in Israel. . . .
> How good are your Tents, O Jacob,
>> Your encampments, O Israel! . . ."
>>   (Num. XXIII: 19-21a; XXIV: 5)

The four blessings delivered, Balaam went home, and Balak went his own way.

So unconnected with the major narration is this account of Balaam that one wonders how it originated, and how it chances to be where it is in the Pentateuch. No clear answers are available. Presumably it once circulated as a separate item. Its inclusion in the Pentateuch may well have rested on this circumstance, that we are near the end of our account of the leadership of Moses, and it seemed to the author desirable to include here whatever random materials he chanced to possess; several passages seem to be a gathering of random materials. On the other hand, the Balaam material, to my mind, serves a necessary function which accounts for its inclusion, however tenuous may be its literary connection with the main narrative. In virtually all that we have seen in Exodus and Numbers, the Israelites are invariably portrayed as constant complainers; they have done such things as making the golden calf; they have infuriated Yahve over and over again, and some of them rebelled against Moses' leadership. The Balaam episode suggests that the account of the misdemeanors of the Israelites was not the whole story, and that they possessed gratifying virtues along with their palpable faults. Had there not been this episode of Balaam, the Israelites as depicted in the Pentateuch would have been a worthless people. Indeed, since the ensuing material shows the peoples' disloyalty to Yahve again and again, it may have seemed to the compiler that this was a judicious place for the episode of Balaam.

In the material that follows there comes first a narrative (Num. XXV) which is designed to show the stature of the priest Phinehas, the son of Eleazar and grandson of Aaron. The details are these. The Israelites began to mingle with the Moabites, especially their women, and they succumbed to the worship of their gods (recalling the warning in the passage Ex. XXXI:14-17, see pp. 136-37), especially the god Baal of Peor. (Thus, the very first contacts with alien peoples led promptly to apostasy.) Yahve in anger ordered Moses to slay the leaders of the people and to hang their bodies in the sun. Even while the people were mourning this punishment, a certain Zimri ben Salu openly and flagrantly brought a Midianite woman to his tent. Thereupon Phinehas entered the tent, and, with a single thrust of his spear, he slew the two of them. For this deed, which assuaged the divine wrath, the rights of priesthood for Aaron's descendants was confirmed by a covenant. (To a modern reader, Phinehas' act perhaps smacks of vigilantism.)

The Wilderness journey nearly over, a census was taken (for a second time) so as to allot the land to the tribes (Num. XXVI: 1-65). Five sisters, the daughters of a man who had died without sons, asked Moses for something unprecedented, the right of women in such a case to inherit the allotment their father would have had. Moses consulted Yahve, who directed Moses to inform the people that women had the right to inherit where there were no sons (Num. XXVII:1-11).[22]

Now Yahve instructed Moses to go to the hilly region known as Abirim, and to look from there to the land which the Israelites were to possess; thereafter Moses would die. Moses asked Yahve to designate his successor, and Yahve selected Joshua, who was to be presented to all the people in the presence of the new high priest Eleazar. This Moses did: he laid his hands on Joshua, and gave him his mandate (XXVII: 12-23). The remainder of Numbers (XXVIII-XXXVI) does not carry on the account of Moses; rather, it is a series of miscellaneous appendices. The direct sequel of the story is found in Deut. XXXIV. Moses ascended the peak of Mount Nebo and he looked over the Promised Land, seeing as far as its northern, western, and southern boundaries. There he died, and was buried, though no one now knows where his grave is. His years numbered a hundred and twenty; his eyes had not dimmed, nor his vigor diminished. The people mourned him for thirty days. Then Joshua succeeded him.

Since that time, the account goes on, no prophet has arisen like Moses; him God knew face to face; he did the divine signs and wonders in Egypt, and he showed his mighty power in many deeds in the presence of Israel.

The preceding has been, in brief summary, the account about Moses that is in the third person. The original writing was only the four books, Genesis, Exodus, Leviticus, and Numbers. The death of Moses was once the conclusion of Numbers. It was moved to the end of Deuteronomy, thereby both adding Deuteronomy as the fifth of the five books, and also detaching Deuteronomy from Joshua, Judges, Samuel, and Kings, of which it was once an integral part.

In retrospect, we should recall that the author has dealt essentially with three characters: Yahve, Moses, and the Israelites. It does not at all reduce the importance of Moses to notice that the Deity is truly the central character; it only sets matters into a proper perspective. Moses, we may say, is the most eminent of all the men of ancient times through whom and by whom the Deity accomplished His divine purpose. Hence, it was Yahve, not Moses, who redeemed Israel from Egypt, and Yahve, not Moses, who led Israel through the Wilderness, but it was Moses who, on behalf of Yahve, was the leader, teacher, prophet, and lawgiver to the people. In the beginning, in Egypt, the Israelites had been without laws, without ceremonial ritual, without organization; through Moses they acquired all these. But Israel was a reluctant, stiff-necked people, resisting the leadership of Moses even to the point of direct rebellion. Though Moses in the Wilderness age taught Israel its array of law and religious practice, there ensued repeated disobedience and apostasy to the point that Yahve would have cast off His people except for Moses' earnest intercessions.

Yet an assessment, affirmative or negative, of this people was possible only when one considered what the expectations, the obligations, incumbent on them were, for they were to be judged by a unique standard, beyond the standard of ordinary peoples. They fell short only because more was expected of them than of ordinary peoples. Even their leaders at times fell short, Aaron flagrantly so, and Moses, too, though in an infinitely lesser degree. Yet, fallible as even Moses was, it was he who under Yahve fashioned a formless mob into His unique people.

Surely the remarkable conception in the Pentateuch, of creation, of the rise of men and of nations, of the origin and expansion of the Hebrews, is greater than any of the details, even the remarkable portrait of Moses. While we have reserved our discussion of the laws for a later chapter, we can make the essential observation here that the author, free from any tendency toward abstractions, uses Moses as a means of making abstract matters specific and definite to the ultimate degree. The Ten Commandments are specific; the laws, which we might divide (as the Bible does not) into the ritual and ethical, are precise. The implication throughout these laws is that man is a free agent, able to choose whether or not to obey the laws. The collective covenant at Sinai demands obedience, but man's own conscience, not the covenant, determines whether he obeys or not. The laws are such as to suggest that the organized priesthood, beginning with the consecration of Aaron as High Priest, arose within the Wilderness period. Indeed, the special interest of P, as distinct from the interests of the authors of the older strata, is to attribute to the Wilderness period the origin of an elaborate, hereditary organization. At places this interest of P leads to a noticeable tendency to raise Aaron almost to the high rank of Moses, and to make the priests, as in the case of Phinehas, the most loyal adherents of Yahve. Modern scholarship for well over a century has concluded that the supposition that the priestly institutions originated in full array during the Wilderness period is romance, rather than history. If this is the case (as I believe it to be), then our admiration for the imaginative mind behind the Pentateuch should rise all the more, for the conception of the Wilderness and its new institutions is the crowning proof that the author was no mere pedestrian copyist, but rather a writer of creative insight. On the one hand, if his creativity somewhat distorts the actual history, which is already obscure, then it is only history as we today understand it, and not history as the ancient Hebrew mind understood it. On the other hand, such creativity, so it seems to me, was an inescapable necessity, for without it the account of Moses and the Wilderness would have lacked that on-going relevancy which it came to have, since the institutions created there were deemed important not because they were ancient, but because they were regarded as living realities long after the time of their supposed origin.

To what audience can we suppose this writing was addressed? We are in the dark. Perhaps it was primarily and exclusively the priests, as suggested by the emphasis on them in the account. Or perhaps it was they, primarily, who had the literacy which a written work requires. Again, it may be that they alone had the means to own expensive parchment scrolls.

Was the audience possibly broader? There must have been portions of the populace besides the priests who were literate, for otherwise how could the writings of the prophets and those books we call Wisdom literature (Proverbs, Ecclesiastes, and

Job) have been circulated? Perhaps there was a restricted, almost elite portion of the populace in addition to, or instead of, the priests, who were the audience. Again, we are in the dark. But one development is certain: the total Pentateuch, whether addressed to the general populace or not, in due time became the property of the populace; we shall see that the Book of Deuteronomy expects this development. Indeed, the Pentateuch became a vehicle of instruction for everyone, whether composed for that purpose or not; it became everyman's guide book.

V

The Deuteronomic Writings

Besides the Priests, as we have said, there was still another chain of literary creators, whose bent, though never anti-priestly, was nevertheless not priestly. From this chain there has come a long, variegated, but connected writing of some consequence, beginning with Deuteronomy, encompassing Joshua and Judges, and terminating with Samuel and Kings. We call this chain "the Deuteronomic writings."

The Deuteronomic writings have for me a double fascination. The materials compiled, which range from colorful folktales through absorbing chronicles by eye-witnesses, are in themselves a rich literature. Unlike the sequence Genesis to Numbers, which, once completed, underwent only very minor interpolation, the Deuteronomic writings give clear evidence of constant and extensive revision. This was the result of a sequence of events that can be an author's despair—he adopts a thesis and writes his book, and then historical events unmistakably refute his thesis. He can either throw his composition into the wastebasket, or else he can rewrite portions of it to bring it into conformity with the conditions that rendered his first draft obsolete. The Deuteronomist chose the latter course. His first thesis was that the introduction of monarchy would solve the nation's problems; then in 586 the

Babylonians invaded Judah and terminated the monarchy, and his thesis was ruined. When the Deuteronomist rewrote, he did not delete erroneous material; rather, he made additions to play down monarchy, though he retained his first opinion. Also, he carried his account beyond his first stopping point, so as to narrate the end of kingship.

The Deuteronomic writings cover about the same number of pages as Genesis–Numbers, but the period dealt with is infinitely longer, and indeed, long enough for the unity of the totality to have undergone separation into logical, and, at the same time, chronological segments. Much, indeed, most, of what he compiled from earlier sources is colorful and can be interesting and exciting to read. Some of the compilation—such as the series of stories about the prophet Elisha—is neither exciting nor edifying; had the Elisha narratives been lost, we would scarcely be the poorer. The quality of the Deuteronomist's own writing, as distinct from what he compiled, ranges from the superb to the excusably bland and, in a literary sense, dull. The dullness is due to the enormity of his bold endeavor, to write an interpretive history of his people in terms of their kings, and, alas, at frequent intervals he had little more to provide than a bare mention and a thoroughly routine judgment. Where he is tedious, he is exceedingly so; where he is not, he is fresh and vigorous and eloquent. And he preserved excellent old materials.

He began with daring, originality, and imagination, qualities that are clearly evident in the first portion of the work, the Book of Deuteronomy.

1. *Deuteronomy*

Deuteronomy supposes that the Hebrews have traversed the Wilderness and are on the threshold of crossing into Canaan, and that Moses is soon to die; Deuteronomy is the series of addresses which Moses purportedly gave to the people as his farewell testament to them.[1] Deuteronomy reflects the author's familiarity with the contents of Exodus, Leviticus, and Numbers; he constantly alludes to specific incidents, though without narrating them. We are told that we are in the fortieth year of the Wilderness wanderings, and are standing east of the Jordan in the plains of Moab. Moses speaks to us three times.

His first address is essentially a series of reminiscences. Moses had recognized that the total burden of leading the people had become too great for him, because the Hebrews had grown to be so numerous (a reminiscence of Num. XI: 14-17). Thereupon officials and judges were selected, the judges being strictly charged to judge fairly, whether for Israelites or aliens; they were to bring to Moses only the cases that were beyond them. From Kadesh, spies were sent to look at the land of Canaan, but despite their favorable report, the people rebelled against moving forward (Num. XIII: 1-XIV: 38). Hence, all that generation were to die without seeing the land, except Caleb and Joshua. Moses said, "Even at me was Yahve angry because of you, telling me, 'You too will not enter there.'"

The recollections proceed; we need not review them here. But the words spoken about the past lead on to a view of the present and the prospect for the future. The people had already seen the consequences of infidelity at Peor (Num. XXV: 1-9), where the unfaithful had perished, but those who had cleaved to Yahve and His statutes had survived. Those same statutes and ordinances were to prevail in the future in the land of Canaan, for they were of such high quality that Gentile nations would laud Israel as a wise and understanding nation in possessing them. Since Israel had seen no physical form of Yahve at Sinai, it should beware of making any images and abstain from the worship of the heavenly bodies, for Yahve was a jealous God. Were these trespasses to arise in the future, divine punishment, such as exile[2] and a diminution in their numbers, would result. In exile, the Israelites would be forced to worship statues made by men. In such a time of tribulation, the people would come to repent and return to Yahve and obey Him.

Israel's past experience was unique; its God spoke to them from the midst of fire at Sinai, with the people surviving a supernatural occurrence which might have killed them. "Has any other god gone to take for himself one nation from the midst of another nation, this by wondrous and terrifying deeds? To you there was given the means of learning that Yahve is the only Elohim, for there is none besides Him."

While the author portrays Moses as speaking to the generation reared in the Wilderness, the words are more cogently addressed to later generations, long settled in the Promised Land. That is, the author not only vividly portrays the great Moses as speaking, but, indeed, as speaking for all subsequent time, even for the late age of the author.

The second address begins with a repetition of the Ten Commandments, which differs from the version in Exodus XX only very slightly,[3] and this is followed by a hearkening back to the events of their bestowal. The address continues with the statement that Moses is teaching the statutes and ordinances which the Israelites should observe without deviation, so that they may "live long in the land" which they are to possess.

We have reason now to expect these statutes and ordinances. First, though, there is a skillful hearkening back to the many Wilderness instances of disobedience and rebellion, and to the golden calf. This serves as a prelude to a warning for the future against repetitions of such faithlessness, and it leads to these words (X:12): "And, Israel, what does Yahve your God require of you? To revere Him, to walk in His ways, to love Him, and to serve Him with all your heart and all your soul." Then come the statutes and ordinances (XII-XXVI). After a section (XXVII) on divine blessing for obedience and divine curse for disobedience, a fervid exhortation to loyalty (XXVIII) concludes the second address.

The third address enjoins a renewal of the corporate covenant already made at Sinai. There is a recitation of Yahve's mighty deeds in the past, followed by these words (XXIX:14 Eng., 13 Heb.): "It is not alone with you that I make this sworn-to covenant, but both with him who is here, today, standing before Yahve, and with him who is not here with us today."

The third address repeatedly speaks of matters contained "in this book," or "in this book of the divine teaching." That is, the ability of future generations to be faithful was to be facilitated by the possession of a written book, though just which book this is is never told us directly. We read a little further on (XXX: 11-19): "This commandment which I enjoin upon you today is not obscured from you, nor is it far off. It is not in Heaven, for you will not need to say, 'Who will ascend to Heaven to bring it to us, and have us hear and obey it?' It is not beyond the sea, for you will not need to say, 'Who will cross the sea for us and bring it for us and have us hear and obey it?'" Perhaps Deuteronomy itself was the book that was meant; perhaps, though, the passages provide a commendation of Genesis–Numbers.

We might assess the import of Deuteronomy, and its inclusion within the Pentateuch, in this way: whereas Genesis through Numbers seem primarily antiquarian, Deuteronomy, through its repeated emphasis on a future, turns the entire Pentateuch into a continuous present. The account is no longer simply a record of ancient events; it is an invitation for those events to become the vivid experience of even the latest generation. Yahve's wondrous deeds are not alone a record of past glories, they are available for renewal and repetition at all future times, and are available to read and reread!

We must inquire, now, into its significance to the succeeding writings, of which Deuteronomy was once the introductory work. Two passages provide the clue. Deut. XVII: 14-20 envisages a future when the nation would be ruled by a king, and this would be long after Moses and Joshua, neither of whom was a king. The passage assumes that the emergence of a king would be quite in order, provided he behaved properly, in conformity to the laws. Second, even though Israel would have the heritage of a written book of laws, some direct communication with Yahve would still be necessary after Moses and Joshua died. Deut. XVIII: 14-22 gives the assurance that prophets would arise to

whom Yahve would communicate His will in the future. Kingship and the office of the prophet are a prime concern of the Deuteronomic writer, and Deuteronomy sanctions these.

Moreover, Deut. XXVII:1-XXVIII:68 supposes that blessings
or curses could ensue from fidelity or infidelity to Yahve; hence
specific blessings and curses were now recorded as substance of a
new covenant made by Moses in the land of Moab. This new
covenant supplemented the older covenant at Sinai. Covenant,
written law, monarchy, and prophecy are the themes by which the
Deuteronomic author explored his review and interpretation of
the ensuing history.

In the Book of Deuteronomy, we encounter the highest point
in the author's imagination and daring. From his conviction that
Moses had bequeathed laws and standards to his people, the author proceeded to something entirely without precedent: he presented this heritage from Moses in the first person, as a legacy of
the spoken words of Moses himself. He did this with so great a
sense of authenticity that we can credit him with tremendous
persuasiveness. The iconoclastic opinion that Moses had not
written Deuternonomy came rather late in the modern scientific
scholarship, simply because the author of the book wrote with
immense and convincing skill. Indeed, it was some aspects of the
legal materials, not the style or the conception which was the
clue, for comparable legal materials in Exodus–Leviticus–Numbers
were noticed to be different in import from what is in Deuteronomy. Deuteronomy alone stresses that only one sanctuary was to
be legitimate[4] after the land of Canaan was conquered; we know
that the future temple in Jerusalem was meant, though Jerusalem
is not specifically mentioned. Also, the prescription for the treatment of the officiants, the priests and Levites, at that prospective
temple is different from the prescription in the other books, and
the terminology itself about them is different. Had it not been for
the close study of the material on the temple and the priests, there
would have been, and would be now, little surface reason to suppose that the Moses described in the third person in Exodus–

Leviticus–Numbers was not the actual person who spoke in the first person in Deuteronomy. Such, then, is a general statement on the imaginative skill of the author. He did not create a Moses, he recreated one, brilliantly.

2. *Joshua*

The first half of the Book of Joshua describes the Conquest of Canaan—from the Deuteronomist's viewpoint—and the second half describes the division of the conquered territories among the tribes and closes with still another renewal of the Covenant and then the death of Joshua.

A certain lack of balance inheres in the Conquest, for a full half of it is devoted to a single event, the capture of Jericho, whose walls fell at the sound of a long blast on the horn as the Israelites marched about the city. The Israelites were defeated when they attacked the town of Ai, but the defeat was caused by a disobedient Israelite who, against Joshua's instruction, took booty for himself at Jericho.

The Canaanites, fearful of being conquered and totally exterminated, banded together to oppose the Israelites. The city of Gibeon did not join this confederation; instead, the inhabitants resorted to cunning. They equipped themselves with worn-out saddlesacks, worn-out wineskins, patched sandals, and moldy food, and then they approached Joshua, identifying themselves as people from a great distance away. They thereby tricked Joshua into making a covenant with them. Because of the covenant, the Israelites were barred from destroying the Gibeonites, but they made them slaves, hewers of wood and drawers of water. (This story is intended to explain the survival of some Canaanites in Canaan, despite Yahve's repeated injunctions to destroy them or drive them out.)

The Book of Joshua is scarcely the factual account of a military expedition. Rather, Joshua achieves the Conquest in an account so compressed that it suggests little more than a single expedition.

The second half of Joshua describes the division of the conquered lands among the tribes (XIII-XXIII), and then tells of still another renewal of the covenant with Yahve.

The author here had little desire to trace the tortuous steps that the actual conquest could well have involved; he preferred instead to abbreviate it and to show the action of Yahve. Fortunately, he balanced this concise summary by citing an ancient document, found in Judg. I:1-II:5; this gives a corrective to the supposition that there was a single military campaign.

3. *Judges*

The supposition in the Book of Judges is that the Settlement of the land was quite different from, and a later stage than, the Conquest. The author begins this book by quoting an old document, with attendant details quite different from those of the same matters in Joshua. Here, the Conquest appears to have entailed local battles, under many leaders; moreover, against the Book of Joshua, with its view of a completed conquest, we read in Judges of the Israelites' inability to conquer certain particular areas. Hence, Judges simply assumes that Canaanites persisted in the land, and that, as a consequence, the worship of the god Baal, and his female consort, the Ashtoret, persisted. As a result, the Israelites forsook Yahve and joined the Canaanites in their worship of these deities, and neighboring nations thereupon marched against the Israelites.

In all the accounts provided in Judges, ancient materials are brought into a later framework, so as to suggest the pattern whereby Israelite prosperity led to apostasy, and apostasy to domination by foreign foes, this requiring the rise of a Great Redeemer, through whose achievement prosperity was restored. This cyclical pattern is repeated again and again. We saw above the accounts of Ehud, of Jeptha's daughter, and of Samson. We cannot here reproduce the content of Judges in detail. We can notice that one of the Judges was a woman, Deborah, of whom we have two accounts, a very ancient one in poetry (V), which is often regarded as the most ancient writing in Scripture, and a later version in prose (IV). The true heroine of the Deborah story is a woman, Jael, the wife of a certain Heber the Kenite, into whose tent the fleeing enemy general Sisera came. Jael slew Sisera while he was asleep, by driving a tent peg into his head! Still another redeemer was Gideon, an able and wily general, who declined the offer to become the king of the northern tribes. The office was usurped by his son Absalom, who perished when the Israelites were assaulting a city. A woman threw a millstone down from a tower, and it hit him. Besides the accounts of five of the twelve Judges, there are two appendices, one of which, the story of the Levite and his concubine, we have already seen (pp. 17-18). Just before that story is another account which is significant for its revelation of the realities of priesthood in ancient times. A man named Micah stole money from his mother, but he returned it; in her gratification at the return of the money, she had him build what we might call a chapel. A wandering "Levite"—here meaning a priest, rather than the member of a tribe—was persuaded to remain on as the officiant. Then the tribe of Dan wandered by, searching for a place to settle; they wanted to relocate from the south to the north. The tribe simply took this Levite away from Micah so he would become their priest.

These appendices are not edifying. Our author knows this, and he tells us that he is presenting this "negative" material as part of his thesis, that anarchy prevailed in the period of the Settlement for the reason "that there was no king of Israel, and every man did what was right in his own eyes." Thus the literary purpose in the Book of Judges is to lead us to the origin of the monarchy, and to justify the need for it.

Not all of the material in Judges and in the early chapters of the next book, I Samuel, fits congruently with this significant thesis; there are a good many anomalies, and far, far more loose ends than the few we saw in the Pentateuch. The introduction of monarchy rotates about the figure Samuel, and while this is clear enough, the old material vies with the new material to provide us with sources that are not smoothly integrated. Also, within the new material there is a noticeable diversity of viewpoint.

4. *Samuel, Saul, and David*

We saw at the beginning the touching account of Hannah, whose prayer for a child was answered. She bore Samuel. In accordance with the vow she made, the boy was entrusted to Eli, the priest of Shiloh, to help him in the service of Yahve. As Samuel grew up he came to be known throughout the land as "a prophet." In the narratives about Samuel as a prophet, there is a somewhat curious verse; it tells that "Eli *judged* Israel forty years (I Sam. IV:18)." Similarly, another verse (I Sam. VIII:15-17) relates that "Samuel *judged* Israel all the days of his life. He would go on a circuit annually to Bethel, Gilgal and Mizpah; he *judged* Israel in all these places." These two summaries, which resemble those found in the Book of Judges, have led to the belief that our present Book of Judges is a shortened version of a once longer book which, at one time, included accounts of Eli and Samuel as Judges. (The only importance in this observation is that it reveals how the whole sequence of writings grew.) Samuel seems to be conceived of by the author in three different ways: as a judge; as a somewhat usual prophet; and also as an extraordinary person, of a stature quite beyond that of the ordinary prophet.

Some old material relates the misfortunes that followed the Philistines' capture of the Ark of the Covenant. Once this old material is concluded, we read that Samuel was at Mizpah, explaining to the people that it was their infidelity to Yahve which had allowed the Philistines to harass them.

This is the point at which there occurs the summary, mentioned above, of Samuel's achievement as a judge, as if it concludes a body of material. But the narration immediately proceeds: Samuel had become old, and had designated his two sons as judges, but they were avaricious and they accepted bribes. Thereupon "all the elders of Israel" came to Samuel and asked him to appoint "a king to rule over us like all the nations." The author has now proceeded to the inauguration of kingship.

But above (pp. 151-52) we spoke of divergency in the younger materials. There are strands which favor the institution of monarchy, and strands which oppose it. We encounter first an anti-monarchy strand: The request for a king, so we are told, displeased Samuel. He prayed to Yahve, Who replied that it was He, not Samuel, whom the people were rejecting by wanting a human king; hence Samuel was to accede to their request, but he was to attest to the people what the evil ways of a king would be. Samuel said to them (VIII): "This will be the habit of the king who will reign over you: He will take your sons and assign them to his chariots as his horsemen, to run in advance of the chariots. He will designate for himself officials, commanders of thousands of people, or commanders of fifty, to do his plowing, to gather his harvest, and to carry out his warfare and to make his military weapons. He will take your daughters as pharmacists, or butchers, or bakers. He will seize your best fields, vineyards, and olive groves and turn them over to his agents. A tenth of the produce and vineyards he will grant to his officials and agents. He will seize the best of your male and female servants and of your cattle and asses to do his work. He will take a tenth of your flocks, and you will become his servants." (Seldom has royal tyranny been described so graphically.)

Chapter IX, on the other hand, is pro-monarchy; it begins by introducing one Saul ben Kish, a handsome Benjaminite, taller by a head than any of the people. Some asses belonging to Saul's father, Kish, a wealthy man, were lost. Kish sent Saul to look for them, and Saul took a servant along. The search took them through the territory of Ephraim and Benjamin, but they did not find the asses. The servant proposed that they consult the prophet Samuel. Our author, aware that he is here describing a procedure already antiquated by his time, inserts a note: "In olden days, in Israel, a man intending to consult God, would say, 'Let us go to the *seer*,' for he who is now called a *prophet* used to be called a seer."

Now on the previous day, Yahve had disclosed to Samuel that He was sending a Benjaminite to him, and that Samuel should anoint him prince over Israel. At dawn the next day, Saul came to Samuel, and when the two were alone, Samuel poured oil on

Saul's head, kissed him, and said, "Yahve has anointed[1] you prince over His possession." The anointing of Saul, as I Sam. IX:27 makes clear, is here a private matter between Samuel and Saul, and it is without direct sequel. (Note that it is important to the author that every man who becomes king legitimately does so through some prophet.) On Saul's journey homeward, he met his uncle, and he told him of searching for the asses, and even mentioned his visit to Samuel, but he said nothing about the anointing.

As the account continues, Samuel then gathered the people at Mizpah. First he scolded them for wishing a king, and then he proceeded to select their ruler by casting a lot (quite as if the anointing of Saul had never taken place). The lot fell first to the tribe of Benjamin, and next to the clan to which Saul belonged, and then to Saul. Saul, however, was apparently not present, and the people ran to fetch him. Samuel then presented him as the choice of Yahve, and the people shouted, "May the king live!" Samuel then told the people about the evils of monarchy, and he even wrote about these in a book which he deposited before Yahve. (We do not know what this writing was; perhaps the speech against kingship, made earlier, is meant.)

Saul returned to his home, apparently to some privacy. There were warriors who supported him, but there were also worthless people who were skeptical. To be king, Saul had to prove himself in battle. The people of Gilead, east of the Jordan, were beset by the Ammonites, and they appealed to Saul for help. Saul led an onslaught against the Ammonites and defeated them. Then Samuel proposed that the people should assemble and there *renew* the kingship (apparently a more public, and more broadly witnessed ceremony, in contrast to the unknown, private anointing.) We encounter hereafter continuing approval and disapproval of monarchy, and, moreover, some passages in which Saul is a great hero, and others in which he is a completely despicable person.

The brief account of the public ceremony is followed by still another denunciation of monarchy by Samuel. Though this reads like a farewell address, Samuel's activities go on thereafter. In the address Samuel defends his own leadership, speaking as if he has been king. Samuel, after a long reign, is now old and gray. "Here I am. Bring your allegations before Yahve and the *king*. Whose ox have I seized? Whose ass have I seized? Whom have I cheated, whom oppressed? From whose hand have I received a bribe to blind my eyes—I will return it."

After the recounting of the address, there is a curious sentence (XIII:1) which apparently aims to provide a summary of the duration of Saul's reign, but the sentence that has been transmitted is defective, and it is completely enigmatic.[2]

Earlier, at the conclusion of the private anointing, Samuel had instructed Saul to go to Gilgal and there await Samuel's arrival (X:1-8). Intervening material (the defeat of the Ammonites, and Samuel's farewell address) provides some minor measure of confusion; the sequel to the earlier injunction to go to Gilgal is now narrated (XIII:2ff). Saul waited at Gilgal for Samuel, but Samuel delayed. Thereupon Saul determined to sacrifice some burnt offerings, rather than continue to wait for Samuel to come and do so. When Samuel arrived, he upbraided Saul for having usurped to himself the offering of the sacrifices: "You have not heeded the command of Yahve, Who would have established your dynasty forever. Your kingship will not abide. Yahve will seek a man after his own heart and make him the ruler of His people." (These words come surprisingly early; they are from the hand of an extreme opponent of Saul.) The episode seems to have no sequel, direct or indirect. Instead, there follows an incident that disparages Saul. The Philistines attacked, and Saul's noble son Jonathan embarked on a "commando" raid against them. Saul put a curse on any Israelite who would eat that day (for the people needed to be dedicated to battle). Jonathan, away, did not hear the curse; he dipped his staff into some honey, and ate it. Saul was prepared to allow Jonathan to be killed for this trespass, but the people intervened to stop the execution.

There now ensues a short passage in high praise of Saul: "He fought against all the enemies on every side, Moab, Ammon,

Edom, Zobah and Philistia. Wherever he turned he defeated them. Valiantly he smote the Amelekites. He delivered Israel from its plunderers." (The author has used sources here which contradict his own low opinion of Saul.)

Throughout Saul's days, we read, there was bitter warfare with the Philistines, and Saul attached to himself any strong or brave man he saw. This sentence allows the author to foreshadow the emergence of David. There intervenes, however, another long passage (XV) disparaging Saul: Samuel had bidden Saul utterly to destroy the Amalekites, and to kill all their animals. Saul proceeded to conquer the Amalekites, even capturing their king, Agag, but he killed only the poorest of the animals, and spared the good ones. Our author now comments that Yahve repented elevating Saul to king. Samuel arrived; Saul told him that he had King Agag in his custody. He ascribed to the people, not to himself, the sparing of the good animals, these for sacrifice to Yahve. Samuel then denounced Saul, who asked for forgiveness, but Samuel would not give it. As Samuel turned to leave, Saul grasped his cloak, and it *tore*. Samuel said, "Yahve has *torn* the kingship from you, to give it to a better person." Saul pleaded to escape public humiliation, and this Samuel was willing to grant. (First, though, he had Saul bring Agag to him, and Samuel—this passage shocks me at every reading!—hewed him into pieces! Then Samuel left, never to see Saul again [XV: 1-34]).

To the author, David was the authentic king chosen by Yahve, as Saul was not. The rise of David to the throne was, both historically and in the author's perspective, possible only through Saul's loss of it. While the author has related that Saul has learned from Samuel that he was to lose the throne, he portrays Saul as nevertheless holding on to it tenaciously. After David is introduced, Saul is almost invariably portrayed as a villain, as the obstacle to the rise of David to the throne which the author believed was properly his. So preoccupied is the author with David, and so much attention does he give him, that his thesis on the importance of kingship is submerged in the abundance of material he presents. This includes sound factual data, mostly taken from old materials; indeed one long section, II Sam. XII-XXII, is reasonably regarded as an eye-witness account. He also gives us legends, some possibly directed toward children.

The anointing of David by Samuel is related in a charming episode (I Sam. XVI). Yahve sent Samuel to Jesse, a man of Bethlehem, one of whose sons was chosen to be king. When Jesse and seven of his eight sons met Samuel, Yahve vetoed each of these seven in succession. The eighth son, David, who was the youngest, was away watching the sheep. David was summoned, and at Yahve's behest, Samuel anointed him.

The author now proceeds to develop the relationship between Saul and David. To do this, he intertwines two legends. In one legend, though war had receded and conditions had become stabilized, Saul began to suffer from depression, for Yahve's spirit had left him, and an evil spirit began to torment him. Saul's servants advised him to seek out someone who played the harp skillfully and who, through his music, could perhaps bring Saul out of his depression. A young servant mentioned David as a skillful musician. Saul asked Jesse's permission to allow David to come and stay with him indefinitely. Whenever Saul was depressed, David's playing drove out the evil spirit, and Saul recovered. Thus they now know each other.

In the other legend, Saul and David have not met. The Philistines mobilized their forces, and Saul arrayed the Israelites against them, the armies facing each other, separated by a valley. From the Philistine camp there came forth a gigantic warrior, Goliath of Gath, in full armor, taunting the Israelites to designate a man to fight him, this in place of the armies battling. David (as if we have not met him!) was the youngest of the eight sons of Jesse, an old man whose three oldest sons were in Saul's army. Jesse sent David to these sons with some food. David heard people saying that whoever might oppose Goliath and kill him would receive riches from the king, and his daughter in marriage. The account now turns to the assumption that Saul and David have already met, as if through David's music. Saul, hearing that David has already volunteered to fight against Goliath, sent for him, to dissuade him. David persisted, so Saul dressed him in armor, with a helmet and a coat of mail. Then David tried to move forward, but he could not, so he shed the armor. He took only his staff, and five smooth stones which he selected from the brook. With his slingshot in his hand, he approached the Philistine. He chose a stone and flung it, striking the Philistine on the forehead, so that Goliath fell prone. David then cut off Goliath's head, and the Philistines all fled back into Philistia.

Again our account veers back to the supposition that David and Saul have not met. When Saul saw David go out to the Philistine, he asked his general, Abner, who the lad was, but Abner did not know. After the combat, Abner brought the lad to Saul, who asked, "Whose son are you?" David said, "I am the son of your servant Jesse of Bethlehem." (The author is giving his audience material they already know. For that reason he is quite content to give single episodes, in themselves amusing or moving or tragic, and to fall far short of smooth connection in the sequence of the tales.)

Our author knows that his auditors know of the deep friendship that existed between David and Saul's son Jonathan. He tells of it, but seems to feel no need to tell how it began; it is sufficient that it did begin. This friendship was to complicate an inevitable rivalry between Saul and David. That rivalry became complex, for we read that Saul at that time had made David a member of his own household.

Saul sent David out on a number of expeditions. Each time David was successful, he won popular acclaim, even from Saul's servants. (The author has not told us very much of Saul's exploits; he had condensed these into the short paragraph which we discussed above, pp. 162-63.) When David returned to Saul from an expedition, the women danced in David's honor and sang a song:

> "Saul has slain thousands,
> But David has slain ten thousands."

The repeated song offended Saul.

Our author provides a series of episodes in which David's fame grew, as did Saul's jealousy and insane hatred. The affection between David and Jonathan also increased. In these episodes, some legendary and some historical, there gradually emerges an open rivalry for authority between Saul and David. At last David left the court to become a freebooter, or even an outlaw. New characters, and striking incidents—gory, or funny, or even humorously coarse—follow in some profusion, and complications increase; for example, Saul gave to another man his daughter Michal, whom he had given to David as a wife. Indeed, David began to acquire wives other than his lost Michal. Again, Saul continued to try to find David, to kill him, but David was able to evade Saul and, twice, magnanimously spared Saul's life when he could easily have killed him. The narratives uniformly describe David's ascendancy, and Saul's decline.

The climax in Saul's disintegration is presented as linked to a new Philistine invasion. Frightened, Saul went to a place named En-Dor, and there had a medium (often called a witch) summon the prophet Samuel from his grave. Samuel told Saul that he was to lose his throne to David. (This eerie scene at En-Dor is the extreme in the disparagement of Saul.) Thereafter battle with the Philistines was joined, and both Saul and Jonathan were killed, Saul by his own hand after he had been severely wounded. When an Amalekite messenger brought David the news of the death of Saul and Jonathan, he lied to David, saying that he had administered Saul's death blow. David mourned for a day, and then killed the Amalekite.

Our author then reproduces a poetic lament by David, citing it from an old source, "The Book of Yashar."

> Your pride, O Israel, is a corpse on your hills.
> How came the mighty to fall? . . .

The poem turns to curse the mountain where the battle took place.

> You hills of Gilboa,
> May you lack dew and rain,
> May your fields have no yield of grain,
> For on you the shield of a hero was defiled,
> The shield of Saul, left without its anointing oil. . . .

Now the poem becomes a eulogy:

> At no time did Jonathan's bow turn back,
> Or the sword of Saul return empty,
> From slaying the foe,
> From entering the body of enemy warriors.
>
> How came the mighty to fall in the midst of battle!
> Jonathan lies dead on your hills!
> I grieve for you, my brother Jonathan,
> Sweet have you been to my taste,
> Your love for me more wondrous than a woman's.
>
> How came the mighty to fall,
> Their weapons to perish?
>
>   (II Sam. I: 19, 21-22, 25-27)

One does not expect so fervent and laudatory a eulogy over Saul, in view of the repeated disdain of him which we have met before; the denigration of Saul seems much more literary than historical.

From here on, however, the legendary and the theological largely recede from the account of David, and we emerge into the nearest equivalent we have of pure history. After Saul's death, some northern people, loyal to Saul's survivors and partisans, rose against David. David's intention appears to have been to pacify, rather than defeat, the north. After Saul's son Ishbosheth was assassinated (and the assassins were executed by David), the warfare ended, and David became, like Saul, the king of all Israel. His capital for seven and a half years was Hebron. He then captured Jerusalem, thereafter known as the City of David, and he made it his capital. He rebuilt the city, and he arranged for the

Ark of the Covenant to be brought into it. He also built himself a sumptuous palace.

The author knows that, though David was the great monarch, it was not he, but his son Solomon, who built the great Temple to Yahve. Why did David, who had built a palace, not build the Temple, especially after bringing the Ark to Jerusalem? The author feels that he must answer this question: He begins by ascribing to David the observation that he, David, lived in a house of cedar (a precious wood), but the Ark was housed only in a tent. The prophet Nathan understood David's hint about a temple and approved his intention, but Yahve appeared to Nathan with a message for David, that Yahve was content with David's intention, for He was giving him an everlasting kingdom through his children, and one of them would instead build the Temple.

David was succeeded by Solomon, the son of David and Bathsheba. The account of David and Bathsheba is one of the most masterly passages in Scripture, and its inclusion in a work which adulates David is a tribute to the author's integrity. It is worthwhile to pause over it, to observe how it was narrated.

The story begins with Israel's continuing wars with the Ammonites. David sent his general, Joab, with an army to beseige the Ammonite capital, Rabbah, but David remained in Jerusalem. One afternoon, while on the flat roof of his palace, he chanced to see a beautiful woman bathing herself. He learned that she was Bathsheba, the wife of one Uriah, a man of Hittite extraction, who was a soldier with Joab's forces in Ammon. David had Bathsheba brought to the palace, and, even though she was as yet not fully purified after her menstrual period, he had intercourse with her. David then summoned Uriah home to Jerusalem. (His motive is not explained. It appears that he was curious about the man with whose wife he was involved.) On Uriah's return, David asked him about Joab, and how the seige of Rabbah was progressing. He then suggested that Uriah go to his home to wash his feet, that is, to rest and relax. Uriah left the palace, and David sent a gift for him to his home. But Uriah did not go home;

instead, he slept near the palace gates. Learning this, David sent for him: "You have had a long journey. Why have you not gone home?"

Uriah said, ". . . My lord Joab and his army are encamped in the open. How can I go to my home, to eat and drink, and lie with my wife? I will not do so." David said, "Stay one more day, and go back tomorrow." The next day, David invited Uriah to eat with him, and he plied him with drink, but Uriah nevertheless did not return to his home, but slept with David's servants again.

David then wrote a letter to Joab, sending it by Uriah: "Put Uriah into the thick of the battle, and then fall back from him, and let him be killed." Joab, observing the siege of the city, set Uriah where he knew there were formidable Ammonite soldiers. The people of the city attacked, and Uriah died, along with others of Joab's troops.

Joab sent back a full report of the fighting. He said to the courier: "When you finish your report to the king, and he becomes angry and asks why our men approached so near the city, say, 'Your servant Uriah was among the slain.'" (Joab's words disclose his keen perception of David's mental processes and at the same time contribute an added depth to the narration.) When David heard this, he sent a message to Joab, "Do not be troubled. Such things happen in battle."

The tone of the narration is bitterly ironic, especially in the contrast between David's indifference to religious ritual and Uriah's earnest and constant fidelity to it. The irony rises even higher. When Uriah's wife, Bathsheba, learned that her husband was dead, she went into mourning, but when the rites of mourning were ended, David brought her to his palace. She became his wife, and she bore him a son. The masterly story is well worth frequent rereading, especially for the sudden religious note, "But David's deed was evil in the eyes of Yahve."

Yahve sent Nathan the prophet to David. Nathan said to him: "In a certain city there were two men, the one wealthy, the other poor. The rich man had flocks and herds in abundance. The poor man had nothing but one tiny ewe lamb. He had brought it and raised it, and it had grown in his home with his sons. It ate from his own food, and drank from his own cup, and slept in his arms —it was like a daughter to him. A visitor came to the rich man. Too stingy to feed his guest from his own herds or flocks, he seized the poor man's ewe and served it to his guest."

David became furious at the rich man. "I swear by Yahve that that man should be executed! Let him pay four times the value of the ewe for this pitiless deed.

Nathan said, "You are that man."

The son Uriah's wife had borne to David became very ill, and died. Later, they had another son, Solomon.

Presently there comes a long section (II Sam. XIII-XX) which is quoted by the author from an old source. It is so vividly told that many scholars believe it to be a long account by a chronicler who was one of David's court followers; one scholar has called it the Israelite "Iliad." It is tough, hard, and realistic, for it entails rape, murder, and revolution; but, when occasion warrants, it becomes tender. Its barest outline runs as follows:

Among David's many children from his many wives were a brother and sister who had the same mother. A half-brother, Amnon, raped the girl, Tamar, and he scorned to marry her. Thereafter her full brother, Absalom, nurturing his hatred, killed Amnon. Absalom fled eastward, fearing David's punishment. Three years later Absalom contrived to return to Jerusalem, though he was barred from the court. He managed, however, to be re-admitted, for David loved him.

Absalom—blessed with beautiful long hair—determined to rebel against his father and seize the throne. He found henchmen, and he attracted followers, so that David found himself confronted with a most formidable foe, and, indeed, had to flee from Jerusalem, which he could not protect against Absalom. The rebellious son entered Jerusalem and publicly slept with David's concubines, to show that he had usurped his father's authority. But David still had to be bested in battle. Here Absalom fell prey to the divided counsel of a certain Ahitophel, who had become his partisan, and a certain Hushai, an agent of David's, who had been planted in Absalom's entourage. Absalom led his army against David and was defeated; as he was fleeing on a mule, his long hair became entangled in the branches of a tree, and David's men put him to death. When the report reached David, he was saddened by the death of his son Absalom more than gladdened by the end of the revolt.

What makes this account—it is complicated by an abundance of characters and innumerable episodes—rise above a routine story of upheavals in an unstable oriental court is the skill of the narration. In fact, the theme is not Absalom's revolt, but David's love for his son. The artistic presentation of how this love impedes David from disciplining Absalom and blinds him to the boy's misdeeds provides an added dimension of depth and makes it memorable as one of the highest points in scriptural narration. The characters, both the minor and the major ones, are examined searchingly; we see Absalom's ruthlessness and David's extravagant love for his wayward son. Subordinate incidents are woven into the main line of the story with unusual dexterity. Profoundly moving is the end of the story, where David's grief is expressed in his tearful words over his dead son: "O Absalom, my son, Absalom my son, my son, Absalom, would that I had died in your stead!"

Next there is a series of somewhat disjointed appendices, apparently gathered for insertion here simply because we are near the end of the long account of David. We are told that David became old and frail. Despite the many clothes his servants put on him, he could not get warm, and the servants proposed that there be sought out some virgin, to lie in bed by him to keep him warm. After searching throughout all Israel, they found a beautiful maiden named Abishag. David, so we are told, had no sex relations with her.

At that time, David's oldest son, or oldest surviving son, Adonijah, tried to seize the throne. He gained the support of Joab, the general, and Abiathar, one of David's two priests. Nathan, the prophet, informed Bathsheba that if she wished to save both her life and Solomon's, she should remind David of an oath which he had taken, that Solomon was to succeed him. She did so; thereupon David instructed Nathan, a warrior named Benaiah, and David's other priest, Zadok, that they should take a royal bodyguard and escort Solomon to a spring named Gihon, where they should anoint Solomon king, and then have a trumpet sounded. After this sounding of the trumpet, the son of Abiathar arrived with the news that Solomon had been anointed and had already ascended the throne, with David's blessing, and Adonijah's supporters slipped away from him. David then died, after reigning seven years (elsewhere it was seven and a half years) in Hebron and thirty-three years in Jerusalem.

If these figures are correct—there is no reason to doubt them —then long as the account of David is, it is surely as incomplete as it is in places disordered. Yet enough has been told to give us a full portrait of the man; even though the partisanship of the Deuteronomist for him often intrudes, the basic realities—all the violence and the hideous misdeeds—are presented with remarkable fidelity and clarity. Surely a fuller account of David's activities was not necessary, for enough has been told us that the essential facts are not at all obscured by the interpretation and the obvious legends. We can see the rise to full power of a local chieftain to the rank of king; his acquisition of Saul's crown; his defense of the newly acquired total kingdom, and thereafter the nasty court intrigues, conspiracies, and maneuverings which went on until his death.

The material on David exceeds in length that on any other biblical character, including Abraham, Jacob, and Moses. If it is read in a modern translation it amounts to a colorful biography of a man of high significance, and gives a well-rounded reflection of a whole age and culture. (To read the account as it is found in the Bible is an antidote to the saccharine versions taught to children in Sunday schools.)

There are present in the writing unresolved inconsistencies and trivial anomalies, but these defects are overbalanced by a double honesty, in that the author does not expunge from his account materials unfavorable to David. In this account we have inherited a remarkably full and vivid portrait of a man and an era. Though there was stability in the land, there was none in the palace.

Our author has adhered well to his intention: to provide an interpretive, theological history of kingship. I have read scholarly works which attribute to the Deuteronomic author artificiality and even pious fraud. That the author does make the events which he reproduces from ancient documents conform to his thesis is true, but I would myself prefer to describe his procedure by the word *patterned* rather than the word *artificial*. I would find the charge of fraud convincing if he had tampered with the ancient sources which he reproduced. For example, he told the legend that David had slain Goliath; if the author were a fraud, he would not have reproduced the ancient source which records that it was, rather, a certain hero, Elhanan ben Yaare-Orgim, who slew Goliath (II Sam. XXI:19). I do not hesitate to speak of the stories of David's youth as legendary, as tales for children, rather than history. But this is far removed from being fraudulent; had the author been intent on deliberately deceiving the reader, we would have heard nothing about Elhanan. I am not contending that the author's theological interpretation of events is the interpretation which I, or any other modern person, might make of them; I am saying, rather, that it is no great chore to separate the legendary material from the factual, and that we can have a sense of full reliability in the facts about David that the author reproduces.

Compare sections of Chronicles which repeat material in Samuel and Kings. The Chronicler does distort; the Chronicler does omit what he might have included; the Chronicler does varnish matters. Indeed, the Chronicler so narrates the building of the Temple that, in his view, it was David who had the architectural plans drawn up, the materials provided, and work force arranged, and all that Solomon did was to act somewhat as the unimportant foreman of a construction gang. The Chronicler tampers with his sources, even grotesquely. Not so the Deuteronomic author. We cannot trust the Chronicler; we can trust the Deuteronomist respecting the history he reproduces, when once we grasp his pattern.

5. *Solomon*

David is a character in full dimension as Solomon is not, for the quality of the writing declines after the narration of David's death. The defects are to be observed best, and typically, in the treatment of Solomon. Solomon reigned for forty years (I Kings XI:42), but we are told relatively little about him, and that little is essentially a series of summary notes; most of the attention in the chapters about Solomon (II:12-XI) is devoted to the building of the Temple (VI-IX). We can be a bit offended when we read that, on coming to the throne, Solomon arranged the execution of Adonijah and his supporters. The author seems unsure whether Solomon was a worthy man or a villain. He tells us (III:1) that Solomon married an Egyptian princess, and that the people were offering sacrifices at high places. At Gibeon, Solomon himself sacrificed at the great hill-shrine there, an evil thing. On the other hand, Yahve appeared to Solomon in a dream, asking what gift Solomon desired. Solomon asked for wisdom. Pleased that Solomon had asked neither for longevity nor wealth, nor the death of his enemies, Yahve gave him a wise and intelligent mind, unequaled before or after.

We get a sample of his wisdom. Two women, harlots, appeared before him. They, and only they, occupied the same house; both had been pregnant. One gave birth to a son, and three days later the other also bore a son. One baby died. In the middle of the night the mother exchanged her dead baby for the live baby. Now, each woman claimed the living baby as her own. Solomon gave the verdict: let a sword be brought and the baby cut in two, with half for each claimant. One of the women said, "Give her the baby—do not kill it!" The other said, "It will belong to neither of us—divide it!" Solomon said, "Give the baby to the first woman; she is its mother." All Israel heard of this, and stood in awe of the wisdom of God which was in Solomon (III). His wisdom, so we are told, exceeded that of some of the proverbial sages. He spoke three thousand proverbs and his poems numbered a thousand and five. His literary subjects ranged from the lofty cedar to lowly shrubs, and included beasts, birds, reptiles, and fish. From all parts of the world people came to listen to his wisdom (as, later, the Queen of Sheba came).

What the author admires most about Solomon is his building of the Temple. Solomon continued the friendly relations of David with king Hiram of Tyre. With peace and great prosperity prevailing, he was prepared to begin the building of the Temple, with Hiram's help. The construction of the Temple and its dedication (VI-VIII) are described in great detail. The first act was to bring the Ark from Mount Zion into the Temple, and with it the sacred vessels from the portable Tabernacle. Thereafter there ensues a long passage characteristic of the Deuteronomic author, Solomon's prayer to Yahve. Here is a portion:

"Will God really dwell [in the Temple] on the earth? The Heavens, and Heavens above the Heavens, cannot contain You. How much less this Temple I have built! But give attention, Yahve my God, to Your servant's prayer and supplication, hearkening to the cry and prayer Your servant utters this day. . . ."

The lengthy account of the dedication of the Temple completed, the author sets the stage for future events, narrating that Yahve appeared to Solomon for a second time, and urged him to abide by His commandments so as to ensure the perpetuity of his throne. Solomon, however, did not remain faithful to Yahve. He loved many women, and married many alien women, even though marriage with these foreigners was expressly forbidden. (His wives numbered seven hundred, all princesses, and his concubines three hundred!) When Solomon became old, these wives seduced him away from true fidelity to Yahve, for he paid homage to the false gods of his wives. Therefore, Yahve announced to him that He would tear the throne away, but out of consideration for David, Yahve would defer this act until the reign of Solomon's son. (The author here is making the events fit his theology, however incongruently; he does this from time to time.)

The author now introduces us to an Ephraimite, Jeroboam ben Nebat, who would challenge the right of Solomon's son to the throne. A prophet, Ahijah of Shilo, encountered Jeroboam alone, and, taking a new garment which Jeroboam was wearing, he tore it into twelve pieces. Jeroboam was to take ten of the pieces, symbolic of his future rule of the ten northern tribes. (Again, a king of a new line needed the approval of a prophet.)

We then encounter for the first time a formula that occurs throughout the Book of Kings: "The rest of the acts of Solomon . . . *are recorded in the Book of Acts* of Solomon." It is the practice of the author to give such a formula again and again. No such "Book of Acts" (or royal chronicles) has survived, to our great loss. The author, by repeatedly alluding to the royal chronicles, thereby implicitly admits that his version of the reign of particular kings is abridged and selective.

6. *The Divided Monarchy*

When Solomon died, his son Rehoboam came to the throne. He went to the north, to Shechem, where there was a gathering of people, among them Jeroboam ben Nebat. The assembly set before Rehoboam the complaint that Solomon had put a heavy yoke on them (either through taxes or forced labor.) They asked Rehoboam to lighten the burden. His reply was: "My father punished you with whips, but I shall punish you with scorpions." Thereafter, open rebellion broke out in the north. The northerners made Jeroboam their king, while Rehoboam retained the southern throne in Judah. Thereafter, for as long as the northern kingdom of Israel endured, there were two kingdoms and two kings. The author ordinarily gives us the years of the reign of the northern king in terms of the southern king, and vice versa. This can be fascinating to one whose interest is history; as literature it is unexciting.

It is beyond the scope of this book to follow in detail each of the kings, and the intrigues, rebellions, and assassinations. The material becomes repetitious, and it loses clear differentiation of one king from another, for most of the kings were evil, even though there were prophets who appeared to warn them of the punishment that would come from Yahve.

The prophets are usually anonymous, though here and there a prophet is given a name. About two of the prophets, Elijah and Elisha, cycles of stores are provided. Those about Elijah are marked by a dimension of profundity and consequence which make his character quite clear, and admirable. The king to whom Elijah was opposed was Ahab, who is clearly portrayed as a most wicked man. Ahab's queen was the Phoenician Jezebel, who was even more wicked than Ahab. When Ahab spoke in passing of wanting to trade a vineyard he owned for one belonging to a man Naboth, and Naboth declined to suit the convenience of the king, Jezebel arranged for Naboth to be arrested and tried for cursing God and the king. Naboth was executed, and his vineyard confiscated by Ahab. Elijah appeared before Ahab, and said to him, "At the place where dogs have licked up the blood of Naboth, dogs will lick up your blood." (Ultimately this happened.) A stirring account is given a bit earlier, in the account of Elijah's personal despair at the misfortunes he has gone through in a contest with some prophets of the Baal. He then went to the Wilderness, and even to the cave on the Sacred Mountain. A powerful wind passed by, but Yahve was not in the wind; there came an earthquake, but Yahve was not in the earthquake; then there came fire, but Yahve was not in the fire. After the fire there came "a still, small voice." The intention seems to be to assert that the Deity is not to be discerned in the phenomena of nature, but as an inner voice within a person.

Elijah closed his career by ascending to Heaven in a whirlwind. His successor was Elisha, who was much more of a mere wonder-worker and magician than a spokesman for exalted religion. Some of the stories about him have a limited charm, but some are reprehensible.

The center of attention is usually some monarch, on whom

the author passes a summary judgment, often adding some small or large bits of information—how grateful we can be for these bits! From such incidental historical material, we learn, for example, of the conquest of the northern kingdom by the Assyrians in 722 or 721, the deportation of its people eastward, and the importation of easterners to their domain (the Samaritans were later regarded as descendants of the people imported from the east; these people merged their pagan religion with the Yahvism of the North, but in addition to not being descended from Abraham, their worship was scarcely proper). In general, the detail about individual kings is brief or extended depending upon the extent to which the author involves the king with some particular prophet. He provides more detail about Ahab and Elijah, and about Hezekiah and Isaiah, than he does about the usual king.

What has been called the first edition of Kings came to a climax in Josiah, whom the author regards as the king most exemplary of the finest fidelity to Yahve, this being exhibited in a great religious reformation which Josiah instituted in 621 (see p. 64). That reformation had two main purposes: the first, to destroy all the temples in the land, preserving Solomon's temple in Jerusalem as the only legitimate sanctuary, and the second, to concentrate the priests in Jerusalem. The first edition ended with Josiah still on the throne, having achieved his reformation. But Josiah, meritorious a man as the Deuteronomist regarded him, perished in battle against the Egyptians about 608. After his time there came the Babylonian invasion in 598/97, the destruction of the Temple in Jerusalem in 586, and the exile of the Judean king Jehoiachin to Babylon. Hence, kingship was not a boon, but a liability. If the first edition did end with Josiah, then the extension of the account through king Jehoiachin could be called merely a supplement. The anti-monarchy portions in I Samuel which we noticed above (pp. 160*ff*) are thought to have been written in disillusionment, at the time that the account was prolonged from Josiah to Jehoiachin; it is for this reason that scholars speak of a second edition of Samuel–Kings, rather than of a supplement.

In retrospect, the process was this: The Deuteronomic author arrayed Judges and the early chapters in I Samuel so as to depict the chaos which had arisen through the absence of monarchy. He thereupon introduced monarchy, beginning with Saul, and traced its passing to David and to David's descendants, assessing the individual monarchs either through the mouth of some prophet introduced into the account or by his own comments. But after he wrote his favorable assessment of monarchy as an institution, admiring David and Josiah, a succeeding Deuteronomic author, persuaded that monarchy had not solved the problems at all, prolonged the account beyond Josiah, and also inserted the eloquent interpolations which expressed his reservations about, and disdain for, monarchy.

In view of various changes of mind discernible in the complicated editorial process, we may ask how well the chain of Deuteronomic authors did their work. Perhaps we should give the highest praise to the writer of the Book of Deuteronomy, and the next highest to the writer who preserved so much stirring historical information about David. Of the description of other monarchs we need to say, on the one hand, that the author was relatively stingy with his information, and that he did little to reduce the occasional tedium involved in his repetitious formulas and in the manipulated speeches of the succession of colorless prophets who appear. On the other hand, we should be sympathetic to the basic literary problem. The monarchy endured for at least 400 years; a full account of that period would have been interminably long. The author, accordingly, seems to have decided to abbreviate the account of the kings as much as he could; I find it hard to see how he could have reduced it any more than he did. Despite inevitable gaps, through him we possess a rather good history of the pre-exilic period, while we are almost entirely bereft of knowledge about the post-exilic period, simply because there was no Deuteronomic author to do for the late period what was done for the earliest period.

I find a peculiar, even enigmatic, shortcoming in the Deuteronomic author. It puzzles me beyond comprehension that his work, dedicated to the on-going phenomenon of prophecy, mentions none of the literary prophets except Isaiah, and that even in the case of Isaiah, he speaks about Isaiah's actions rather than about his teachings. Indeed, one must say forthrightly that from the passages in the Deuteronomic writings one would scarcely infer the range, profundity, and high uniqueness of the literary prophets and their teachings. I find myself admiring Deuteronomy, the tales in Judges, the accounts of David and Elijah, so much that I am prone to forgive all the blemishes of the work. Yet I could wish that the Deuteronomist had treated the prophets more adequately.

VI

The Laws

How can one with pleasure read the laws which occupy so much of the Pentateuch? It might be done when the reader has some special interest; otherwise collections of laws are more matters to look up or study than to read. One might have a particular concern, as for example, in the question, Does Pentateuchal law distinguish, as does modern law, between murder (deliberate, intentional killing) and manslaughter (accidental killing)? (It does.) Again, inasmuch as there were law codes among the ancient Babylonians, such as the Code of Hammurabi (*c.* 1792–50 B.C.), does biblical law owe any direct or indirect debt to such codes? At least indirect debt is owed, in both content and form. It should be noted, though, that the Code of Hammurabi is only the most famous of many pre-Mosaic collections. Others, which are even older, include that of the Sumerian king Ur-Nammu (21st century B.C.); that of the Amorite king Bilalama (20th century B.C.); and that of Lipit-Ishtar of Isin (19th century B.C.). It is set forth in the Code of Hammurabi that the code was given to King Hammurabi by the god Shamash, because the king was designated by the god to rule over the god's territory. In its content, the code is similar to the biblical laws in a great many particulars, though the Code of Hammurabi pays more attention to laws concerning property than the Bible does, and the Bible pays more attention to laws concerning persons than the Code of Hammurabi does. Biblical law appears also to have had some antecedents in the oral tribal laws of the early nomadic Hebrews.

Still another kind of curiosity could center in the question of the quality of the biblical laws. We today make a distinction, which the Pentateuch does not, between civil and religious law. The biblical civil laws are, in any fair-minded appraisal, relatively enlightened, their sense of justice is high, and the idea that laws are to protect the citizen not only from a wicked neighbor but even from what we would today call the state is notable. Naturally, much that became the glory of western law, especially the laws concerning personal freedom, does not appear at all. There is also no explicit statement of general legal principles: we find, rather, specific regulations for specific cases. In what we would term religious law the demands and procedures can well seem exotic and alien to us—for example, laws about the "leprosy" of a house or a garment (some frightening rot?)—or the trial by ordeal of a woman suspected of adultery. Biblical law gives more attention to the control of blood feuds than we now give. More significantly, the biblical regulations deal sparingly with what we might call "due process," that is, legal procedure. Yet, all in all, on scrutiny we find the biblical laws to be quite humane, enlightened, and praiseworthy.

There are obvious layers of biblical law; one can readily see repetitions, some items repeated without basic change, and others given with significant differences. The scholars have noticed all these phenomena and have attempted to separate the layers from each other. Often a given layer is alleged to be associated with one of the four major strata, J, E, D, and P, of the Pentateuch, but such a procedure works reasonably well only with D and P, but not as well with J and E.[1]

Scholars have noted the variety of Hebrew terms for law: *mishpāt* ("judicial precedent"), *mitzvāh* ("commandment"), *ḥūq* ("decree," that is, royal pronouncement), *tōrāh* ("teaching," a P term for an individual bit of legislation), *piqqūd* ("precept"), and *'ēdút* ("testimony"). The variety of terms may suggest a different *origin* for aspects of the laws, but most scholars believe that so advanced is Hebrew law beyond its primitive origins that these different terms are now without different import.

Some laws are presented with great brevity: "Who strikes a man fatally surely shall be put to death." Other laws are not stated so briefly, but include a clause such as "When a man does X, then the rule is A. If, however, Y takes place, then the rule is B; if Z takes place, then the rule is C" (see, for example, Ex. XXI: 7-11). The very brief laws normally lack any explanation of why the law is as it is. The longer formulations, with the alternate possibilities, often provide some kind of explanation or rationalization. This is especially the case in the laws found collected in Deut. XII-XXVI. Scholars have generally termed these laws "prophetic," because an explicit humanitarian basis is given as the reason for the law. A later collection constitutes much of the Priestly Code. Within the P writings survivals of earlier, even of quite ancient, laws are presented, and those laws which the P author himself composed he evidently took from ancient materials. P, thus, is not entirely a single stage of legislation; indeed, within P there is a section, Lev. XVII-XXVI, which is called the Holiness Code, and which was recorded a little earlier than the rest of P. Also there are tiny bits of legislation appended to and inserted within the basic P code.

The range of biblical laws can perhaps be discerned by listing some of the major topics which are dealt with: slavery, murder, assault and battery, rape, damages resulting from an ox that gores, damage to crops, theft, burglary, loans and pledges for loans, inheritance, marriage, divorce, incest, "levirate" marriage, and kidnapping. Problems of judicial procedure, such as bribery and the calling of witnesses, are briefly dealt with.

The ritual laws cover the sacred days of the annual calendar (Sabbath, New Year, Day of Atonement, the three pilgrim festivals of Booths, Passover, and Weeks), the mode of various types of animal sacrifices (whether burnt up entirely, or only burnt in part), the occasion and manner of the various sacrifices, forbidden foods, ritual impurity, the sabbatical year of no planting, the "jubilee" year of the reverting of property to previous owners, and prohibitions of idolatry. An account of the investiture of Aaron as high priest is given in Lev. VIII, and an account of the inauguration of the priestly functions of Aaron and his sons is given in Lev. IX.

In both the priestly writings and the Deuteronomic writings there is an emphasis on the need for the entire people to conform to the highest ritual and ethical standards. This emphasis occurs in the so-called Holiness Code, in Lev. XVII-XXVI, in the repetition of the phrase, "You shall be holy, for I, Yahve your God, am holy."

That aspects of the priestly ritual are ancient, and began in the Wilderness period, is not doubted by modern scholars. What is doubted is that the full array, including the institution of Aaron and his children as a hereditary family of Priests, is that early. To put this in another way, modern scholars tend to hold that the elaborateness of the priestly system, despite its ancient roots, developed over a period of centuries, and came to fullness only in the post-exilic period; in this later time the conception arose, and was recorded, that the matured priestly functions and organization were actually inaugurated in the Wilderness period. The mention of priests and of rituals in the Deuteronomic writings (which are earlier than P) are such as to imply that there was no ancient, Wilderness priestly organization, system, and regulations. The practices described in Samuel and Kings are often out of conformity with the Pentateuchal requirements, yet they are not conceived of in these writings as improper or abnormal. Most scholars hold that priesthood before the post-exilic period was never confined to a family such as Aaron's; the latter development is the end result of a trend toward system and uniformity which came to a climax in the post-exilic period. I myself subscribe to this view. It is my opinion, however, that the view of the Wilderness origin of the priestly system is not the result of deliberate falsehood; it is the result, rather, of the unconcern with precise history which marks biblical writings.

Far more important than the details about compilation or composition is another matter. We might lead into it by noticing two items. First, there was the old tradition, that the Deity revealed Himself to Moses, and thus to the people, at Sinai/Horeb, and that there the Deity and the people entered into a covenant with mutual obligations. In a sense, the obligations on men specified in the covenant were divine law, as in the Ten Commandments (these, of course, make no mention of courts or of punishment). Second, there was the tradition that monarchy prevailed from the time of Saul (11th century B.C.) to the time of Jehoiachin (about 550 B.C.), and that during this period monarchs promulgated laws. After the Babylonian exile, there was no restoration of monarchy. The ruling authority was assigned by the Persians to priests, indeed, to the high priest. Legislation which before the exile was *royal* law persisted in force after the exile as *religious* law, as compiled and recorded by P. The recollection of Moses and Sinai paved the way for the view that all of the immense body of accumulated law had been enjoined at Sinai or in the Wilderness, either through Moses, or through Moses and Aaron. Hence the accumulated law ceased to be conceived of as having any royal and therefore human origin, but instead the laws were deemed to have been *revealed* to many by God, their author. The Hebrew word for that revelation is Torah.

This word *torah* can refer to a single item in the Priestly Code; more generally, though, Torah has the overtone of something in which men could be instructed; indeed, some modern scholars render *torah* in this broad sense as "divine instruction." This divine instruction, through the work of the priests, now became something unique: a Book. It became a Book to refer to, a Book to read, a Book to meditate on. Laws were the direct impetus for creating the Book, but the Book was more the laws, for it included narration, as we have seen. The Book emerged as a repository of a religion which could live, thrive, and be transmitted. In time, Jews extended the use of the term Torah so that it became their way of speaking of the totality of The Five Books of Moses, the divine instruction to live by.

After the time of Alexander the Great (*c.* 325 B.C.) Jews settled in the Grecian Mediterranean lands in great numbers, lost their ancestral tongue, and therefore needed a translation of Scripture in order to perpetuate their Jewish loyalty. We know of no other book (as distinct from royal decrees) that was translated in ancient times. Other peoples had writings they deemed sacred; the Bible differed from them in that it contained divine laws to regulate and to sanctify *every man's daily life*. This was its chief distinction from other sacred writings.

VII

Verse and Poetry:
Canticles, Lamentations, and Psalms

We have seen in passing some random specimens of Hebrew verse and poetry. Now we shall look more closely, recalling the essential differences in any literature between verse and prose. Verse is a form of writing which conforms to certain external characteristics, normally either meter or rhyme; in biblical literature it is meter, never rhyme, which distinguishes verse from prose. There are a number of distinctive meters which we shall notice.

Poetry, even while adhering to the form of verse, rises above prose and verse by its heightened expression, through capturing some intensely emotional mood or feeling, often expressed through felicitous words and phrases, such as figures of speech. (Naturally, there are passages which to some tastes would be verse and to others poetry, for the line of demarcation is not always clear-cut.)

Because verse and poetry conform to a metrical pattern, there is often, or always, a potential artificiality in them, but the better the versifier or the poet, the less evident the artificiality. We tend to tolerate the artificiality in verse and poetry because the greater effectiveness of the total compensates for the departure from prose. The nature of the Hebrew language, and of Hebrew syntax, tends to reduce artificiality to the vanishing point. For example, what we call a verb in Hebrew can contain the action, the subject, and the object; thus, *re'ītíkā*, a single word, means "I have seen you." Hebrew verse, accordingly, is relatively free of glaring disruptions of word order or of syntax, as when a poet writes, in English, "Him I saw." In Hebrew the usual word of a sentence, even in prose, is normally the verb, the subject, and then the object. Thus, "God remembered Noah" (Gen. XIII:1) is: "remembered God Noah." In Hebrew, where the writer desires to indicate an emphasis, he accomplishes this by putting that word first in the sentence or poetic line, so that the Hebrew, "Noah remembered God" would denote that it was Noah, *not somebody else*, whom God remembered. On the other hand, the order, "God remembered Noah," would denote that God, *not somebody else*, did the remembering. The flexibility available in Hebrew word order dissolves the artificiality.

A peculiarity in Hebrew (and in some other languages) is the ability to dispense with the verb "to be" in the present tense. In Psalm XXIII, the best-known of the Psalms, the literal rendering is: "Yahve my shepherd," though the meaning is inescapably "Yahve *is* my shepherd." Grammarians of Hebrew call this kind of construction a "noun clause," simply because no verb is directly expressed. Indeed, we must note the verb tenses in Hebrew. An English verb has six tenses: I see; I saw; I shall see; I have seen; I had seen; I will have seen. A Hebrew verb has only two. We give the two tenses names comparable to those some grammarians have given Indo-European tenses, calling them "imperfect" and "perfect." However, a Hebrew verb, whether "imperfect" or "perfect," lacks a clear and definitive sense of time, such as past or future; the two Hebrew tenses express the completeness or incompleteness of the action, without respect to time. Thus, "I *went* to the store yesterday" would in Hebrew mean that I went there and finished my going; in such a case one would use what is called the perfect tense. But suppose that yesterday, on my way to the store, I met a friend, stopped to talk, and forgot to go on to the store; that is, I left the going uncompleted. In such a case, the Hebrew, in saying "as I *went* to the store yesterday," would use the imperfect tense, not the perfect, and mean, "as I *was going*." It follows, then, that there is a certain suppleness in the tenses of the Hebrew verb, despite the lack of a full system of tenses.

Psalm XLI:2 reads, "Happy the considerer of the poor," meaning, "Happy is he who considers the poor." Analysts call the Hebrew form for the word "considerer" a participle. In Hebrew, a participle is part verb, part adjective, and part noun. When a participle is used along with a noun, it is an adjective; for example, "The man, *seeing* the cloud, knew it would rain." As a noun it denotes "the one seeing" or even "the see-er." We can translate a participle by a noun like "see-er," or even use a roundabout English expression, "the one who sees . . ." There are times,—for instance, in our use of the present tense—when the Hebrew participle acts like a verb. We might illustrate this from the well-known verse: "Yahve *visits* the sins of fathers on the children." In the sentence, a perfect tense ("visited") would mean that the action was completed, as if, "Last year, God *visited* the sins . . ."; an imperfect would mean, "Yahve was *in the act of visiting* the sins . . ." but did not complete the act. The sense of the participle is that "Yahve *continually* (or *customarily*) visits the sins. . . ."

The time factor (past, present, or future) of a Hebrew sentence is dictated largely by context. A kind of convention has existed among earlier translators whereby an imperfect has come to be rendered into English as a future; often this is right, but just as often it can be wrong. The sentence, "Yahve is my shepherd, I *shall* not *want*" (understanding "want" as "lack") illustrates in "shall . . . want" the way in which an imperfect can become a future in English. It is just as accurate to render this, "I *do not* want." Had the verb been a perfect, it would have meant, "I did not lack"; had it been a participle, "Yahve is my shepherd, I *continuously* do not lack." The Hebrew imperfect means, "now, at this time, I do not lack."

Why should we spend this space on the verb forms? To make the point that the Hebrew language, despite its paucity of tenses, is able to express subtleties in meaning.

The opportunity for subtlety is increased by a characteristic Hebrew mannerism, used both in prose and in verse. The usual Hebrew sentence is composed of two parts, so that we speak of an A and a B part of a verse. In prose, this is a typical sentence: "In the beginning God created heaven and earth" (the A part); and "the earth was waste and void" (the B part). While there are some occasional short sentences which are not in two parts, most Hebrew sentences are, even in prose.

In verse, where meter enters in, the two parts are ordinarily of the same length metrically, consisting, in the most usual pattern, of two three-beat half-sentences:

$$- - - \, / \, - - -$$

Whereas in prose, devoid of meter, the two half-sentences are only loosely tied to each other, in verse they are intimately bound together.

For example:

Le-yáhve hā-áretz u-melóah / tēvél ve-yóshevé-hāh
(A:) The earth is Yahve's, and its contents; (B:) the world
and those who inhabit it.

(Ps. XXIV:1)

Here B essentially repeats A, extending it somewhat. Again:

(A:) He has me graze in grassy fields; (B:) He leads me
beside tranquil waters.

(Ps. XXIII:2)

Here, too, B extends A.

But there are instances in which B adds to A by providing a contrast:

(A:) Sons have I reared and raised; (B:) but they have
sinned against Me.

(Isa. I:2)

So close, then, is the relationship between A and B in verse that
the sense of A carries over into B, and without A, B is often
incomplete or unintelligible or absurd. Here is an example:

> (B:) And righteousness like a mighty stream.
>
> (Amos V:24B)

This is fragmentary; it lacks a verb. The verb, though, is in A;
it carries over to B.

> (A:) But let justice flow like water.
>
> (Amos V:24A)

Putting A and B together, we have: "But let justice flow like
water, and righteousness like a mighty stream." ("Mighty" is
the figure for a watercourse which, when the dry season is over,
fills and rushes.) A and B are so tightly intertwined here that
they are in effect inseparable.

The term for the relation between A and B in verse is "parallelism." Sometimes in scholarly analysis adjectives are added to
modify the term, such as "balancing" parallelism, or "intensify-
ing" parallelism, or the like. It is sufficient for us to know the basic
term without these various shadings. More important is our grasp
of the utility of parallelism. Hebrew lacks all but a few adverbs,
and its stock of adjectives is not abundant. It possesses only a
few synonyms in its verbs. Moreover, Hebrew has no common
words that are compounds, as do Indo-European languages. (In
Hebrew only proper names are compound.) Thus, in English
(from Latin), we can say transfer: to carry across; refer: to carry
back; prefer: to carry in advance: confer, to carry with. That is
to say, compound words, especially when prepositions are joined
to verb roots, can lead to the expression of a precise meaning, or
a subtlety in meaning; in this sense both Greek and Latin (and
thus English) are richer than Hebrew. But in many ways parallelism gives a comparable subtlety to the Hebrew, for the A and
the B combine to provide precision and shade of meaning. Parallelism also helps make good the lack of adverbs.

Most of us would, I think, regard what we find in Proverbs as verse, rather than poetry, for the figures of speech are more restrained and the emotion less intense than they would be in poetry. Indeed, the proverbs usually possess the parallelism of verse, while they do not always have the usual or expected metrical regularity. The following, though, exhibit both the 3/3 meter and the parallelism:

> A soft answer turns wrath away,
>   A paining word raises anger.
>
> (XV:1)

> The memory of the righteous becomes a blessing,
>   But the fame of the wicked rots away.
>
> (X:7)

Other passages in Proverbs diverge from the 3/3 meter, but almost never from the parallelism:

> Hatred stirs up strife,
>   But love covers all sins. (3/4)
>
> (X:12)

> Whoever heeds advice is on the road of life,
>   But whoever abandons prudent counsel goes astray. (4/3)
>
> (X:17)

Poetry, in contradistinction to mere verse, combines parallelism and elasticity of word order to provide an emphasis which can heighten the poetic expression that is accomplished in other languages by the use of adverbs or adjectives. When verse moves into genuine poetry, these resources are employed to wondrous effect, as we shall see. Indeed, the resources of Hebrew can turn even unlikely passages into high poetry. The form of verse called an alphabetical acrostic, in which the first line begins with A, the second with B, the third with C, and so on, is in other languages highly artificial, and almost always wooden; in Hebrew the use of the acrostic is no barrier to poetic eloquence:

A. Aleph   Whoever finds a worthy woman, beyond pearls is her
                value.

B. Beth   Her husband's heart relies on her, and he does not lack
               gain.
C. Gimmel   She requites him with good, not evil, through all the
               days of her life.

(Prov. XXXI: 10-12)

The poem continues, as do many Hebrew poems, through all
twenty-two letters of the Hebrew alphabet.

Without figures of speech, metaphor, simile, or personification,
there can seldom be poetry. Hence, figures of speech are abundant in Hebrew poetry. Personification is what makes Psalm
XXIII so vividly beautiful:

> Yahve is my shepherd, I lack nothing.
> He has me graze in grassy fields, He leads me beside
>   tranquil waters.

Both simile and metaphor are exemplified in the allusions to the
adversaries normal in life:

> Who have sharpened their tongues *like a sword,*
> They aim *their arrow,* a bitter word.

(Ps. LXIV:4)

Or:

> Would that someone would give me the *dove's wing;*
> I would flee away and [there] settle down.

(Ps. LV:1)

Or:

> The heavens tell of God's glory, the sky relates
>   His handiwork.
> One day tells it to the next, and night hands on the
>   tidings to the next night.
> There is no telling, there are no words, no voice at
>   all is heard.
> Yet the sound of these permeates all the earth, and the
>   words reach to the end of the world.

(Ps. XIX:2-4)

The figures of speech are normally strong and vivid:

> After Israel came out of Egypt, the house of Jacob from
> the foreign land,
> Judah became His sanctuary, Israel the seat of His reign. . . .
>
> The sea observed—and fled; the Jordan flowed upstream.
> The hills danced like rams, high places like kids.

The poet now turns to the second person:

> What has happened to you, O sea, that you flee,
> O Jordan, that you flow upstream?
> You hills that you dance like rams, you high places
> like kids?

(Ps. CXIV:1-4)

Such shifts in person are not infrequent in Hebrew poetry. The
Hebrew grammar, with different forms for singular and plural,
and for first, second, and third person, is the clue that such a shift
in person is occurring; that is, the poem itself lacks the direct stage
direction; it is the sense of the poem, as buttressed by the unob-
trusive grammatical forms, which reveals such shifts. This shift
occurs in individual Psalms. In a long poem or group of poems
such as Canticles, it occurs to the point that we are not told who,
of a range of possibilities—the boy, the girl, the friends—is speaking;[1] we ourselves must supply this from the content.

Scripture tells us virtually nothing about the poets; there are
allusions to David, and there are references to what we might call
certain "guilds" of poets, such as is likely meant in allusions in
Psalms to "Asaph" and "the sons of Korah." An ancient book of
poems is mentioned, and even quoted from, and in a way this
causes a problem, for the title given is at times "The Book of *yšr*"
(II Sam. 1:18), but at one point the Greek translation (there,
I Kings VIII:54, diverging from the Hebrew) suggests that the
word should be *šyr*; if the latter, the title was "The Book of the
Song," but if the former, "The Book of the Upright." We do not
know what "Upright" connotes. Elsewhere (Num. XXI:27)
mention is made of *mōshlím*, for which a possible translation
might be "minstrels." In the absence of any direct information
about poets, we are left completely dependent upon the poems.

That some of the verses are alphabetical acrostics clearly reveals some conscious intent on the part of someone to write a poem; on the other hand, there are bits here and there, like the song of Lamech (see p. 77) and an incantation to a well (Num. XXI:17-18) which suggest folk poems. A single short citation is made from a book called "The Wars of Yahve" (Num. XXI:14); we know nothing about this book. The citation seems to come from a folk poem, describing briefly the boundaries of Moab. Perhaps ultimately every folk poem was created by a person, and hence some poet lies behind a folk poem too, but Scripture gives us no information to help us. Other types of poems, some seemingly liturgical hymns, and some reviews of Israel's history, appear to have been composed deliberately. Meter and parallelism suggest that these poets were craftsmen. One would need to conclude, too, that the people were receptive to the poems; some high status of the poet is certainly to be inferred from the epithet applied to David, that he was Israel's sweet singer.

Canticles

The Book of Canticles is known in Hebrew as *shír ha-shírím*, from the first two words of the book. The literal meaning is "Song of Songs"; the import is, "The very best of all songs." The Book is also known as the Song of Solomon. Canticles is a collection of love poems, and is at places very frank in the descriptive praise of the female anatomy. Ancient bowdlerizers, both Jewish and Christian, declared these poems to reflect either God's spiritual love for Israel, or Christ's for the Church, on the premise that the physical description was unseemly. Such was not the view of the early poet, nor should it be our view.

The first line is spoken by a girl, probably a bride; the A part is spoken *about* her beloved, but the B part is spoken *to* him, as are the subsequent verses.

> Would that *he* would kiss me with kisses of *his* mouth! . . .

> For better than wine is *your* love.
> Your perfumes are excellent in fragrance;

Your name is sprayed fragrance;
Hence, the maidens love you. . . .

The attendants speak:

We rejoice and delight in you.
We regard your love as better than wine,
Your caresses as beyond song.*

The bride speaks again:

Dark am I but pleasant-looking, O daughters of Jerusalem,
Like the [black] tents of the Kedar desert,
The draperies of Shalmah.*
Do not look askance at me that I am darkened,
That the sun has browned me.
My brothers were annoyed at me,
They made me the watcher of the vineyards—
My own vineyard I have not tended. . . .

Tell me, O you whom I love,
Where is it you are grazing [the sheep]? . . .

The attendants speak:

If you do not know, O fairest of women,
Go, follow the footprints of the flock. . . .

(I:2-3, 5-6, 8)

Another poem is addressed by a young man to his beloved:

Behold, you are beautiful, my love!
Behold, you are beautiful.
Your eyes behind your veil are doves.
Your hair is a flock of goats
Trailing from Gilead.
Your teeth are a flock of sheep ready for shearing,
Emerging from their washing,
All of them fertile,
Not a sterile one among them.

* An asterisk indicates that the translation rests on an alteration of the Hebrew text. Such alteration, frequent in modern translations, emerges from studying Hebrew Bible manuscripts or ancient translations. The alterations made sense out of otherwise difficult or puzzling passages.

Your lips are like a thread of scarlet
And your mouth is pretty.
Your cheek behind its veil is red
Like a piece of pomegranate;
Your neck is like one of David's towers,
Built for a fortress,
Hung about with a thousand shields
All of them bucklers of mighty men.
Your breasts are like two fawns,
Twins of a gazelle.
Until the day breaks and the darkness departs
I will betake me to the mountain of myrrh
And the hill of incense.
You are altogether beautiful, my love;
There is no flaw in you.

(IV:1-7)

The girl replies:

I am my beloved's; it is I whom he desires.
Come, beloved, let us go into the field,
    Let us lie among the bushes.
Arising early to the vineyards,
    We will see if the vine has budded,
    If its blossom has opened,
    If the pomegranates are in flower,
If the mandrakes have given off their [lusty] fragrance,
    And are precious fruits at our door—
        New ones and even old ones—
        These I have saved up for you!

(VII:1-12)

These apostrophes to love, to physical love, are eloquent because they are so genuine, for

Love is as strong as death,
    And jealousy domineering like the grave.
    Its flames are fires like those of Yahve.
For abundant water cannot extinguish love,
    Nor can rivers flood over it.

(VIII:6B-7A)

The poems exalt youth and vitality, in direct and unabashed expression. One can almost feel the springtime and hear the chirping of the birds—the turtledoves, not the turtles, as the King James has it—and smell the fragrance as the new blossoms appear and the flowers unfold. What a lovely, and happy, series of glowing poems!

Lamentations

Notably different, though in its own way equally moving, is the mood of sorrow reflected in the harrowing lines of Lamentations. The sorrow is far beyond mere grief. In the background lies the fact of desolation, of some devastation caused by a merciless invading army. Tradition ascribes Lamentations to Jeremiah, and identifies the calamity as the destruction of Jerusalem and the Temple by the Babylonians in 586 B.C. The tradition seems untenable to some, but in Lamentations III we encounter a man of sorrows like Jeremiah, if not the prophet himself. Throughout the five poems (all but the fifth are alphabetical acrostics) there hovers a sense of despair which only a major calamity, like the Babylonian invasion, could inspire. The poet believes that the disaster came because of Israel's sinfulness; hence even the glorious city of Jerusalem, once thought invincible, has come to degradation. The meter here is 3/3/2 : 2/2/2—that of the *dirge*:

E-cháh yāshváh vādád / hā'ír rabbátī 'ám / hāytáh k'almānáh /

Rabáti va-gōyyím / sāráti ba-m'edīnót / hāytáh lāmás.

How sits she bereft, the city once populous!
She has become like a widow.
    She has been eminent among the nations,
    A princess among the provinces!—
        She has become someone's tributary. . . .

Bitterly she weeps by night, her tears on her cheeks.
No comforter has she from among those who loved her;
Her friends all became traitors,
    Turning into enemies. . . .

> Gone into exile is Judah from affliction, and abundant
>   forced toil.
> She dwells among the nations, but has found no rest.
>   All her pursuers overtake her
>   In narrow passage-ways. . . .
>
> The roads of Zion mourn;
>   No one travels for festivals.
> Her law-courts are desolate, her priests are in grief;
>   Her young girls are raped—and she herself is
>   engulfed in bitterness.
>
> (Lam. I:1-4)

This graphic picture of a battered and beaten people arises from specific events. The poem is an alphabetical acrostic, yet it sounds spontaneous enough as to have emerged even prior to meditation on the disaster; indeed, the poem reflects a lingering sense of calamity.

The third poem heightens the emotion by letting us view the experience of one man who lived through the divine wrath and punishment. (The meter is not regular.)

> I am the man who has experienced misery
>   At the rod of His wrath.
> Me did He lead, but He made me walk in darkness,
>   Not in light. . . .
> He has wasted my flesh and skin,
>   He has broken my bones. . . .
> He has set me in darkness, like those long dead. . . .
>
> (III:1, 3, 6)

Yet the poet cannot be content with what has happened. It is his axiom that Yahve has caused the calamity; his question is, Why?

> A great sin did Jerusalem sin,
>   So that she became a thing of filth.
> Those who had honored her despise her,
>   For they have seen her naked.
>   She only groans, and turns about.
>
> (I:8)

The Lord has swallowed without pity all the dwellings of Jacob.
In His wrath He tore down the strongholds of Judah's daughter,
He brought them to the ground; He desecrated the kingdom
    and its princes.

(II:2)

Thus, beyond the vividness of the calamities is the poet's lament, as if to say, here is the dreadfulness we brought on ourselves.

Psalms

In turning to the simple beauty and recurrent majesty, the alternating heartfelt loneliness and security, of the Psalms, we must begin with the full awareness that since Psalms is a collection of 150 poems, all of them cannot be masterpieces; some are only routine; and the spirit in some is a dreadful, raucous call for vengeance. Our gratification is that so many of them are excellent.

What is it in man that stirs him to religious emotion, and then into expressing it? The immediate answer is that man knows the transiency of his life, and the delicate and fragile nature of life itself. None of us is born to escape death; few of us avoid all sickness; all of us are tied to parents and brothers and sisters whose sufferings become our own. We grow from the weakness of babyhood into the vigor of adolescence and maturity, and then we all begin to decline. Even at the height of our vigor an accident can befall us; at the pinnacle of our strength a boulder which we have not the power to move is readily pushed about by an earthquake, as if to scorn such strength as we have. We are prone to fears, and even terror, and we all long for some unshakable security. We are puny, for the trees are taller than we, and the mountains immensely greater. To the Hebrew, it was God who moved the boulder, and gave the trees their stature, and the mountains their grandeur. He made the mighty seas rough, and He calmed them. He always existed; He will always exist; it is we who are here but for a moment. It is He alone who is man's security.

Yet there are times when He seems to ignore man, to withhold His concern and protection, and man is moved to ask, Why is He silent? or even, Why has He abandoned me? Indeed, Israel is His people; has He at times abandoned His people? The individual who feels abandoned is prey to accentuated fears, not alone of what is unknown—he is often prey to terrors brought on by the hostility of one's fellowman which all men encounter. The collective people, Israel, could feel abandoned to the appetite for conquest of neighboring peoples (and hence they could feel recurrent hatred and desire for revenge).

The Psalms reflect such personal and collective moods: fear, anxiety, dread—but they also reflect their opposites: assurance, confidence, and utter security. A portion of Psalm LXVIII seems to me useful as a prologue to the entire book, for in it we can see reflections of a variety of moods:

> Out of the press of woes on me, I called to Yahve,
>   He answered me in His boundlessness.
> Yahve is with me; I do not fear.
>   What can man do to me?
> Yahve is a help to me,
>   I shall look triumphantly at my adversaries.
> Better is it to take refuge in Yahve
>   Than to put trust in princes. . . .
> The Lord is my strength and song
>   And He is my Salvation:
> Joy and deliverance are heard in the tents of the righteous;
>   Yahve's right hand works valiantly.
> Yahve's right hand is exalted,
>   Yahve's right hand works valiantly.
> I shall not die, but shall live,
>   And relate the deeds of the Lord:
> The Lord has greatly chastened me,
>   But He did not give me over to death.
>
> (CXVIII:5-18)

The allusions in this poem to the hostile nations are not always certain; possibly they are at times figurative, and refer only to one's personal adversaries and not to some foreign foe. The rest of the poem is unmistakably clear; the fear that arises in distress gives way to confidence in Yahve's saving power, a confidence which is unshakable, since it is placed in Yahve, not in man, who is unworthy of confidence. The transition here, from perilous distress to the inner assurance of rising out of the danger, is not directly paralleled in other Psalms, but aspects of danger, or of confidence despite it, are. The poetic greatness of the Psalms rests on the manner in which these moods are expressed, and in the way in which, in an individual Psalm, the mood is retained, and its emotion constantly deepened. Here is a similar poem:

> I love it when Yahve hears
>   My voice, my supplication!
> For He has inclined His ear to me,
>   Whenever I have called out.
> The cords of death have bound me,
>   And the pressure of the grave has encountered me:
>   I meet trouble and sorrow,
> But I call on Yahve's name:
> "I beseech You, O Yahve,
>   Rescue me!" . . .
> Gracious is Yahve and righteous;
>   Our God is compassionate.
> Yahve preserves the ordinary man.
>   I was brought low; He became my deliverance.
> Return, O my soul, to your tranquillity
>   For Yahve has been generous to you.
>   (CXVI: 1-7)

So old are some of the Psalms that they reflect some aspects of early folklore. This is evidence of a long outgrown polytheism,[2] in which Yahve was the chief among many gods. In early folklore, His control of the sea was expressed through his victory over a sea-creature, Rahab.

> Who in the sky compares with Yahve,
> Who among the sons of the gods is like Yahve?
> He is God, regarded with terror in the great council of
>   the [heavenly] saints,

Awesome over all those about Him. . . .
You [O Yahve] rule over the arrogance of the sea.
When its waves arise, You still them. . . .
You broke Rahab into pieces, as a corpse;
You scattered Your foes with Your strong arm.

(LXXXIX:7-11; 6-10 English)

Vestiges of what appear to be ritual processions occur in the Psalter:

Open for me the gates[3] of righteousness,
  I will enter them, I will thank Yahve. . . .
This gate is Yahve's,
  [Only] the righteous enters it.

(CXVIII:19-20)

Raise your heads, O gates,
  Be raised, O eternal portals,
  And let the glorious King enter. . . .
Who is the glorious King?
  Yahve strong and might, a hero in battle!

(XXIV:7-8)

Man's dependence on God is total, and hence his despair is total when he seems to be unanswered:

My God, my God, why have You forsaken me?
  [Why are You] far from my help, from the words of
    my outcry?
O my God, I call upon You by day but You do not answer,
  By night, and there is no relief. . . .

(XXII:1-2)

Another voice speaks:

Let him turn to Yahve, He will save him,
  He will deliver him, for He delights in him.

(XXII:9)

The first voice resumes:

It is You who drew me out of the womb,
  You entrusted me to my mother's breasts.

> Upon You have I been cast from birth,
> From my mother's womb You have been my God.
> Do not be far from me, for trouble is at hand,
> With no one to help. . . .
> I am poured out like water,
> My bones are disjointed. . . .
>
> (XXII: 10-12, 15A)

> But You, O Yahve—do not be far!
> O my Help, hurry to my succor. . . .
> Rescue me from the lion's mouth,
> Answer me, when the horns of wild oxen [threaten me].
>
> (XXII: 20, 22)

In another mood, a poet sings of God's greatness:

> Shout to Yahve, O all the earth;
> Break forth, sing, and be melodious.
> Sing to Yahve with the lyre,
> With the lyre and the sound of song,
> With trumpets and the sound of the ram's horn;
> Shout before the King Yahve! . . .
>
> (XCVIII:4-6)

Still another mood is that of thanksgiving.

> I extol You, O Yahve, for You have raised me up,
> Thus preventing my adversaries from gloating over me!
> O Yahve, my God, I cried to You; You healed me.
> O Yahve, You brought me out of Sheol;
> You preserved me alive from the grave. . . .
> Out of His wrath comes smiting;
> Out of His favor comes life. . . .
> Weeping was there at evening to lodge for the night,
> But in the morning there was rejoicing! . . .
> You turn my mourning into a dance,
> You take off my sackcloth, and gird me with joy!
>
> (XXX: 1-6, 12)

There are occasional poems which come out of historical events, such as this song of the exiles:

By the rivers of Babylon,
There we sat and wept
When we remembered Zion.
On willows there we hung our lyres,
For there our captors demanded songs of us,
And our oppressors entertainment:
"Sing to us one of the songs of Zion."
How shall we sing Yahve's song on foreign soil! . . .
If I forget you, O Jerusalem, let my right hand
      [wither and] be forgotten.
Let my tongue cleave to my palate
If I fail to remember you,
If I do not raise Jerusalem above my own joy.
                                              (CXXXVII:1-6)

Quite apart from God's great deeds of deliverance was His revelation to man of His divine laws. The act of that revelation, and the laws themselves, were a source of rejoicing:

Happy is the man who reveres Yahve,
And finds great delight in His commandments.
                                              (CXII:1)

Yahve's revelation is perfect, reviving the soul.
Yahve's instruction is reliable, making the simple man wise
Yahve's precepts are direct, rejoicing the heart.
Yahve's commandment is clear, illuminating the eyes. . . .
                                              (XIX:8-9 Heb.; 7-8 Eng.)

In some Psalms there is a spirit somewhat kindred to that found in the Book of Proverbs, in that the divine laws and personal wisdom combine to lead a man to live the righteous life so pleasing to God. We find this in Psalm I:

Happy is the man who has not taken the counsel of sinners,
Nor stood in the path of sinners,
Nor sat in the company of scorners.
Rather, he finds delight in the instruction of Yahve,
And he meditates on His instruction day and night,
So that he becomes like a tree planted near pools of water,

Which produces its fruit in its proper time,
Nor does its leaf dry up,
But all that he does prospers. . . .
This is not so with the wicked.
They are like chaff the wind blows away.
Hence, the wicked cannot withstand [divine] judgment,
Nor can sinners [withstand] the assembly of the righteous. . . .
Yahve takes care of the way of the righteous,
But the way of sinners perishes.

(I:1-6)

No short selection such as here given can do justice to the range found in the collection of 150 poems, for only a bit of the flavor, not its totality, can be conveyed. The reader needs some measure of guidance in his reading, for the text in some of the Psalms had been transmitted with uncertainty and faults. The inherited division is not fully reliable: in certain cases two different Psalms have come to be presented as a single one. Yet in reality little guidance is needed, provided the reader understands that a psalm is an emotional utterance, not a logical one. The reader who either totally disbelieves in God, or is so strong himself that he is not aware of human weakness or human limitation, simply ought not to read the Psalms. For others, though, the Psalms still can speak of man's fears and doubts, of his hopes and, indeed, of his attainment of inner tranquillity.

VIII

Wisdom Literature: Proverbs, Ecclesiastes, Job

In every society, in every age, problems arise, whether at the palace, in a family, or in an individual life. Will the solution offered today reasonably anticipate what can arise in the future? Ancient men often resorted to various types of magic and divination to learn in advance what the outcome of some decision would be. The early prophet was a holy man who, it was believed, could reveal what would happen in the future.

In almost every society there has also existed the sage, the wise man. No king of consequence failed to have a staff of counselors who could presumably gather the facts, make an analysis and a synthesis of them, and then recommend what appeared to be the best advice. This advice was deemed to be the result of wisdom.

But what is this elusive quality, wisdom? Is it a knowledge only of facts? Obviously not, for we all know students and professors whose learning is tremendous, but whom we should never judge to have wisdom. Wisdom, then, is different from learning, for an unschooled person may possess it, out of rich experience. On the other hand, there are people with rich experience to whom we would not attribute wisdom, for even that experience does not necessarily lead them to it.

It is a very ancient truism that wisdom, whatever it may be, is the most precious possession a man can acquire. But exactly what is it? And how can men attain it? The ancient Hebrews, like other peoples, asked such questions. Out of their asking these questions, three books came to be written or compiled, and these made their way into the Hebrew Bible: Proverbs, Ecclesiastes, and Job. Proverbs is a book which presumes to offer the sound counsel which wisdom provides; Ecclesiastes is a commentary on the experience of men, as seen by one man; Job asks the question, can man truly arrive at that profound understanding of life which implies wisdom?

The ancient Hebrews, though they were unable to state exactly what wisdom is, recognized that it does not come automatically from book-learning, nor, necessarily, from experience. Wisdom was, in their view, a gift which God graciously bestowed on the rare individual. The proverbial sage in Hebrew history was Solomon (see p. 175), who happily had bequeathed a legacy of the wise things he had said. Hence there was in existence a body of transmitted wisdom, surviving long after the wise man who expressed it had died. That is to say, wisdom was something that was detached from the man who produced it.

Proverbs

While the Book of Proverbs, attributed by the Hebrews to Solomon, may indeed contain some examples of that monarch's personal wisdom, it also cites the names of other wise men, Agur (XXX) and Lemuel (XXXI), and thus we know that it is a collection, an anthology, of the wise sayings of many men. The proverbs of Solomon himself are, in fact, confined to two sections, X:1-XXII:16 and XXV:1-XXIX:27, and they seem not at all reflected in the opening of the book, for there the phrase "The Proverbs of Solomon" appears to apply to the total book, but not particularly to what immediately ensues. Especially is this the necessary conclusion if by the term "proverb" we mean a short, pithy statement, such as "a stitch in time sometimes saves nine." There is no dearth of such pithy sentences later in the book, though there are by no means as many as the three thousand which Solomon was reputed to have spoken (I Kings IV:32). But the Hebrews did not limit the *māshāl*, "proverb," to the pithy statement. *Māshāl* has a variety of denotations. Its root meaning is "to be like," or "compare." It is used in the Hebrew Bible at times, just as in the Gospels and rabbinic literature, for an anecdote which illuminates some point or conveys some teaching. There are additional Hebrew terms, such as *melītzāh*, which might be translated "metaphor," or even "allegory," and *ḥīdāh*, which at times means "riddle," and at times "analogy"; these two terms occur in Prov. I:6, along with *mashal*, to suggest that the ancients were enough concerned about the forms in which wisdom was expressed to divide them into categories.

Most of the Book of Proverbs is in verse, in the usual three-three meter and with the usual parallelism.

The Book, after the superscription, "The Proverbs of Solomon," moves on to a statement that it was compiled in order to convey wisdom, so as to provide fools with shrewdness, and a youngster with knowledge and discretion (I:1-6). That is to say, a person can be trained in wisdom and, if by chance he does not himself become personally wise, he can at least absorb the wisdom in the book well enough to live prudently.

To live prudently is to live without unnecessary risk. In past ages, when the Bible was usually the only subject that people were taught, Proverbs was deemed the most useful of the biblical books, for its counsel was safe and reliable, and fostered the virtues of thrift, hard work, foresight, and piety. One who followed the advice in Proverbs would find his life well organized and ordered. A frequent scholarly phrase correctly characterizes Proverbs as a repository of "prudential" wisdom.

According to the author, the beginning of true wisdom is religious piety, for it is precisely this identity of piety and wisdom which fools scorn. The world is full of sinners who entice the young to sin and even violence; the young should be assured that the greatest damage which sinners do is to themselves (I:8-9). Folly and sin are interchangeable.

Wisdom, in the Hebrew view, was an entity that existed apart

from man, just as chemistry can exist independent of chemists.
Hence wisdom can be personified:

> Wisdom cries aloud in the streets;
>   In the open squares she puts forth her voice.
> At the head of the noisy thoroughfare she calls out;
>   She speaks her pieces at the gates of the city:
> "How long, O foolish ones, will you love foolishness,
>   And scorners, will you delight yourselves in scorning
>   and fools, hate knowledge?
> Turn about at my rebuke; see I shall put my spirit on you
> And I will make my words known to you. . . .
>
>   (I:20-24)

The person who searches for wisdom, we are told, is able to
move from having piety to receiving wisdom as a gift from God.
Such a man is preserved from evil, devious men. He is saved, too,
from the evil woman, unfaithful to her husband, who entices men
with smooth words. Moreover, the upright prosper and the
wicked are cut off from life (16-22).

Since wisdom is a gift from God, one needs to rely upon Him:

> Put all your trust in the Lord,
> And do not rely on your own understanding. . . .
> Do not think how wise you are,
> But fear the Lord and turn from evil. . . .
>
>   (III:5, 7)

God Himself had had recourse to wisdom, thereby setting an
example for man:

> In wisdom the Lord founded the earth
> And by understanding He set the heavens in their place;
> By His knowledge the depths burst forth
> And the clouds dropped dew.
>
>   (III:19-20)

Wisdom is as old as the world itself, as she herself proclaims:

> God made me as the beginning of His ways,
>   The earliest of His works of olden times.
> Aeons ago I was fashioned, at the beginning,
>   Even before earth. . . .

> For whoever finds me finds life
> And wins favor from God,
> And whoever misses me wrongs himself;
> Those who hate me love death.
>
> (VIII: 22-23, 35-36)

The proverbs, that is, the pithy sayings, including the following:

> Treasures gained by wickedness do not profit,
> But righteousness delivers from death.   (X:2)

> Hatred stirs up strife,
> But love covers all offenses.   (X:12)

> When pride comes, then comes disgrace,
> But with the humble is wisdom.   (XI:2)

> Whoever loves discipline loves knowledge,
> But he who hates reproof is stupid.   (XII:1)

> A prudent man conceals his knowledge,
> But fools proclaim their folly.   (XII:23)

> He who withholds the rod hates his son,
> But he who loves him is diligent to discipline. (XIII:24)

> Better a dinner of herbs where love is
> than a fatted ox and hatred with it.   (XV:17)

The last portion of the book seems to be advice to daughters: it presents a portrait of the ideal wife and mother that a Hebrew girl should become:

> When one finds a worthy wife,
> Her value is far beyond that of pearls.
> The heart of her husband is confident about her
> And he does not lack gain. . . .
> She rises while it is still night,
> Giving food to her household and a portion to her
> maidens. . . .
> Mere grace is delusive and beauty is empty;
> The woman who is reverent toward God is worthy of
> praise. . . .
>
> (XXXI: 10-11, 15, 30)

Ecclesiastes

Ecclesiastes is completely different in tone. Unlike Proverbs, it is not a book of instruction, but rather a series of exceedingly penetrating comments about the unvarnished realities of life. The book is properly described as "cynical." It seems to deny the idealism affirmed in Proverbs. A troubling question which affects the understanding and therefore the enjoyment of Ecclesiastes is whether this cynicism is bitter, as some suppose, or gentle and amused, as others believe. If we could only hear the tone of voice of the author, we could readily solve the problem. We cannot, so each reader must make up his own mind. But it is not enough merely to notice that Ecclesiastes sets forth what the realities of living are, in contrast with the prevailing sentimentalities of the pseudo-wise; rather, one must move on to consider the presuppositions behind the book. At the time when Ecclesiastes was written, there had not yet arisen some doctrines which flowered in later ages. One of these later doctrines was resurrection; another was immortality.

What was it that led to the rise of a belief in an afterlife? First, the premise existed in Hebrew religion that God was just. Yet if one observed that men suffered injustice, that the righteous suffered and the unrighteous prospered, one might retain a belief in God's justice only by supposing that ultimately the observable injustices would be righted. If so, when?—especially in the case of those who chanced to die prior to the rectification of the injustice? The answer was that the inequities in this life would be straightened out in an afterlife.

The very absence of a belief in an afterlife, the belief that man is born, lives, and dies, and this is the whole story, raises the questions, What importance or significance is a man, or his life? To believe that there is nothing awaiting man beyond his ultimate grave is to make life a tragic struggle of helpless man against the terrifying certainty of oblivion.

The author of Ecclesiastes, as we have said, lived before the rise and wide acceptance of a belief in an afterlife. His book, on the one hand, meditates on what man can and should do in his progression from birth to death and oblivion. On still another level, he speaks—and here is where those who believe the book to be cynical find some justification—of the universality of death and oblivion whether a man has been poor or rich, foolish or wise, insignificant or important. On yet another level, he speaks with the tongue of the gifted poet on the tragic nature of the disappointments which inevitably come to every man, and, if man lives long enough, of the horrendous infirmities of old age.

It is surely wrong to follow a rather frequent line of interpretation, which sets Ecclesiastes over and against the later Jewish and Christian views of an afterlife, to the detriment and disparagement of Ecclesiastes. There is in this book a perception of reality which is pertinent even in the context of a later age which adopted totally different premises. It is this perception of reality which has given the book, despite its occasional gloom and its haunting sense of tragedy, a recurrent appeal. There are what seem "orthodox" additions to the book, such as the last verses, which try to blunt the sharpness of the author's judgment and his unorthodoxy; but even if we were to accept the opinion that these passages are additions, they are of no great consequence. The book does not make for ordinary pleasure in reading, because of its cynicism and gloom. Yet the full honesty of the book and the remarkable poetry in it make Ecclesiastes one of the gems of Scripture.

We are not told exactly who the speaker in the book is. He is called, simply, "Koheleth ben David, king in Jerusalem." Because Solomon was David's son and became king, tradition identified Solomon with Koheleth, thereby going beyond the book itself. Perhaps the supposition that Solomon was its author provided this unlikely book with its entry into Scripture.

The first words set the tone: "Vanity of vanities," said Koheleth, "Vanity of vanities, all is vanity." The bitter interpretation spoken of above is reflected in many translations. I have seen: "Futility of futilities, all is futility." Another equally possible translation is: "Folly of follies, all is folly." There is some merit in this latter, for Ecclesiastes is often a commentary on the follies of men and their pretensions.

The author seems from some standpoints disillusioned, but he is by no means surprised or startled at being disillusioned. He has not been shocked by some event or personal tragedy into a rejection of the usual attitudes of the pious, but rather has grown into this rejection as a perceptive spectator of life. Some have described him as world-weary; perhaps. Yet we should not attribute literal weariness to him, for his mind and speech are always fresh, alert and incisive, and free from physical fatigue. He may be an old man, as some infer from his allusion to his many experiences, but he is far removed from senility or from some apathetic wait for his approaching death. Though he is resigned, his spirit is young enough to be rebellious.

His unorthodoxy does not lie in some capricious denial of God or of sin; indeed, he is always on the side of piety, justice, and the good. It is rather that, as things work out, there is no difference, so he asserts, in what happens to a man, whether he is pious or impious, righteous or wicked, for the same grave awaits all men, good and bad, rich and poor, eminent and lowly. What Ecclesiastes denies is the viewpoint repeatedly expressed in Deuteronomy —for example, Deut. XXVI:16-19 or XXVIII—which promises that obedience and fidelity to Yahve will bring blessings and prosperity, while disobedience and infidelity will bring curses and dire want. There is in the Deuteronomic view a causal relationship between a person's conduct and what thereafter happens to him, in that he is rewarded or punished. Ecclesiastes does not directly deny this theory of reward and punishment; rather he asserts that there is no permanence even in them, any more than there is in any other aspect of man's existence, for all is transient, and once a man is dead, he will be forgotten. Since every man, whether he triumphs or is defeated in life's struggles, nevertheless ends in the grave and oblivion, all is essentially vanity.

Now this could be treated as a most lugubrious and despairing viewpoint. Yet Ecclesiastes seems not to regard his viewpoint as gloomy or despairing, but rather as the truth. His contention is not that life is not worth living; to the contrary; he believes that life has to be lived in terms of reality, not illusions. What is true in life must be accepted, since man cannot change things. Man must respond to life as it is, and enjoy it insofar as he can, until the time when death and oblivion overtake him. Ecclesiastes is a philosopher, in the sense that he seeks to peer beyond mere appearances and to penetrate into the underlying realities.

His opening words, that all is vanity, are both the introduction to his book and its unifying theme. He then turns to the question, What *yitrón* is there for a man out of his lifetime of toil? *Yitron* has two possible denotations which ought not to be separated as if distinct from each other. One denotation is best expressed in the word *plus*, that is, What *plus* is there, beyond food or wealth, or eminence, in a lifetime of toil? The other denotation is *remainder*, that is, What is there *that abides* after a lifetime of toil? Ecclesiastes is not denying that hard work and thrift can bring a man economic sufficiency; he does not deny the beneficial results to a man of the homely virtues. Rather, he is asking, What is the *yitron*, the plus, the abiding nature in what man accomplishes through his toil? (The words *advantage* or *profit*, by which some translations render *yitron*, are not wrong, but the overtones of the Hebrew do not seem fully contained in them.) The reality, according to Koheleth, is that man is impermanent, for only the physical universe is permanent:

> What profit is there for man in all his exertions,
> In all the things that he exerts himself for under the sun?
> A generation comes and a generation goes,
> But only the land remains forever.
> The sun rises and the sun sets,
> And hurries to its rising place.
> The wind blows to the south
> And then circles back to the north.
> Circling, circling goes the wind,
> And on the circuit the wind returns.
>
> (I: 3-6)

Yet even nature occasions its own weariness, for nature is endlessly repetitious and produces no novelties:

> All the rivers flow into the sea,
> Yet the sea is never filled up.
> They flow back to whence all streams flow,
> So as to flow again.
> All things weary [a man]
> And a man is not able to describe it,
> [For] the eye is not satisfied with what it sees,
> Nor is the ear adequately filled with what it hears.
> What has been is what will be,
> And what has been done is what will be done,
> For there is nothing new under the sun. . . .
>
> (I:7-9)

Hence, man is of no real consequence:

> There is no recollection of the men who were earlier,
> And as for those who will be later,
> There will be no recollection of them
> On the part of those who will be even later.

The reliability of this judgment seems to require a statement of how the author knows it to be so:

> I, Koheleth, was a King over Israel in Jerusalem. I set my mind to investigate and to explore by wisdom every thing that has been made under the sun. It is a bad business that God has given man to be concerned with. I saw everything that was being done under the sun and the whole matter is emptiness and a striving after wind. That which is crooked can never be made straight and that which is lacking can never be counted.
> I searched my inward self, telling myself that I have grown in wisdom beyond all that existed before in Jerusalem, for I had been dedicating my mind to discerning both wisdom and also silliness and folly. Yet this too is useless. More wisdom brings more trouble and whoever increases his knowledge increases his pain.   (I:12-18)

Indeed, he turned from his inquiry into wisdom to a comparable inquiry into alternatives—pleasure, and laughter and folly—and such inquiry too was useless.

Possessing royal power, Koheleth embarked on providing great edifices, and parks and orchards, and irrigation pools. He acquired endless wealth, slaves, herds and flocks, silver and gold, and court entertainers. The reward for all this toil was a pleasure in doing these things (II:10). Yet once they were all accomplished, it was all vanity, for there was no *yitron* in anything.

Granted, he proceeds, that wisdom is superior to folly, the fact is that the wise man and the fool meet the same fate. Indeed, what Koheleth had personally accomplished as a wise king could be ruined, if his successor, inheriting all this accomplishment, were to be a fool. Hence, accomplishment, too, is transient and futile.

There is nothing at all better for man than eating, drinking, and enjoying his work. For a man to have even these limited boons is a gift bestowed by God (II:24). The righteous man gets the gifts of wisdom, knowledge, and joy, while the sinner simply does menial toil, and others benefit from his labors (II:25).

But now a new lament arises. Man is powerless to change things, for all that takes place in the world happens in a regular, immutable pattern, as if on schedule. There is:

> A time to be born, and a time to die.
> A time to plant, a time to pluck the planted.
> A time to kill, a time to heal.
> A time to tear down, a time to build.
> A time to weep, a time to laugh. . . .
> A time to love, a time to hate
> A time for war, a time for peace.

> (III:1-4, 8-9)

Then what *yitron* is there for a man in his toil?

Look at man's labor. True, God made all things skillfully for their proper occasion; He has even let man come to understand the world. But man does not succeed in coming to understand God Himself.[1]

Again, when one turns to the courts, Ecclesiastes discerns the reality of injustice over justice. Perhaps one can suppose that God, rather than man, is ultimately to be the judge. Perhaps, also, God intends man to learn that he is essentially an animal. But the reality is that man and the animal meet the same end, and die in the same way, and man has not *mōtấr* (a word related to the root of *yitron*, with a similar meaning of advantage) over the animal at all. No one knows whether the life-force in humans goes up or the life-force in animals goes down (III:16-22). So, too, one can move on from witnessing injustice into witnessing oppression. The dead are better off than the living who undergo oppression. But best of all are the as-yet unborn, who have not experienced the evils of the world (IV:1-3).

Envy of a neighbor can spur a man to work and exert himself. This is foolishness; it is better to have a mere handful of tranquillity than both fists full of futile striving. The envious become self-centered and alone (IV:4-12). For a few passages, the author speaks very much in the manner of Proverbs, offering his wise counsel to his readers. He advises a king to accept advice (IV:13-15); he tells what the proper attitudes should be in religious observance (V:1-7); he comments on wealth and the silliness of those who so pursue it that they enjoy nothing and even fail to enjoy the wealth they acquire (V:8-VI:12).

There comes next, in verse, a series of four proverbs which have the common thread of piquantly reversing the usual human viewpoints:

> Better is a good reputation than precious ointment, and the day of death than the day of birth.
> Better is it to go to a house of mourning than a banquet hall; the former is the fate of all men, as the living should understand.
> Better is anger than laughter, for the heart is gladdened by the sight of an angry face.
> The attention of the wise is for the house of mourning, the attention of fools is for the house of rejoicing.
>
> (VII:1-4)

Man, the author persists in saying, cannot change things ("Who can make straight what he [God] has made crooked?"). Thus, one can observe a righteous man dying before his time, and a wicked man living on beyond his. Then what should one do? His answer is: "Do not be over-righteous, do not be over-wise; why destroy yourself? Do not be over-wicked, do not be foolish; why die before your time? (VII:13-17)."

As admirable as wisdom is, it is elusive, and man is unable to penetrate to the ultimates (VII:18-29). Man, moreover, must make peace with the real demands of life, even the distasteful obligations (VIII:1-9). Man will never understand why it is that the wicked, as one can see, go unpunished and the righteous unrewarded (VIII:10-17). The race is not to the swift, nor is victory in battle to the strong, nor is food provided for the wise, nor is wealth given to the intelligent, nor grace [achievement] to the experts. Timing and chance influence everything! Accordingly, one might as well enjoy himself as much and as long as he can (IX:1-12).

There follow next a series of suggestions or admonitions for prudent living (X:1-XI:7). Koheleth then counsels that one should enjoy his youth, for it is very short and what comes later is very long (XI:8-XII:7). What seems to be the real end of the book (XII:8) repeats the beginning: "Vanities of vanities," said Koheleth, "all is vanity."

There ensues a short passage (XII:9-14) which many scholars believe to have been added; it praises Koheleth for what he taught, and for his adept arrangement of Proverbs; it commends him for seeking to bring to light delightful words and eloquent writing, always truthfully. Yet admirable as are the words of the wise man, it is the Shepherd, God, who has provided them. One should be warned against endlessly producing too many books, for excessive study confers only fatigue. The final matter is this, that all that can be [said and] heard can be expressed in the following: revere God and observe His commandments.

I have left for last the author's desperate injunction to enjoy youth, for this passage seems to me one of the most powerful, and shattering, in all poetry:[2]

> Rejoice, young man, in your youth;
> Let your heart cheer you when you are young.
> Walk as your heart directs you,
> In the light of what you see. . . .

[Do this] before the days of sorrow come,
And the years arrive about which you say,
"I have no desire in them."
[Do this] before the sun darkens,
As do the light of the moon and the stars,
And the clouds come back when the rain seems over.
[Do this before] the day when the guardians of the body [the
   hands] tremble,
And the men of valor [the legs] bow themselves down,
And the grinders [the teeth] come to naught for they are few
And those who look through the windows [the eyes] are
   darkened.
When the doors of the market [the lips] are closed,
And the sound of grinding [chewing] is low
When one rises at the sound of the bird [a short night's sleep]
And the daughters of song [the hearing] are brought low. . . .
Then a man is afraid of the height,
And of the terror of a journey.
The almond puts forth its [white] blossoms [the hair]
And the grasshopper drags along (?)
And the food provides no health,
For man is on his way to the eternal home
And the mourners circle about the mountain . . .
[Do this] before the silver cord is broken,
And the golden bowl is shattered,
And the pitcher is broken at the fountain
And the pully is broken at the well.

(XI:9-10A; XII:1B-7)

How dismal is this picture of old age, when all the machinery of
the body fails!

Job

Ecclesiastes does not reflect any specific event or incident. Job, on
the other hand, reflects the experience of calamity and disaster.
When we read Ecclesiastes we tend to be, like him, spectators of
life; when we read Job we become participants in his human misfortune. Especially is this the case if we personally have experienced some undeserved misfortune, or have been the victim of

some gross injustice, and have found no alleviation of pain and anger.

The author of Job writes from a background similar to that of Ecclesiastes in that he does not suppose that there is an afterlife where the injustices of this life can be corrected. It is in the here and now that Job is convinced that he has suffered unjustly, and hence whatever alleviation might come must appear, if at all, in the here and now. While Ecclesiastes has commented that he has observed injustice in the courts of law, the injustice which Job has experienced and which he so deeply laments has come not from man, but from God. Therefore the injustice to Job seems that much the greater, and Job's protest is that much more soul-searing. Since Job is thoroughly persuaded both that he himself has suffered from injustice and that the injustice has come from God, he must seek to try to understand those ultimates in existence which have brought this irrational and bitter fate about. The central poem which is the body of the Book of Job is the dialogue between Job and three friends who have come ostensibly to comfort him; actually the dialogue, in part, is a debate in which Job's assertion that God has dealt with him unjustly is challenged by his friends and then eloquently reasserted by Job. Quite beyond the debate itself is the self-revelation of Job in his soliloquies, which are addressed less to the friends than they are to God.

The central poem, then, is in dialogue form, and it brings the theater to mind. Some interpreters think that the theater was actually in the mind of the author, and that he knew it, or knew about it, from the Greeks; most interpreters discard this possibility, both because of chronological difficulties, since Job seems in origin too early to have been touched by Greek influence, and also because there is very little dramatic progression, as there is in Greek plays, through exposition, mounting action to a climax, and resolution. Job, rather, is essentially static, for it supposes an established situation which the characters discuss; it does not portray a protagonist engaged in mounting action. Nevertheless, there is in the dialogue a constant tension which makes it kindred to the dramatic.

The central poem is followed by an epilogue of no great literary significance and, in my judgment, of little insight and minimal value. On the other hand, the prologue to the poem, which leads directly into it, is a masterly work of prose, at the same time eloquent and striking—and a source of some fascinating problems, extending even to the question of whether the prologue truly conforms with the poem. But before we consider that question we need to look at the prologue.

A man there was in the land of Uz, Job by name. He was pious, upright, reverent, and never bent on evil. There were born to him seven sons and three daughters. His wealth was immense; he was the most important man in the east.

When his sons gave festive parties, each in turn, they invariably invited the three sisters. When the occasion for a festive party came around, Job would remind them of their religious consecration; he would arise in the morning to offer holocausts conforming to the number of his children, for he thought that possibly his sons might have sinned or been impious to God. Job always did this.

Now, in heaven on the [annual judgment] day, the angels, the "hosts of heaven," arrived to congregate with Yahve, and to fill the heavenly court room. Satan, too, was among those present. Yahve said to Satan, "Where have you been?" Satan answered, "Strolling about, hiking on earth." Yahve said, "Did you notice my servant, Job? There is no man on earth like him, for he is pious, upright, reverent, and never bent on evil!" (The dialogue is as if between two mortals. The Deity, instead of being omniscient, asks Satan where he has been. So far it is all quite casual.)

Satan said, "Is it strange that Job is reverent? You have shielded him and his household and possessions on all sides. You have blessed his works. For a change, put Your hands out and touch what is his. I swear, he will curse You to Your face."

Yahve said to Satan, "I give you sway over all that is his, but not over his person." Then Satan departed from the presence of Yahve.

One day, when all Job's children were gathered at the home of the oldest son, at a party, a succession of messengers came to Job, telling him of destructive assaults on his beasts, and of the murder of their keepers, and of the deaths of all his children.

Job thereupon tore his cloak [in mourning], and cut his hair, and fell prone to the ground. He said:

> Naked came I from my mother's womb; Naked do I end my life.
> Yahve gave; Yahve took away.
> Blessed be Yahve's name.

Job in no way trespassed, and ascribed no fault to God.

On the next judgment day [a year later], the divine beings again arrived to congregate with Yahve, as did Satan also. Yahve said to Satan, "Where have you been?" Satan answered, "Strolling about, hiking on earth." Yahve said, "Did you notice My servant Job? . . . He has preserved his piety; you enticed Me to injure him for no purpose."

Satan said, "A man will give anything, even his skin, to live on. But, make a change; put Your hand out and touch his person, his own self. I swear that he will curse You to Your face."

Yahve said, "He is in your sway. But do not kill him." Thereafter Satan smote Job with foul boils from the sole of his foot to the top of his head, so that Job took a piece of broken pottery to scratch himself, as he sat in the ashes. His wife said to him, "Do you maintain your piety? Curse God so that you may die."

He said, "Will even you speak like some of the silly women? Shall we accept good from Yahve, and not accept evil?" In no way did Job trespass in any of his words.

Three friends of Job, Eliphaz the Temanite, Bildad the Shuhite, and Zophar the Naamathite, having heard all the evil that had befallen him, left each his home and met to journey together to Job to lament with him and to comfort him. When from the distance they saw Job, they did not recognize him. They wept and tore their mantles, and threw dust onto their heads. They sat on the ground with Job for seven days and seven nights, no one speaking a word, in recognition of Job's acute distress.

This ends the prologue (I:1-II:13). Prose though it is, it verges on poetry, especially in the symmetry of the narration, as the second episodes recapitulates so much of the precise wording of the first. In the first episode, the climax in the succession of the messengers' reports is a rare touch, for disaster strikes in turn the cattle and donkeys and their herdsmen, then the sheep and the shepherds, then the camels and their drivers, and then the children, but Job's reaction is deferred until the last report, creating in us the suspense of wondering how he is taking these successive calamities. The casualness of the origin of the disaster to Job, that is, the off-hand conversation of Yahve and Satan, intensifies the awfulness of it. A man of highest eminence, in good health, has lost all that he has had, even his health, in a rapid series of disasters. He is no longer in his mansion, but an outcast from his city, sitting in the place of refuse.

Few passages in Scripture appeal to me more than this prologue to Job. This is so even though two related problems cannot help but arise, touching on the relationship of the prologue to the central poem. On one level, Satan never appears in the poem and the illness of Job in the poem is different from the boils of the prologue. On another level, the implication in the prologue is that something unheard of, unusual among men, has happened so as to test the faith of a single man; in the poem, the implication is that Job has undergone an ordeal which is not unknown among men, however unparalleled Job's particular ordeal has been. In the prologue Job is the unusual case; in the poem he is every man who has suffered strangely and undeservedly. The prologue, then, does not completely fit the ensuing poem.

Now the poem is such that even without some prologue the setting would eventually become relatively clear to a persistent reader. Yet the beginning of the poem strongly suggests that we need some introduction, so we can grasp right from the start what the situation is. Surely some prologue was needed. Did the present prologue replace some older prologue? Many scholars think so. Their first basis for this argument is that the poem requires an introduction of some kind. They then note that, in the later development of the Hebrew religion, there was a tendency to shield the Deity from being the direct source of evil. That is why the figure of Satan emerged in the religion (and grew in dimension and depth until he became a formidable rebel against Yahve). In the interest of shielding Yahve from being the source of man's evil, the prologue makes Satan responsible; but this assignment of responsibility to Satan seems to be a stage later than the poem itself, for the greatness in the poem is its challenge of God. Hence, according to scholars, the present, remarkable prologue replaces a different original prologue. I think this opinion is right.

Artistic as the prologue is, it cannot compare in depth and poetic fervor with the poem itself. The debate and self-revelation in the poem disclose that the author had a mind of penetrating acuteness and sympathy for the travail of men that is unmatched in any literature anywhere. We must remind ourselves, and constantly recall, that it is not alone that Job has suffered injustice, believing that the injustice has come from God, but that he is desperate to understand the why of it. He seeks to understand even the ways of God.

The reading of Job is materially eased, and its full flavor savored, when the reader has available annotations which can readily guide him through some minor difficulties, and through exotic and hence unclear allusions. Also, the third round of speeches exhibits some problems, suggesting that a small part of the book has disappeared. The poem on wisdom, Chapter XXVIII, is possibly an interpolation; the speeches of Elihu (Chapters XXXII-XXXVII) are an afterthought, possibly written by another author. Only the professional scholar needs to be preoccupied with such problems in their fullest dimension; he who reads for pleasure should take only enough note of these matters to ensure his fullest response to the total content. The challenge to the reader lies not in his comprehension of the contents, but rather in his ability to share in Job's emotions.

Emotion becomes an issue with the very opening words of the dialogue. The author of Ecclesiastes, as we saw, declared that life was not worth the living of it, and even before Job the prophet, Jeremiah had cursed the day of his birth. The passage here goes far beyond Ecclesiastes in reflecting the sorrow and dismay of the human heart, and far beyond Jeremiah in probing the full extent of a man's despair. Can we share fully in it? That is the challenge.

> Perish the day whereon I was born,
> And the night which announced,
>   "A male child has been conceived."
> Would that that day were darkness! . . .
> Would that thick darkness would seize my birthday,
> So that it not be numbered in the days of the year,
> Nor come into the tabulation of time. . . .
> Why did I not die at the womb,
> Perish when I came out of the belly?
> Why did knees greet me,
> And breasts which I could suckle?
> [If I had died] then now I would be inert and be quiet,
> I would sleep in tranquillity. . . .
>
> (III:3-4A, 6, 11-13).

He asks:

> Why is a new day given to the man in travail,
> And life to the embittered? . . .
> My anguish replaces my solid food,
> And my liquids are my cries of distress.
> What once I truly feared has come now upon me;
> What I was frightened of has overtaken me.
> I have no ease and no quiet,
> And I do not rest, for turmoil prevails.
>
> (III:20, 23-26)

The response of Eliphaz begins calmly and even considerately:

If one were to try to speak to you, would you hear it—
For how can one restrain some comment?
You are the one who used to counsel the many,
Who used to strengthen weak hands,
Your words lifted up those who had stumbled
And you stiffened wobbly knees.
Yet now when it is you whom [disaster] has touched,
    You go into panic.

When it has touched you, you become confused. . . .
Try to remember: Has an innocent person ever gone to destruction?
Has there been any place where the upright has been ruined? . . .
God has no confidence in His [divine] servants,
And ascribes frailty even to His angels.
How much the more is this true of mere men,
Whose origin is dust,
And whom He can crush like a moth. . . .

                                                (IV:2-5, 7, 17-19)

It is normal, then, for men to succumb to evil, and in various
ways, but men do not succeed in deceiving God. He chastises
men, so as to bring them back to righteousness. The man whom
God chastises should be grateful, for God proceeds to bind up the
wound He has inflicted. In view of the benefits that can accrue
to the person who responds affirmatively to the divine punishment
he has merited, Job should accept his merited punishment, turn
back to God, and relish all the advantages of such a return.

   This speech of Eliphaz is extraordinary. It is, as the author intends us to understand, a goodly array of clichés, pompously delivered. Moreover, Eliphaz is blithely oblivious of what he is in
effect saying, that Job has deserved what he has gotten. Eliphaz's
clichés rest, so it would seem, on his experience of observing the
affairs of men (see, especially, IV:8 and V:3), whereas, when
Bildad will speak, he will base his on something quite different.

   Job does not reply directly or immediately to Eliphaz. Probably
the author wishes us, with Job, to ignore Eliphaz's arguments at
this point as irrelevant. Job now agrees with Eliphaz only in one
point, that it is God who has caused his distresses. It is the depth
of these which Job first reasserts:

              Were my distresses accurately weighed,
              Or my anguish put onto a scale,
              It would outweigh the sand of the seashore;
              Therefore my words are extreme.
              It is God's arrows that have struck me;
              My spirit has drunk their poison.
              God has arrayed His terrors against me. . . .
                                                (VI:2-3)

Now Job turns directly to Eliphaz's intimation that he is guilty of trespass and needs to repent:

> He who is faint wishes support from a friend,
> Even when he abandons his reverence for God.
> My brothers have betrayed me. . . .
>
> (VI:14-15A)

He proceeds to challenge his friends to document Eliphaz's contention that his suffering comes because he has sinned, for he knows that the charge is baseless. Having by implication asserted his innocence, Job goes on to lament how transient and miserable life is, and how permanent death is:

> Is there not a burden for men on earth?
> Are not his days like those of a hired man? . . .
> The legacy of months of emptiness has been forced on me,
> And nights of toil have been designated for me.
> If I lie down, then I say, "When will I arise?"
> Every night, and until dawn, I become sated with tossing about.
>
> (VII:1, 3-4)

Momentarily he mentions his illness:

> My flesh is clothed in worms and dirt,
> My skin has broken out and become loathsome.
>
> (VII:5)

He goes on, in great boldness, to speak directly to God, on the very premise, which he has denied, that he has been guilty of something:

> I shall not restrain my mouth,
> But shall speak in the bitterness of my spirit,
> I will murmur in the bitterness of my soul. . . .
> When I say, "My bed will comfort me,
> My couch will bear my complaint,"
> Then You frighten me with dreams,
> And You terrify me with visions,
> So that I should choose to be strangled,
> [Choose] death, rather than my sorrow[3] . . .

> What is a man that You raise him to the importance of
>   Your notice,
> That You should set Your attention on him,
> That You visit him every morning,
> And try him constantly? . . .
>   (VII: 11, 13-15, 17-18)

Bildad is shocked by Job's bold words:

> How long will you go on saying such things?
> [How long] will your words be a powerful wind?
> Does God pervert justice?
> Does the Almighty distort what is right? . . .
> But you—[just] seek Good constantly. . . .
> He will answer your prayer,
> He will prosper your righteous habitation.
>   (VIII: 2-3, 5A, 6B)

Whereas Eliphaz has appealed to his own experience for wisdom, Bildad appeals to the collective wisdom of men:

> Ask of the former generation,
> Give attention to the quest of our fathers:
> We are of yesterday and know nothing,
> Our own days on earth are a shadow.
> But they can teach you, and tell you
> And speak their words intelligently.
>   (VIII: 8-10)

This solid guidance from the past teaches the dependency of all men on God. The guilty He brings to ruin; the righteous He preserves.

In his reply Job concedes that all men are dependent on God, for men are weak and God all-powerful. But the fullest tragedy in man's weakness is his inability to enter into a genuine interchange with God. Since God has so much power no one can effectively say to Him, "What are you doing?"

> Even if I speak, and choose my words with Him,
> If I am in the right, I will not be answered* . . .

[Or] if I call and He answers, I cannot believe He has
   heard my voice,
For He looks at me stormingly,
And gratuitously increases His wounds on me. . . .
If I am in the right, His* mouth can convict me;
I can be perfect—yet He can distort me.
I am guiltless. Do I not know myself?
I despise my life! . . .
For He is not a man like me, for me to speak to Him,
Or for us to come together for a trial. . . .
I say to God, Do not [merely] condemn me,
But show me the basis of Your quarrel.
Does it benefit You to oppress,
To hate what You created? . . .
Have You eyes of flesh?
Can You see like a man?
Are Your days like a man's,
Your years like a human's?
Why must You inquire into my sin
And search into my transgression? . . .
If I sin, You observe me,
And You will not acquit me of my transgression!
If I were truly guilty, woe unto me;
But if I am innocent, I still cannot raise my head. . . .
For You renew Your toil against me!

(IX: 14-15A, 16-17, 20-22, 32;
X: 2-6, 14A-15A, 16B, 17B)

Zophar heaps scorn on Job as a mere babbler of words. It would
be well, he says, if God Himself would reply to Job's words. But
Job, he goes on, errs grievously in supposing that Job or any man
can understand God. Despite this assertion, Zophar goes on to give
his understanding, that God knows who the sinners are, and does
not overlook sin. Accordingly, if Job would only admit his guilt
and repent, he would harvest great blessings of security and
tranquillity (Ch. XI).

Job, in reply, makes direct assault on his visitors for stupidity,
and for arrogance in deeming it wisdom:

> You, indeed, are the knowing ones
> And when you pass away, so will wisdom! . . .
> Is wisdom a matter of old age,
> And is length of days the equivalent of understanding?
>
> (XII:2, 12)

He cannot join them in their distortion of the truth:

> Would you speak falsehood on behalf of God,
> Or for His sake talk deceitfully?
> Will you show partiality to Him? . . .
>
> (XIII:7-8A)

He goes on with firmness:

> I take my flesh in my teeth[4] and I put my life in my hand;
> Behold, He will slay me; I have no[5] hope.
> Yet I will defend my ways to His face. . . .
> Behold now, I will set forth my case,
> For I know that I am right.
>
> (XIII:14-15, 18)

Job then addresses God directly:

> Either You call out, and I will answer,
> Or else let me speak and You answer me.
> How many sins and transgressions are charged to me?
> Let me know exactly what my transgressions and sin are. . . .
> Man, born of a woman, allotted only a few days,
> And these full of trouble,
> Comes out like a flower and is cut down,
> And has no permanent place as though he is a shadow.
> On such a being do You fix Your stare
> And bring him into judgment with You!
>
> (XIII:21-22; XIV:1-3)

We cannot here follow the two remaining cycles of speeches as we have the first. Indeed, these remaining cycles in one sense repeat the substance of what we have seen, though by constantly deepening the probing they add rather than merely repeat; the same material is progressively examined from an increasing number of angles of sight and poetic vision. To choose but one example, the frustration of Job that he cannot enter into litigation with God keeps recurring:

> Would that I knew how to find Him! . . .
> I would fill my mouth with arguments.
> I would grasp what He answered me,
> Understand what He said to me.
> I go forward but He is not there,
> And backward, but I do not discern Him.
> I look for Him on the left but do not see Him,
> I turn to the right but I cannot observe Him.
>
> (XXIII: 4B-5, 8-9)

Even in the confusions that mar Chapters XXIV-XXVII, we can with Job lament his experience of what he charges is God's unresponsiveness to the prayer of the righteous (XXIV:1-12). Especially pitiable is Job's speech in the last cycle, in his summary of his personal experience of catastrophe:

> Would that I were back in those months of long ago
> In the time when God preserved me,
> When He had his lamp illumine my head
> And by His light I traversed the darkness—
> In the days of my vigor,
> When God protected my tent,
> When the Almighty was still with me,
> And my children were about me.
> When my paths were washed in milk,
> And the rocky hills were streams of olive oil . . .
>
> (XXIX:2-6)

He thought, in those days, of a tranquil growth into old age in peace and strength:

> But now men much younger scorn me,
> [Men] whose fathers I would not let join my sheepdogs. . . .
> They stay far from me, abominating me,
> And do not refrain from spitting at seeing me.
>
> (XXX:1, 9)

This moving lament of his fall from eminence to lowliness and even contempt leads on to a stirring denial by Job of his friends' allegation that he has sinned, and the juxtaposition of the fall and the denial lends force to the denial. He gives in his defense a list of possible sins which his opponents have failed to give, and thus he denies succumbing to lust (XXXI:1-4), dishonesty (5-8), adultery (9-12), mistreatment of his servants (13-18), neglect of the poor, faith in wealth (24-25), idolatry (26-28), vengefulness and inhospitality to strangers (29-34), and unconcern for his farmlands. Negative as all this is since it is a denial, it is nevertheless an impressive list of the qualities that should characterize the righteous man. That Job in the midst of his dismay and distress should be able to affirm the life of righteousness adds its own force to the constantly deepening nature of the exploration of the issue of God's justice.

Yet we must not let a fascination with the beauty and force of individual passages make us forget that the author is pursuing an inquiry into the ultimate question, Can man understand the meaning of life, the profundities, which lie below the surface of our daily routines? Chapter XXVIII, a poem on wisdom, in one sense intrudes, for its position and its language support a frequent judgment that it is an interpolation from a hand other than that of the author; in another sense, though the chapter's position is indeed questionable, the substance is not. The poem[6] has considerable power. Its first portion describes how ingeniously men can carry on the pursuit of fine metals in their mines, bringing buried precious metal and stone from darkness into the light (1-11). Exactly is the opposite with wisdom, for neither men nor beasts nor birds of the air, not the sea itself, can tell where it is to be found. Wisdom is more precious than fine metals and stones (12-19). Yet no one but God knows where wisdom is to be found (20-27; verse 28 is apparently an interpolation).

The presence of this poem attributing wisdom only to God accentuates the necessarily indecisive character of the debate of Job and his friends, who search for understanding but do not find it. The direct sequel is the Deity's reply to Job, described as coming out of a whirlwind. In the reply, the Deity first upbraids Job for his presumptuousness in supposing that he can comprehend the ways of God:

Who are you who are obscuring [God's] counsel by words
  devoid of knowledge?
Gird your loins like a mighty man and let Me ask you and you
  reply to Me.
Where were you when I made the foundations of the earth?
If you have true understanding, then tell me!
Who fixed its measurements so that you seem to know them,
Or who stretched the [measuring] line over it? . . .
Do you know, because you were alive then,
And the number of your days is great?

(XXXVIII:2-5, 21)

Not only is God the creator, but He rules over nature: the sea,
Sheol, the rainfall, indeed, over the wild beasts. Hence, how can
Job set his knowledge against God's?

Will the would-be reprover contend with the Almighty?
Let him who argues with God answer!

(XL:2)

To the Deity, Job replies very briefly:

Behold, I am of small account; what shall I answer You?
I will put my hands over my mouth.
One time have I spoken, but I will not do so again;
Yes, twice, but I will not do so further.

(XL:4-5)

The Deity then speaks again:[7]

Do you deny Me justice,
And condemn Me in order to be justified?

(XL:8)

There is no alternative for Job but to acknowledge that man
cannot understand the ways of God:

I know that Your power is unlimited,
And no plan is impossible to You. . . .
Therefore I spoke, but really did not understand,
Things too wonderful for me, which I did not comprehend. . . .
Therefore I reject my words,
And I repent, [sitting] in dust and ashes.

(XLII:2, 3B)

Indeed, it is not only Job, but the author, too, who faces this need to acknowledge man's inability to understand.

For some this ending is unsatisfactory, as if some other outcome were possible. Yet no other can be envisaged, granted the premises of God's power and man's finiteness. The supreme tragedy in the book, then, is the concession that even the man who experiences tragedy, however resigned to it he becomes, can never come to understand it, boldly and honestly as he may try.

Even in ancient times there were those who yearned for a different tone in the book. There is a poem, less to be admired than the central poem but still a gifted writing, in Chapters XXII-XXXVII. It purports to be the speeches of one Elihu, a character who joins the company without any introduction. He is portrayed as speaking up because he is dissatisfied with the inability of Eliphaz, Bildad, and Zophar to persuade Job; indeed, he likens this failure to their joining Job in indicting God.[8] Hence, Elihu proceeds to recapitulate much of the argument used by the visitors, but he does so without comparable eloquence.

The prose epilogue succumbs to sentimentality. In it, God is irked with the three visitors for not conceding, as we saw Job do, that God was in the right (XLII:7-9). Thereafter, circumstances all become reversed, and Job receives twice as much from God as he had originally had. He even has a new crop of children (10-17). One ought to read the epilogue for completeness, but dissociate its bathos from the elevated quality of the central poem.

Nowhere in any literature is the literary quality of the Book of Job surpassed. Imagination, eloquence, delicacy, profundity, and the ring of real authenticity have been combined in what even in the days of the ancient rabbis was recognized as a work of creativity, not as a record of a historical man. The poet has illumined the experience of men through a poem about a man.

IX

The Literary Prophets

The literary prophets to me represent the pinnacle of artistic writing in the Bible. Do I regard the quality of prophetic literature as even beyond that of the Book of Job? I would say that Job is a single book, while the literary prophets were written by a chain of men. Again, is their greatness truly literary, or is it only religious? The answer must be that it is both, and that the literary is no less worthy than the religious.

We should begin our inquiry into the literary prophets by reverting to the Book of Kings, for we must divest our minds of a prevailing conception there of the nature of prophecy. Thus, the countless prophets in Kings are presented either as a resource to whom a monarch could turn, supplying an alternative to consulting a diviner or a priest in order to learn before an event what the outcome would be, or else the prophets appear so as to provide repeated castigations of the monarchs for tolerating or abetting the distasteful Baal worship. Very little differentiation was made in the personalities or messages of these prophets. Two exceptions were Nathan and Elijah. Nathan's scolding of David for the Bathsheba incident (pp. 170-71), and Elijah's denunciation of Ahab and Jezebel for stealing Naboth's vineyard (p. 178), can serve as our clue to an initial grasp of the literary prophets.

There are two formidable obstacles to reading the literary prophets with esthetic pleasure. One is the way in which the prophetic writings appear in Scripture. For the most part, one segment of a given prophet follows another, usually without any clarifying statement as to when and why each segment was spoken or written. We learn the when and why from the content alone, sometimes with some clarity, but often without it. Accordingly, simply reading a prophetic book from beginning to end without some introduction and clarifying annotation can give us the impression that we are reading confused and vague passages. And this impression would be a true one if each and all the texts of the prophetic books had been transmitted with gratifying accuracy and orderliness. The opposite turns is the case. The disarray within many prophetic books adds its own bit toward impeding an easy reading. Is some work involved on the part of the reader of a prophetic book? Yes. Is the gain commensurate with the effort? Assuredly.

There is a second difficulty. The literary prophets speak in the light of presuppositions which are assumed, and seldom specified. Without some idea of what these presuppositions were we can remain mystified by the prophets even when we possess annotations which suggest the time and occasion of a particular passage. Here are the main presuppositions, especially of the earliest literary prophets: Israel was Yahve's people, and He and they were bound to each other by a covenant made long before, in the Wilderness period. The covenant involved mutual responsibilities, the people being obligated to fidelity to Yahve, and He being obligated to protect and safeguard them. Fidelity was conceived of as having a double aspect. The first was an exclusiveness of the worship of Yahve. The second was the matter of ethics in human behavior, in that honesty, decency, integrity, and social concern were deemed as fully incumbent on Israel as was fidelity in the worship of Yahve. In prophetic thought these two, fidelity and social ethics, are inextricably bound to each other. If we were to say, as we might, that the essence of all religions is the matter of man's relation to God, we must add that in Hebrew thought the substance of that essence is man's obligation to his fellowman. Other ancient religions either lacked entirely a bond between ethics and religion, or else lacked the full measure which the Hebrew religion demanded. As a consequence, cheating one's fellowman, or committing murder, was as much a violation of the covenant with Yahve as worshipping the Baal was. If and when the behavior of Israel exhibited an accumulation of instances of infidelity or social transgression, the accumulation could signify a rupture of the covenant, with the implication that the covenant was either on the verge of being canceled, or else was already abrogated. The consequence of the abrogation of the covenant was that Israel was bereft of Yahve's concern and protection. Hence, when world empires, such as Assyria or Babylonia, extended their sway westward toward the land of Israel, the lack of Yahve's protection could be a matter of tangible consequence, since the invader could conquer. A protected Israel did not need to fear a foe, an unprotected Israel had much to fear.

From Amos through the early years of Jeremiah, a persistent message of the prophets was based on the conviction that the ancient covenant was indeed ruptured and that shattering consequences were about to ensue.

It was men, not Yahve, who had ruptured the covenant, for it was inconceivable that Yahve would be faithless, as men were. Yahve, rather, was characterized by his *ḥésed*, his reliability. Moreover, He was unlike man in that He was not to be conceived of as arbitrary, or as inclined to respond to man's misdeeds hastily or in some mechanical way. Rather, He was forebearing, merciful, slow to anger, and, above all, cognizant of human frailty, and therefore He was willing and even ready to defer the abolition of the covenant, and to withhold the consequences of that abolition, in the hope that man, exercizing his ability to choose, would prefer to repent and turn back from the accumulated evil, rather than undergo dire punishment. Yahve neither punished immediately, nor did He hasten to irrevocable acts; instead, He bided His time, to discover whether or not Israel would come to its senses.

Since Yahve had the ability to shield Israel from foreign invaders, He had power over such foreigners. In prophetic thought we can trace an enlargement of this view, from that in which foreign nations are thought of quite passively, in terms of Israel's need for protection from them, to the view that Yahve actively controlled the foreign nations and guided what they did. Such views about foreign nations are related to a larger question: Is Yahve the god of Israel alone, with power limited to the land of Israel, or is He the sole true God of the world, with power unlimited? We shall not usually find such questions dealt with explicitly; rather, we shall encounter inferences which the basic views led to.

The messages of the prophets involve abstractions, and Hebrew, as we have said, has few abstract nouns. The manner of the prophets, accordingly, is to express abstractions in concrete terms. That is, a prophet charges not that Israel *was unjust*, but that Israel *had acted* unjustly. Furthermore, it was the manner of the prophets to use symbols to clarify the abstractions, or, indeed, to act out a symbol, so that the message was unmistakably clear. Isaiah, for example, spoke of Israel as disappointing vineyard; Jeremiah acted out a symbol by walking about with a yoke on his neck, to portray impending captivity.

Certain passages tell us to whom the prophetic message was addressed, for example, a particular king. Other passages lack such information; they seem to suggest that the audience was the people in general. We have no clear information about such general addresses; we do not know whether they might have been delivered in a marketplace, or in some building, such as a temple. Certainly the bulk of prophetic discourse presupposes a broad audience, and often what we read seems to be a later written record of some earlier oral discourse. The question of the prophet's audience, and the possible oral precursor, has this relevancy; we ought to think of a prophet more as an orator than as an essayist. The prophetic words seem calculated to elicit a response promptly on being heard, and we will not gain the full flavor if we do not try to keep the matter of the listening audience in mind.

We are not so much interested here in what the doctrines which the prophets expressed were, but in the literary manner, and the poetic attainment, of their expression. Quite possibly, when a prophet spoke, his speech was in prose; we who now read him discover that when he turned to write, he wrote in verse, indeed, in poetry. Certainly we could assume some forensic skill, innate or cultivated, in the oral delivery. What should impress us, however, is the poetic fervor which the written word so clearly exhibits, for each of the pre-exilic prophets was a poet. Each had his individual style and manner. Indeed, our reading of a prophet, even in translation, ought to carry us to the point at which the man behind the words becomes known to us in some dimension, for no misunderstanding is quite as great as that of forgetting that a mind and a heart and a personality lie behind the words of each of the prophets. Perhaps when we come to know the artist, we will thereby know the artistry, and need no special words of praise.

However God-intoxicated the prophets were, they were flesh and blood human beings. Indeed, the prophet was an ordinary man, in the sense that he was not, like a priest, attached to, or in charge of, a sanctuary. A priest usually inherited his office from his father, but a prophet was someone whom Yahve explicitly summoned for the prophetic responsibility. We have some accounts of this divine "call." Why are we given these? Because by the very fact that the prophet was an ordinary man, not a priest, he needed to make some assertion of his authenticity, or else he could encounter a disbelief in his prophetic message. The accounts of the call partially disclose the personality and character of the individual prophet. Amos tells us (VII:14) that he was neither a prophet nor a prophet's son, but that Yahve had taken him away from the sheep; he was, he tells us, a shepherd and a tender of sycamores, fruit-bearing trees in the Near East. Yahve had said to him, "Go, prophesy to My people Israel." Amos said this in response to the taunt made to him that he was simply a "seer," who ought to rush back to his native Judea, and earn his living there by his divining.

Isaiah's call, one of the best-known passages in Scripture, is most vivid:

> In the year that King Uzziah died, I saw Lord [Yahve] seated on a high and lofty throne; the skirts of His robe filled the temple. Fiery creatures stood above Him, each with six wings, two to cover the face, two to cover the feet, and two to fly with. . . . One of the fiery creatures flew to me. In his hand was a hot coal which he had taken off the altar with tongs. He touched it to my mouth, saying, "See! This has touched your lips; your guilt is gone, your sinful state is atoned for."
>
> Then I heard Yahve's voice saying, "Whom shall I send? Who will go on our behalf?"
>
> I said, "Here am I! Send me."
>
> (Is. VI: 1-2, 6-8)

The account of Isaiah's call is essentially prose, not verse, yet it has all the vividness of poetry. The seraphim we should understand as fiery creatures, to buttress the intent in the figure of speech that Yahve's radiance filled the entire earth. The allusion to the shaking of the Temple walls and the smoke which filled the Temple explains the terror which Isaiah felt as a consequence of his vision of the Deity. The crux is the prophet's "Here am I! Send me." Yet, later, in the prophet's retrospect, he comes to sense that his mission has failed, for he has not been listened to. Hence, he turns the account of his call in such a way as to suggest that even when he was called, it was already fore-ordained that people would not hearken to him: "Make gross the mind of this people, and dull its ears, and avert its eyes, lest, seeing and hearing, it comprehends, repents, and is saved." To what point is this lack of hearkening to endure? "Until cities are destroyed and are bereft of people, and houses are empty of dwellers, and the land itself rendered infertile." This vision of man's experience of the disaster of war, invasion, and conquest, read back by Isaiah into the moment of his call, lends to the call a dimension of awesome significance, for the momentary terror of it becomes overshadowed by the strong assertion of an inescapable doom destined to come to the people who have been untouched and unconcerned.

In the case of Jeremiah, the call comes at the beginning of the book:

> The word of the Lord came to me saying,
> "Before I formed you in the womb I predestined you,
> And before you came forth from the womb I sanctified you;
> I made you a prophet to deal with the concern of nations."
>
>   . . .
>
> I said, "My Lord Yahve, I have no knowledge of how to speak,
>   for I am but a boy."
> Yahve said to me: "Do not say, 'I am a boy,'
> For wherever I send you, you will go, and whatever I com-
>   mand you, you will speak."
>
>   (Jer. I:4-7)

Where Isaiah had pleaded his own impurity as his objection to a prophetic mission, Jeremiah pleaded his youth, but in the context of a contention that he was pre-destined for his inescapable obligation. At this point we might misinterpret Jeremiah's assertion that God had pre-destined him as mere arrogance; we shall see a bit later that the assertion of pre-destination relates to Jeremiah's constancy, for imprisonment and physical punishment were to befall him, as they can befall anyone who dares to speak openly and forcefully words which people do not wish to hear, especially in critical times. The chief characteristic of the call of Jeremiah is its total inwardness, for it lacks all mention of external circumstances, such as are present in the call of Amos and Isaiah.

A fourth example of the call is found in Hosea I:

> Yahve said to Hosea, "Go, marry a wife who will prove prone to infidelity, and bear children adulterously, just as the land has committed adultery away from Yahve." Hosea married Gomer, the daughter of Diblaim. She conceived and bore him a son. Yahve said to [Hosea]: "Call him Jezreel; shortly I shall visit the blood of Jezreel on the [royal] house of Jehu, and bring to an end the monarchy in Israel. . . .

> Again she [Gomer] conceived and bore a daughter. Yahve said to him, "Call her name Unloved, for the house of Israel is unloved by Me." Unloved was weaned, and Gomer then bore a son. Yahve said, "Call his name Not-My-People, for you are not My people and I am not your God."
>
> (Hos. I:2-4, 6-9)

Whether or not Gomer was a real person, a whore whom the prophet married, or only a fictitious symbol used to justify the accusation that Israel, like a lewd woman, had whored away from Yahve, is the subject of an old and unended scholarly debate. Similarly, Chapter III (told in the third person, whereas Chapter I is in the first) continues to seem to some scholars to be a variant of Chapter I, though to others it is an account of a second marriage by Hosea, again to a lewd woman. Whether Gomer is history or mere symbol is all the same, for the point of the matter is that Yahve's experience with Israel is like that of a man who finds the wife *whom he loves* engaging in endless, sordid liaisons. Surely there can be no better figure of speech for extreme disloyalty than that of a repeatedly whoring wife. That Hosea could still love her not only discloses his view of Yahve's basic concern for Israel, but also reveals the man himself, for his disapproval of his people never led him away from his passionate concern for them.

The literary prophets number fifteen books, and it is quite impossible to review here the totality of the thought and writing. Since our primary interest is literary, we must at least glimpse the literary force of the prophets; since their concern was religion, we need to see how they expressed their religious concerns. There is no evidence of a direct influence of one prophet on another, but there is a development which can be presented here, not a direct development from one prophet to another, but rather an expanding of horizons and a deepening of prophetic thought.

Amos and Hosea were the first of the literary prophets. They flourished within roughly the same two decades of the eighth pre-Christian century. Each has an emphasis essentially missing from the other; hence, they complement each other. Amos was a social critic, a rural man from the simple, pastoral south, who wandered to the north where the rich agricultural economy had led to some "urbanization" and to the complexities of city life. He came from a relatively classless society; in the thriving north he observed the very rich, the very poor, and those in between; he observed that the rich were unconcerned for the poor and for the powerless widows and orphans. What he saw was totally out of conformity with the antecedent Hebrew ethical suppositions of social concern, probity, and decency. Hosea, on the other hand, was preoccupied with the purity of worship; that is, the land was filled with the worship of the Baal, and Hosea was thereby profoundly scandalized, not only because the people were unfaithful to Yahve, but because their infidelity inevitably led to conduct which in his eyes was unbecoming to Hebrews, and inconsistent with the covenant.

Here is how Amos speaks, in the name of Yahve, about the northern kingdom:

> For the three sins, yes, the four sins,[1]
>   I shall not withhold punishment:
> For selling an innocent man for silver
>   And a poor man for a pair of shoes.
> [These are people] who crush the head of the needy in the
>   dust,
>   And distort the rights of the humble. . . .
> Yet at altars they stretch out in garments taken in pledge;[2]
>   The wine gained through oppression they drink in
>   their temples to God. . . .
>
> (II:6, 7A, 8)

He turns to the women of the leisure class:

> Hear this word, you cows of Bashan, in Mount Samaria,
> Who oppress the poor, who abuse the needy,
> Saying to their husbands, "Bring us something to drink!"
>
> (IV:1)

To the wealthy men he speaks in this way:

> Woe to those at ease in Zion [to the south]
>   And secure at Mount Samaria [to the north]. . . .
> You are headed to a day of evil,
>   You are bringing near the reign of violence—
> You who sleep in ivory beds, with spreads on your couches,
> And who eat the choicest of sheep, kids taken from the folds,
> Who play the flute like David, and make musical instruments,
> Who drink elegant wine, and eat the best of delicacies—
> And are not sickened by the distress of people!
>
>   (VI:1A, 3-6)

He has this to say about the public worship at famous temples:

> Come to Bethel—and you will transgress!
> Go to Gilgal—and increase your transgression. . . .
> Seek Me, in order to live!
> Do not seek out Bethel, do not go to Gilgal,
> Do not journey to Beer Sheba! . . .
>
>   (IV:4A; V:4B-5A)
> Woe until those who celebrate the [festal] Day of Yahve. . . .
> The Day of Yahve is a day for darkness, not light,
> Thick darkness, bereft of brightness.
> I hate, I despise your festal celebrations,
> I have no pleasure in your assemblies. . . .
> But let justice flow like water,
> Righteousness like a constant[3] stream.
>
>   (V:18A, 20-21, 24)

What is to be the consequence?

> A foe will go freely around your land,
> And take your power from you,
> And make spoil of your castles. . . .
>
>   (III:11B)

The essential message of Amos can be paraphrased in this way: social inequity and injustice have grown to the point at which Yahve has reluctantly abrogated the covenant, so that Israel is a ready prey to an invader who is already on the horizon (that invader, we know from other sources, was Assyria). Yet beyond the social injustice there exists another evil, namely a broad conformity to the worship of Yahve in conventional ritual forms. This ritual fidelity, even if dedicated to Yahve, is meaningless!

The tone of Amos (except for the closing verses, which many believe are an addition) is unrelentingly severe, an expression of shocked surprise and unrelieved outrage. The indictment is directed primarily, indeed almost totally, at the highly placed and the wealthy. Amos is beyond the stage of exhortatory warning in some hope of reform; rather, he views the evil so to have accumulated that he speaks not of what may come about but of what he believes is already on the way. His figures of speech exhibit poetic contrasts, either in irony or in contempt. Moeover, passage after passage utilizes synonyms and synonymous expressions, underlining the depth of his scorn: "I hate, I *despise* your festivals; a refuge will evade the swift; the mighty hero will not replenish his strength; the swift runner will not escape, nor will the warrior on his horse; the valorous among the great heroes will flee naked on the day which will come" (II:4-16). Poetic contrast is employed recurrently:

> In all the streets there will be mourning,
> In all the wide places people will say, "Alas."
> They will summon men from the farm to mourning,[4]
> And professional mourners to a [genuine] lament.
> (V:16)

Since we are told in the text that Amos was a shepherd and a tender of sycamore fruit, we have reason to wonder at the literary skill in the measured verse and high poetry of his expression. Granted that the gift of eloquence is not limited to the educated, what is significant in Amos is the poetic elegance of his eloquence. We cannot explain this.

We must also wonder at the Hebrew mind. Why did the Hebrews preserve, and even cherish, this impressive record of unsavory actions and attitudes? Why should they not, in understandable national pride, have suppressed and destroyed it? Why did they keep alive this indictment of their infamy? We cannot readily explain this; we can only observe that they felt no shame in the shameful record of their past, and, far from concealing it, they glorified the literature which portrayed their shortcomings.

By contrast with Amos, Hosea gives relatively little attention to social injustice. He scolds priests and prophets who have insufficiently guided the people and who tolerate silly forms of alien worship:

> They get their food from My people's sin,
> They direct themselves to [My people's] trespass.
> They will eat, but not be sated,
> They will indulge in sex, but not propagate,
> For they have abandoned heeding Yahve.
> Whoring and drunkenness have erased their understanding.
>   . . .
> My people seek counsel from a piece of wood,[5]
> And a staff of wood then informs them,
> For a spirit of harlotry can lead them astray
> And they have gone whoring away from their God.
>   . . .
> Hence, your [own] daughters will go whoring,
> And your brides engage in sexual orgies.
> [Yet] I shall not punish your daughters for their whoring,
> Nor your brides for their orgies,
> Because the adult men made rendezvous with harlots,
> And offer sacrifices with sacred[6] prostitutes.
>   (IV:8, 12, 13B-14A)

These charges of Hosea's are his much graver accusation of total infidelity to Yahve. The constant figure here is that of Yahve, the husband, betrayed by his whoring wife Israel, through her engaging in Baal worship. The reason for this figure of speech is not only its inherent strength, but also the circumstance that the Baal worship to which Israel has strayed was marked by the use of sacred prostitutes. (The Hebrew Bible looks askance at both general and ritual prostitution, though it exhibits sympathy for individual prostitutes, such as Tamar and Rahab).

Hosea's disapproval of the public trespass is comparable to that of Amos. Hosea, however, stresses Yahve's reluctance to cast off

Israel, while Amos stresses Yahve's stark severity. Amos would scarcely speak as Hosea does here:

> When Israel was a boy, I loved him;
> Out of Egypt I called his sons.
> Despite My calling them, they went far away from Me.*
> They sacrifice to the Baals,
> They make offerings to images.
> It was I [Yahve] who reared Ephraim [the northern kingdom];
> I used to take them up in My arms.
> They never understood that it was I Who healed them
> [from boyhood bruises].
>
>   . . .
>
> How, Ephraim, can I give you over,—
> Give you up, O Israel? . . .
> I shall not put My anger into effect,
> Nor proceed to destroy Ephraim,
> For God am I—not man.
> Sacred am I—I shall not become furious.*
>
>   (XI: 1-3, 8A, 9)

Yet even that reluctance seems to give way to the inevitable divine displeasure.

> Ephraim surrounded Me with falsehood,
> The House of Israel with deception. . . .
> Ephraim shepherds the wind,
> And he pursues the east wind;
> All day long he multiplies lies and frauds.
>   (XII: 1-2A Heb., XI: 12-12.1A Eng.)

There follows then another verse of special import:

> He makes a covenant with Assyria,
> Or despatches a [treaty] gift to Egypt.
>   (XII: 2B Heb., XII: 1B Eng.)

The allusion here is to the international situation, wherein Israel was caught between the two great powers, Egypt to the west and Assyria to the east—and Assyria was now moving westward in conquest. It was natural for the Israelites to seek safety now in one alliance, and now in another; yet to Hosea, to do so was to exchange the sure reliance on God for a reliance on mere man, and, while this may appear useful as practical politics, it too is apostasy, of the worst kind. What Hosea says laconically can be seen in more developed form in the prophet Isaiah; here there is just enough for a glimpse of the deepening concern of the literary prophets for what we might call collective morality.

The prophetic concern, then, came to encompass the very ultimates in the total life of the people, so that the call of Hosea is revealed as something quite beyond a single man and his whoring wife; instead the experience becomes a jolting reminder that an entire value system is being eroded in favor of momentary advantage and accommodation. In Hosea the infidelity in ritual is the symptom of the more fundamental infidelity. Hence, the stakes could not have been higher in the prophet's mind than they were.

The divine reluctance in Hosea, we have said, marks him off from Amos. So does another quality, Yahve's warm love, as distinct from mere concern, for his people, despite their waywardness:

> I will heal their sickly apostasy,
> As an act of free will I will love them,
> For My anger against them has dissolved itself.
> I shall refresh Israel as does the dew.
> He will blossom, like the lily. . . .
>   (XIV:5-6A Heb., 4-5A Eng.)

We have said that, in a sense, Amos and Hosea complement each other. The bill of particulars on the social injustice in Amos and the constant reiteration of the theme of infidelity to God in Hosea contribute to a double perspective which in reality is single. However sternly a prophet spoke to his people or about them, he was motivated by his concern for them. Like the author of the Pentateuch, the prophets expected from the Israelites a standard of conduct which was unique not only in the lofty character of the demand but in the level of conduct required, for it transcended mere obedience of the laws of the land. Not law and order, but a morality more basic and more permeating was their concern. It is in this extra demand that pre-exilic prophecy attains its uniqueness.

The riches to be found in the message of Isaiah repay lavishly the toil involved in the reading of him. Not that the inherent message is difficult to grasp; rather, the Book of Isaiah has not been felicitously compiled; indeed, one might even venture to say that it was not compiled, but thrown together. Modern scholars customarily divide the 66 chapters into sections, separating Chapters I-XXXIX from XL-XLVI, and labeling the latter II Isaiah. They have also found reasons for further subdividing both portions, so that XL-XLVI is in itself a compilation of writings by different people, and I-XXXIX, which contains I Isaiah, also contains more than one man's work. Moreover, if universal assent were to be secured from scholars on which sections in I-XXXIX are authentically I Isaiah and which are not,[7] a residual problem would remain, for chronological orderliness and sensible system are absent. Accordingly, there are very great difficulties to be met in reading this book.

The general reader of Isaiah, so it seems to me, need not immerse himself in all the details which the technical scholars have justly concerned themselves with. If he is prepared to realize that he is confronted by an anthology of materials from different hands and different ages, and has just enough guidance to glimpse reflections of these in what he reads, that could well be sufficient. Perhaps a double clue might be offered. First, some matters of chronology. In Isaiah's career (about 740-690 B.C.), Assyria moved westward, seizing some northern cities from Israel in 734, and then conquering the capital Samaria in 721. Isaiah spoke before 734, and between 734 and 721, and also after 721. Besides the Assyrian invasion, there was the threat of war, and, indeed, war itself, between Israel and Judah, with Israel allied with Aram against Judah. Second, as to the later additions which are not by Isaiah, in quantity there are perhaps a third of the material, and they include some of the choicest literary compositions in the work. They are addressed to the hopes of a glorious future.

The call of Isaiah we have already seen (p. 242). It might be well to turn next to the "Song of the Vineyard," to see how a figure of speech is used and applied.

> I shall sing to my beloved a [troubadour's] love song to
>   his vineyard.
> My beloved had a vineyard in a lush corner of land.
> He put a fence around it, moved the stones,
>   planted it with excellent vines,
> Built a watch tower,[8] and hewed out a wine vat.[9]
> He hoped it would yield grapes—
> It yielded stinking fruit! . . .
> The vineyard of Yahve is the house of Israel,
> The men of Judah are the plant of his enjoyment.
> He hoped for justice, but there was bloodshed,
> For righteousness [but there was] outraged cry.
>
>   (V:1-2, 7)

Not only does Isaiah use a figure of speech verbally; elsewhere (Ch. XX) he acts out a figure of speech. The background story is about rebellion against the Assyrian conquerors by the people of the coastal city of Ashdod; the passage is in prose:

> In the year when Sargon of Assyria sent his *tartan* ("commander") against Ashdod and conquered it, Yahve at that time spoke through Isaiah: "Loose the sackcloth from about your waist, and remove your shoes from your feet." Isaiah did this, going about naked and barefoot. Yahve said, "Just as my servant Isaiah has gone naked and barefoot for three years as a sign, the sign is applicable to Egypt and Ethiopia, for in the same way the king of Assyria will lead away Egyptians as captives, and Ethiopeans as exiles, men and boys, [all] naked and barefoot, with buttocks and sex organs exposed. Those who have looked to Ethiopia and to Egypt's attractive might will be dismayed and humbled. Those who dwell on the coast will say [in chagrin]: "See what has happened to our expectation, to those to whom we turned for help, for rescue from the king of Assyria! Now, how shall we escape?"

All poetic discourse, as we have said, uses figures of speech. In Isaiah such figures are raised to the point of becoming symbols.

This presents a difficulty: regrettably, we are not always able to understand the application of the symbol. What makes symbol occasionally difficult in Isaiah is the high level to which he brings the prophetic interest; that is, Amos and Hosea made comments on international relations, but they spoke as if they were remote from the level of monarchy where decisions were made; Isaiah, and later Jeremiah, on the other hand, spoke directly to kings. While the figures of speech and the symbols in Isaiah obviously relate to eminent foreign nations, often the precise allusion is less than clear, or even totally unclear.

The component elements in Isaiah are not so much altered from Amos and Hosea as they are heightened. That an opinion on the diplomatic machinations of the Judahite crown, as it turns now eastward, now westward, should elicit prophetic attention is not to be wondered at; that the attention is often expressed in lofty poetry is. Here are samples of Isaiah's writing about these matters. First he scorns social injustice:

> Woe to those who annex house after house
> And make field after field adjacent. . . .
> Woe to those who arise early in the morning to pursue
>   alcohol,
> And tarry beyond twilight for wine to inflame them. . . .
> Woe to those who pull iniquity like a bull on a rope,
> Who drag sin as with cart ropes. . . .
> Woe to those who are mighty—at guzzling wine,
> And men of valor—at shaking up a drink.
> They acquit a guilty person for a bribe,
> And deprive the innocent of his innocence.
>
> (V:8-23)

He speaks of infidelity to Yahve in these stirring lines:

> Hear, O heavens, and hearken, O earth, for Yahve has spoken:
> "Sons have I reared and raised up, but they have trans-
>   gressed against Me.
> An ox knows its owner, an ass [knows] its master's stable;
> Israel does not know, My people does not understand!
>   . . .

> "Woe unto a sinful people, a nation heavy in iniquity,
> The scions of evildoers, offspring who are corrupt.
> Yahve they have abandoned, despised Israel's Holy One . . . !"
>
> (I:2-4)

He inveighs against the hypocrisy in ritual fidelity, and declares such ritual observance meaningless:

> What do I care about the abundance of your sacrifices?
>   says Yahve.
> I am overfilled with burnt offerings of ram
> And the fat of well-fed beasts.
> I have no wish for the blood of bullocks, lambs, or goats,
> Nor that you come to see My face.
> Who asked you to trample the [temple] court?
>
>   . . .
>
> I hate your new moons and your appointed festivals,
> They have become a burden upon Me, I am tired of bearing them.
> And when you spread out your hands [in prayer],
> I will cover My eyes from you.
> Even if you multiply prayer, I will not hear,
> For your hands are full of blood!
>
> (I:11-12, 14-15)

The certainty in Isaiah's mind that rampaging Assyria would conquer Israel was based not on his estimate of Assyria's strength, but rather on his view that the conquest was the direct result of Israel's infidelity to Yahve! This becomes clear in these words:

> Woe unto Assyria! He is the rod of My anger;
> He is the staff in My hand of My fury.
> I am sending him against [My] impious people
> And commanding him against the people of My wrath,
> To seize spoil, and grab plunder,
> To tread them down in the streets like clay.
> But he [Assyria] does not reckon it this way,
> And in his heart he does not so consider things!
> Rather, it is in his heart to destroy,
> And to annihilate many nations.
> For he says, "My local commanders were all once kings! . . .

> As my hand subdued [other] kingdoms*
> Shall I not do likewise with Jerusalem*?"[10]
>
> (X:5-8, 10-11)

But Yahve will punish the vaunted arrogance of Assyria, who says:

> By the strength of my hand I have done this
> And by my cunning, for I am skillful.
> I have removed the boundaries of nations,
> I have pillaged their treasuries,
> And, powerfully, have laid low the inhabitants.
>
> (X:13)

Promptly, Isaiah portrays Yahve's comment on Assyria:

> Does the axe elevate itself over him who hews with it?
> Does the saw possess ascendancy over him that plies it?
> Does a rod wield him who raises it?
> Can a staff raise something as if it is not wood?
>
> (X:13, 15-16)

That Assyria was only a tool in the hands of Yahve is a theological expression of considerable importance. Where Amos had said that Yahve would abandon Israel so that Assyria would thereby be enabled to enter the land and conquer it, Isaiah asserts that Yahve was actually bringing in Assyria. Conceived of in this way, Yahve is not the local or national god of Israel, but the universal Deity Whose sway is without geographical limit and Who controls the events of all history.

The many facets of the mind of Isaiah, and his poetic fervor, are all the more revealed when the totality of his writings, impossible to reproduce here, are absorbed. Frequent ambiguities and obscurities are indeed present, but these are of only limited significance, for there is enough clarity to enable us to encounter a perceptive, highly intelligent mentality, with a gift for poetic expression of remarkable beauty and force. To deny Isaiah the authorship of such chapters as II, IX, and XI, as modern scholars do, does not reduce the stature of the man; enough is left to reflect an exceedingly gifted and noble heart.

To Micah we are indebted for an inspired passage in which the
essence of religion is set forth:

> With what shall I visit Yahve,
> And bow before God on high? . . .
> Does Yahve want countless rams,
> With untabulated streams of oil?
> Shall I give my first-born child in place of my transgression,
> The fruit of my body as a sin offering for me? . . .
> He [Yahve] has already told you, O man, what is good,
> And what He asks of you:
> Merely to do justice, To love righteousness,
> To walk humbly before your God.
>
> (VI:6A, 7-8)

Micah, too, speaks against social injustice:

> Woe to those who devise wickedness,
> Planning evil while in their beds,
> And practicing it when the morning is light,
> Because they have the power to do so.
>
> (II:1)

The experience in our day of the unwelcome response of people to scolding and menacing words could reasonably raise the
question, Was there not a comparable resentment in ancient times?
The fullest answer to this question will emerge from Jeremiah,
but Micah too has his comment to make, quoting those who object to his words:

> "Do not prophesy"—thus *they* prophesy—
> "People should not prophesy such things!
> Shameful things will not overtake us!"
>
> (II:6)

Micah rebukes such people in words of scorn:

> A prophet for this people would be a man, going about utter-
>   ing wind and lies, and saying,
> "I will prophesy for you about wine and liquor."
>
> (II:11)

He speaks later of the "false prophets," and concludes with his epitome of the obligation of the true prophet, which all the pre-exilic prophets met:

> . . . To declare to Jacob his transgression,
>   And to Israel his sin.
>
> (III:8B)

Zephaniah seems to me not to rise to the stature of Micah or Isaiah. There is a passage which I find memorable in the vividness with which he portrays the merited punishment which Yahve will visit on Israel:

> Be silent before the Lord Yahve, for the Day of Yahve
>   is near. . . .
> The great day of Yahve is near, it is greatly speeding.
> Swifter is the day of Yahve than a runner, and faster
>   than a warrior.*
> A day of wrath is that day, a day of trouble and distress,
> A day of ruin and destruction, a day of darkness and gloom,
> A day of cloud and thick darkness,
> A day of trumpet blast and signal against the fortified
>   cities and the high battlements.
>
> (I:7A, 14-16)

Nahum has seemed to me a poet, rather than a prophet; indeed, the quality of his poetry is in inverse proportion to his prophetic gift. The main portion of his book celebrates the capture of Nineveh, the capital city of Assyria, which fell to the Chaldeans in 612 B.C. Nahum rejoices vindictively over the downfall of Nineveh, poetically imagining that he has personally witnessed it. First comes the initial attack:

> He who puts to rout has come against you!
> Let the defense be manned, the road be watched,
> Loins be girded, full strength be mustered! . . .
>
> (II:2 Heb., II:1 Eng.)

He proceeds to taunt the Ninevehites for the loss of their power:

> What has become of the lion's den—
> The cave of the young lions
> Where the [lion] returned,
> Where the cubs were unfrightened?
>
> (II:12 Heb.; 11 Eng.)

Then comes the account of the conquest itself:

> Woe unto the city guilty of murder, completely deceiving,
> Full of ill-gotten gains, where rape never ceased!
> Crack of whip, loud sound of wheels.
> Horse gallops, chariot bounces,
> Cavalry charges, sword flashes,
> Spear shines, hosts fall! . . .
> "I am against you," says Yahve of Hosts,
> "I will roll your skirts up, over your face,
> And show your private parts to the nations,
> And your shame to kingdoms.
> I will throw upon you filth,
> I will make you a sight to gaze at in scorn!"
>
> (III:1-3, 5-6)

With Habakkuk there comes a turn in prophecy, much as though there has already been enough of excoriation. Like Nahum, he speaks against the background of the Chaldeans' triumphs over the Assyrians, and their movement westward toward Judea. Far from gloating that the Israelites were receiving merited punishment, Habakkuk was deeply concerned that his people were to suffer. Moreover, he felt that the punishment was undeserved, in the sense that other peoples had been as wicked and had gone unpunished. Most striking of all is that Habakkuk speaks not to the people, but to the Deity:

For how long, O Yahve, shall I cry and You will not hear?
[For how long] shall I call out, "Violence is done!"—
But You will not help?
Why do You permit me to experience evil, and encounter ordeal? . . .

In light of this silence on Yahve's part:

> Revelation has come to a standstill, and true justice
>   cannot emerge,
> For the wicked circumvent the righteous, so that justice
>   becomes distorted.
>
> (I:2-3A, 4)

Then Yahve in reply affirms that it is He who is bringing the Chaldeans against His unfaithful people:

> I am raising up the Chaldeans, a bitter and hasty nation
> Which travels the breadth of the earth to seize dwellings
>   that are not his. . . .
> His people are bent entirely on violence, its terror
>   precedes them,
> And they gather prisoners like sand.
>
> (II:6, 9)

Habakkuk thereupon partly replies and partly muses:

> Are You not more ancient than [Chaldea], O Yahve,
> My holy God, not subject to death?[11]
> You appointed him as an instrument of justice,
> Established him as a means of chastisement. . . .
> Yet why do You countenance treacherous people,
> Keep silent while he swallows the wicked,
> Who are, nevertheless, more righteous than he? . . .
> Is it right that [Chaldea] should wield the sword,*
> Constantly to slay people, without pity?
>
> (I:12, 13B, 17)

Now the prophet turns to speak a highly personal thought:

> I take my stand on my place of watch and station myself
>   on my tower,
> And look forward to see what He will say to me,
> And what He* will reply to my complaint.
> Yahve answered me, "Record the vision,
> Make it plain on tablets, that even one who runs by,
>   will be able to read it.
> The vision will still abide to the appointed time,
> It will speak out at the end, and not lie,

> If it tarries, wait for it; for it will surely come and
>   not too late:
> 'Behold, the wicked; for him there is no uprightness.*
> But let the righteous person abide in his faith.' "

                                                                    (II:1-4)

Against the background of the belief that Yahve controls the events of world-wide history, Habakkuk was presuming to question whether Yahve was fair and just. The question is a natural one, arising from the clash between the axiom that Yahve, a just God, controls all, and the observation that injustice did exist, or at least appeared to.

No other prophet is as vivid, at least to me, as Jeremiah. This is not so much because we have, by chance preservation, more external data about him than we do about others, as it is because we can see the self-revelation in the poetry of the man. Jeremiah suffered because the time in which he lived was perilous: the Babylonians destroyed the power of the Egyptians in 605 B.C., captured Jerusalem in 597, destroyed that city and the Temple after a rebellion in 586, and then drove the leading citizens, including the king, into exile in Babylonia. But he also suffered because the monarchs whom he dared to counsel, Jehoiakim and Zedekiah, did not hesitate to charge him with treason and to imprison him, and to destroy the original written record of his words. They scorned him as a false prophet, preferring to listen to the prophets who foretold only favorable events, so that Jeremiah experienced a deep personal rejection—and scorn and contumely. He loved his people so passionately that he felt an uncontrollable impulse to speak to them plainly, without gloss or deception, and he thereby incurred their animosity. He did not hesitate to speak slightingly even about their reliance on the sacred Temple as a guarantee of their safety; he considered this silly.

He experienced pain and hate and agony. Prudence urged him to silence, but conviction overcame prudence. In poetry that has never been surpassed he tells us of the inner ordeals he endured. Yet it was he, when calamity came, who saw the way to reconstruction. The man who had spoken words of deunuciation before

586 was also the man who spoke words of encouragement and comfort after the calamity.

His life alone would stamp him as remarkable, had there survived only a biographical sketch of him. But what truly overwhelms me in Jeremiah is his poetry. Here is what many scholars believe is an early discourse, notable for its sensitivity and for its being more an appeal to fidelity than a denunciation of infidelity:

> The word of Yahve came to me, "Go and proclaim in the
>   ears of Jerusalem:
> 'I remember your youthful fidelity,
> Your love when a bride, when you followed Me in the
>   wilderness,
> In an unsown land. . . .
> . . . What defect did your fathers find in Me
> That they have moved far from Me?' . . .
> . . . Pass over to the island of Cyprus and look,
> And send to Kedar and consider diligently,
> And see if there ever was anything like this.
> Did any other people exchange their god—
> And those gods are not gods!
> But My people exchanged its glory
> For something which yields nothing.
> O heavens, be appalled at this,
> Shudder and tremble exceedingly!* . . .
> For two evils has My people done:
> Me have they forsaken, a fountain of living water—
> To hew out for themselves broken cisterns which cannot
>   contain water."
>
> (II:1-2, 5A, 10-13)

In the above, often Jeremiah deviates from the normal verse pattern of a three/three meter, using instead a three/two meter; just as often, too, he seems to disdain meter altogether.

His desire is to bring people to their senses, not to denounce them. His words can be harsh:

> Lift up your eyes to the high places,
> And see if there is anywhere that you have not committed
>   adultery.
> You have sat on the roads [waiting for lovers]

> Like a marauder in the wilderness [waiting for passers-by];
> In your whoring and your wickedness you have polluted the
> > whole land.
>
> > (III:1-2)

Yet his plea for their restoration modifies the harshness:

> A voice is heard on the high places,
> The weeping supplications of the children of Israel.
> They have distorted their way,
> They have forgotten Yahve, their God—.
> Return, O wayward sons, and I will heal your waywardness.
> > (III:21-22A)

He knows that disaster lies ahead:

> "I shall cause to disappear from the cities of Judah
> And from the streets of Jerusalem
> The sound of joy and the sound of rejoicing;
> The sound of the bridegroom and the sound of the bride.
> For the land shall become desolate."
>
> > (VII:34)

His mood, though, is one of sorrow:

> For the hurt of the daughter of my people I have been
> > made hurt.
> I am clothed in mourning; dismay has taken hold of me.
> Is there no balm in Gilead, no physician there?
> Why is the health of the daughter of my people not recovered?
> Oh that my head were waters and my eyes a spring of tears,
> Then I would weep day and night for the destroyed of the
> > daughter of my people!
> > (VIII:21-23 Heb.; IX:1 Eng.)

A narrative about him relates that he went to the very gates of the Temple to plead for a life of restored righteousness. There he denounced as a lie the words of those who prated that the Temple would save them: "Is this Temple, on which My name is called, to be a den of thieves?" He goes on to assert that the celebrated temple at Shiloh (which we should remember from the account of Samuel, see p. 14) did not save the northern kingdom (VII:1-15). Later in the book we are told that the priests and the prophets (*false* prophets) and the people responded to Jeremiah's word by seizing him and demanding of the nobles that they execute him. Jeremiah was saved in this crisis, however, by the intervention of a certain man, Ahikam ben Shafan (XXVI:7-24). But danger and personal anguish brought Jeremiah to such a point of distress that he even contemplated desisting from his prophetic role:

All day I am a laughing stock,
Everyone mocks at me.
As often as I speak, I cry out
And I shout, "Violence, Spoil!"
For the word of Yahve has meant for me reproach and derision all
    the day.
And if I say: I will not make mention of Him,
Nor will I again speak in His name,
Then there is in my heart, as it were, a burning fire
Shut up in my bones.
I weary trying to restrain it,
And I cannot.
I have heard the defaming by many.
Terror is all about me.[12]

.   .   .

"You denounce him, and we will denounce him,"
Say all my acquaintances who watch for my stumbling.
"Perhaps he will be led astray and we will prevail against him,
And take our revenge upon him."

.   .   .

Cursed is the day on which I was born,
The day on which my mother bore me—may it never be blessed! . . .
Why is it that I came out of the womb
To see toil and pain,
And for my days to be consumed in shame?

                            (XX:8-10, 18)

Later he speaks these bitter words:

> Woe unto me, O my mother, that you bore me,
> A man of contention, a man of contention to the whole earth.
> I have neither lent money nor have men lent money to me—
> Yet all curse me!

                            (XV:10)

Jeremiah's certainty that disaster lay ahead was borne out by the events of 597 and 586. Jerusalem was laid waste, Solomon's glorious Temple destroyed, and all but the unconsequential people were taken into exile in Babylonia. At this series of tragedies, which he had foreseen, Jeremiah turned from deunuciation. The Exile, he insisted, was not the end (as it had been in the northern kingdom in 721). The Exile, too, fitted in with Yahve's plan. As a father chastises a child so as to discipline and correct him, so Yahve would use the Exile for such purposes:

> "But do not be afraid, O My son Jacob," says Yahve,
> "And do not fear, O Israel,
> For behold, I shall deliver you from the distance
> And your children from the land of their captivity. . . .
> I shall *discipline* you to the point of justice.
> For I will not hold you entirely guiltless."
>
> (XXX:10A, 11B)

At some future time a regenerated people would return to its land:

> Behold, I shall change the fortune of the houses of Jacob
>   and upon his dwellings I will have mercy,
> And a city will be built anew on his own rubble heap and
>   the palace will be restored to what it once was.
> And from them shall come thanksgiving and the voices of
>   those who are making merry.
> I shall multiply them, they shall not be few;
> I will glorify them and they will not be insignificant.
>
> (XXX:18-19)

Not only did he express this hope, but he wrote a letter to the exiles in Babylonia:

> Build houses and dwell in them and plant gardens and eat their fruit. Marry women and beget children and take daughters for wives for your sons, and give your daughters to husbands. Let them bear sons and daughters and multiply and not diminish. Seek the peace of the city whither I have exiled you and pray on its behalf to Yahve, for in its tranquillity you will have peace.
>
> (XXIX:5-7)

Even these words of solicitous counsel brought Jeremiah distress, for a certain prophet among the exiles, Shemaiah, wrote a letter to Jerusalem to denounce Jeremiah, since his letter implied a very long sojourn in Babylonia. (Passages, possibly secondary, depict Jeremiah as supposing that the exile would last for a period of seventy years; see XXV: 11-12; XXIX: 10.)

In view of the covenant background of the prophets, and the clear implication in the conquest by the Babylonians that that covenant was ruptured, we need to ask on what basis Jeremiah could assert that relations with Yahve could and would continue. There is a passage which seems to me to suggest that precisely such questions were thrown up to Jeremiah. His answer leads one to wonder if he came to it out of long meditation, or whether he reached it intuitively; it is the latter view that appeals to me. Here are his incisive words:

> "Behold, days are coming," says Yahve, "When I shall make a new covenant with the house of Israel, not like the covenant which I made with their fathers in the days when I took hold of their hand to take them out of Egypt—a covenant which they broke and over which I was master," says Yahve. "But rather this is the covenant which I shall make with the house of Israel after those days: I shall put My revelation in their innards and I shall write it in their hearts, and I shall be their God and they will be My people. No longer will one man teach his neighbor and his brother, saying, 'Come to know Yahve,' but instead all of them will know Me, from the small to the great, for I shall forgive their sin and their transgression will I no longer remember."
>
> (XXXI: 31-34)

In these few lines Jeremiah charted a new course and provided a higher dimension for the unfolding religion. He emancipated the religion from a bondage to Temple and animal sacrifice; he swept away, not the love for the ancestral land, but all residual thought that only there could the universal God be worshiped; himself a person who turned inward, he gave a sanction for religious piety as more a matter of internal heart than external conformity.

The reader can scarcely become a master of all the prophetic literature without concentrated study. I should not hesitate to recommend that one whose leisure time is restricted should content himself with a mere acquaintance with Amos, Isaiah, and Second Isaiah, and proceed to familiarize himself with Jeremiah alone. To know Jeremiah intimately is better than to know all the prophets superficially.

I find it impossible to turn from Jeremiah to Ezekiel without a vivid sense of disappointment. Here, though, I am in a minority among scholars. I am able to muster some reluctant regard for Ezekiel, but more for his prose than his poetry. He provided in prose a significant statement on individual responsibility, a useful counterbalance to the dominant note whereby the individual seemed negated in the community, for under the earlier covenant one's personal righteousness or wickedness was swallowed up in the corporate righteousness and wickedness. Ezekiel could write prose with precision and even pedantry. He depicted the righteous man: one who avoids idolatry, desists from defiling the wife of his neighbor, abstains from sexual intercourse with a woman when she is menstruous, takes no garment in pledge, does not rob, gives food to the hungry and garments to the naked, and does not charge interest on the money he lends, and, in general, observes Yahve's statutes. We notice that his formulation here is mostly negative. He describes the wicked man briefly as merely the opposite of the righteous man.

Now, let us suppose that a righteous man has a son who is wicked. Can the father's righteousness enable the wicked son to be deemed righteous? Or, if a wicked man has a righteous son, does the righteous son inherit the father's guilt? In each case the answer was a resounding no: "Behold, all souls are mine, the soul of the father as well as the soul of the son is Mine. The person who sins, he [alone] shall die" (XVIII:4).

Similarly, he speaks intelligibly about repentance:

> "As I live," says the Lord Yahve, "I do not desire the death
> of the wicked person, but rather that the wicked person

should turn aside from his way and live. Return from your
evil deed! Why should you die, house of Israel! Now you,
son of man, just say to your people, the righteousness of the
righteous will not save him on the day of his transgression,
nor will the wicked stumble in his wickedness on the day
when he turns aside from his evil. The righteous will not be
able to live because of his past righteousness on the day when
he sins. When I say about the righteous that he shall surely
live, if it is one who has relied upon his previous righteousness
but has done evil, all his righteous deeds will not be remembered, and in the iniquity which he has done, will he die.
When I say about the wicked that he will surely die, if it is
one who turns aside from his sin and does justice and righteousness and returns the pledge taken unjustly, or [returns]
that which he has seized in robbery, and walks in statutes of
life without committing iniquity, then he shall surely live and
will not die. All the sin which he sinned will not be remembered against him. If he has done justice and righteousness he
will surely live.

"Now your kinsmen will say that the way of Yahve is not
right, but it is they whose way is not right. When the righteous turns from his righteousness and does evil, then he shall
die thereby. And when the wicked turns from his wickedness
and does justice and righteousness he shall live because of
these things, and as for your saying 'The way of Yahve is not
right,' I shall judge each man according to his ways, O house
of Israel."

(XXXIII:11-20)

Perhaps my difficulty with Ezekiel is that I have great love for
Jeremiah, and hence I am not fair to Ezekiel. Perhaps, too, I under-
assess Ezekiel the man because his book chances to have been
transmitted with disquieting textual confusion, for which copyists
and not Ezekiel himself could be responsible, and in that I may
become excessively captious. Scholars, spurred by the book's problems, have produced many theories about Ezekiel, as to his period
and his locale. The visions in the book have persuaded some, ab-
surdly, that Ezekiel was an epileptic. Scholars have experienced
much frustration with Ezekiel, and for that reason they have pro-

duced a spate of theories about the book. I fear that it is as hard to made sense of their theories as it is to understand the book itself.

Perhaps much of the difficulty in Ezekiel is the author's impulse, which led to extreme symbolism. Few imaginations have been as vivid as his. The opening chapter, here condensed, relates that he was at the River Chebar in Babylonia with the exiles from Judah. From the north there came a storm-wind, about which there was fire flashing, and in which there was an emanating radiance. He saw four creatures, each with four faces, those of a lion, an ox, an eagle, and a man. Each of these creatures had two distinct pairs of wings, one pair on the upper body and the other on the lower. The creatures moved, going in a chosen direction without veering. In the midst of the creatures there was a bright fire, out of which lightning came. Near each of the creatures there was a wheel, and, indeed, there was a wheel within a wheel. The vision was the Deity's chariot throne; above the creatures there was a plane that was like crystal, and on it there was a throne, on which there sat someone in the appearance of a man. Above the loins of the creature there was visible gleaming bronze, and below there was an intense brightness, for this vision was the fiery radiance of Yahve. Ezekiel fell on his face, and he heard a voice speaking.

This is all very colorful, and it is useful to students of anthropology for its splendid assortment of folk-materials. The vision certainly contains its dimension of awe and of mystery. But what does it really mean? Despite the accumulated explanations which scholars offer, we really do not know. And we can scarcely answer the question, why was there this recourse to so elaborate a set of symbols?

The richness of the symbolism in Ezekiel is beyond cataloguing here. Some of it is explained and clear; more of it leaves one floundering. The passages between the symbolic sections, though in more or less straightforward prose, teem with textual difficulties and present a confused sequence of apparently incomplete paragraphs.

One vision of Ezekiel, however, is as clear as it is vivid. Yahve brought Ezekiel to a valley which was full of dry bones strewn about. The Deity informed Ezekiel that a spirit could enter the dry bones and make them alive, with sinews and flesh added to them. Then there ensued a voice and a commotion, after which the bones came together, with sinews on them. Flesh too came, and also the covering skin. Ezekiel then spoke the right words, and the proper spirit entered into the inert bodies and brought them to life: "The bones are all the house of Israel." The meaning is that the collective Israel, resurrected, would return to its native soil; indeed, both the northern and the southern kingdoms would be restored and be reunited:

> Behold, I will take the children of Israel from among the nations whither they have gone and I will gather them around about and bring them to their soil. I will make them into one single nation (not as in the past, when there were two kingdoms). [A descendant of] my servant David will be king over them, and one single shepherd will they both have. They will walk according to My statutes and they will observe My ordinances to execute them. . . . I shall make a covenant of peace with them, a perpetual covenant will there be with them. . . . My dwelling place will be with them and I shall be their God and they will be My people. All the nations will know that I, Yahve, sanctify Israel through My sanctuary's being in their midst forever.
>
> (XXXVII:21-28)

Most modern scholars believe that the resurrection here is not meant in an individual sense but only in a corporate one; they hold that belief in individual, personal resurrection arose later, about two centuries before the time of Jesus. My own opinion is that while the passage does concern the corporate restoration of the two kingdoms, it actually applies to the corporate body a belief in personal resurrection that was then already known but not universally accepted.

Perhaps this stirring section of Ezekiel is a clue to what all of the Book might have been, had it survived in better form.

We find a great rise in poetic quality in moving from Ezekiel to

Second Isaiah. We should notice also that we are seeing a turn in the prophetic manner, in that Jeremiah, after a long career of denunciation, turned to assuage his people's suffering and distress, and Ezekiel spoke to them of the hope of a return from exile and a resumption, in new terms, of the national life under a worthy shepherd king. With Second Isaiah, denunciation is virtually abandoned. It is replaced by the injunction to the prophet and the leaders:

> "Comfort, comfort My people," says your God.
> "Speak to the heart of Jerusalem and call out to her
> That her term of toil is fulfilled, her penalty acceptably paid,
> For she has received from God double for all her sins."
>
> (XL:1-2)

Perhaps the explanation here should be explicit: when Bible scholars speak of *Second* Isaiah, they are recording a conclusion which was first expressed almost a thousand years ago, that in chapters XL-LXVI we are no longer in the period of the eighth and early seventh pre-Christian century, which chapters I-XXXIX portray. To speak of Second Isaiah is no way to suggest that we know the name of the prophet and poet shown in the latter portion of the Book of Isaiah; we do not. It is strange that so supreme a writer is nameless, and that we have no direct data about him. If we speculate why his words were recorded with those of First Isaiah, the disappointing probability is that a copyist had room in his scroll after he completed Isaiah I-XXXIX, and that he simply used up the parchment sheets that were available to him. Indeed, those scholars who regard XL-LXVI as a repository of diverse anonymous writings are probably correct, though it seems to me a bit heavy-handed to follow their usage of speaking of Third and Fourth Isaiah.[13]

Second Isaiah was written at the time of the emergence of Cyrus of Persia, in 539. He conquered Babylonia, and he gave the Judean exiles permission to return home. But the Judeans had become dispirited through the experience of the Exile; if they were to journey homeward they would have to traverse the eastern wilderness, and face all the difficulties that one could associate with the journey—a frightening prospect. There was need to rally the exiles, to encourage them, to animate them with hope and purpose. The words "Comfort, comfort My people!" reveal the underlying motif of Second Isaiah.

Second Isaiah regarded himself as the spokesman, not for himself, but for Yahve. As he encouraged the people, he explained how the Exile, and now the return, would conform with the will and plan of Yahve. In his explanation he had referred to the role of Israel in the divine plan, for a special reason: in Second Isaiah Yahve ceases completely to be the limited god of the Israelites; He is, instead, the one universal God of the world. As the universal God, it was He who raised up Cyrus to the latter's conquests. But if Yahve dealt with victorious world conquerors, what concern could He, the universal God, have for the small, disheartened, and defeated people of Judah? The answer of Second Isaiah is that so broad and encompassing were Yahve's purposes among men, that the divine will could be carried out only as a human king carries out his purposes, that is, through his servants. Israel was the servant of the universal God.

It must be, or become, plain that Second Isaiah was a poet, not a political analyst, and that he was surely not a realistic philosopher. A member of a small and harassed people, he dared to speak of the great conqueror Cyrus in the light of his people's experience. There is, hence, a certain madness in his conceptions, an extravagance in which his daring impracticality triumphs over mundane facts. He does not lack logic, once his poetic premises are accepted; his mind was acute, his perception sharp, his vision far-reaching, and his profundity unsurpassed. But above all these stand his boldness, and his poetic genius.

The poet expresses his conviction that the past events, like those of the future, are by no means accident, but the deliberate design of God. Moreover, he asserts that the unfolding events were foretold. That they were foretold proves that God, and not some idol, has controlled the events:

I have declared the first things from of old;
They went out from My mouth and I caused them to be heard.
Suddenly I have done them and they have come about! . . .
I told you these things from of old,
And before they came about I let you hear them,
So that you should not say, "My idol has done them,"
Or "My graven image or molten statue has brought them about."

> (XLVIII: 3, 5)

He does not tell us where or when the foretelling took place. We can wonder if such material failed to be preserved. On the other hand, there was by his time an abundant legacy of prophecy from the past, including Jeremiah and Ezekiel, and the predictions of the future return from the exile in those books could have served as Second Isaiah's basis.

The control of world-wide events, in turn, demonstrated that Yahve is the only God:

Hearken unto Me, Jacob, and Israel, whom I have called upon:
I am God. I am the first and I am also the last.
It is My hand which laid the foundation of the earth,
And My right hand which spread out the heavens. . . .

> (XLVIII: 12-13)

Yahve had had no difficulty in exercising His control. The Chaldeans had to be defeated; hence He raised up Cyrus against them:

Thus says Yahve concerning His anointed one,
Concerning Cyrus, whose right hand He* has taken hold of,
To subdue nations before Him,
To loosen the girdles of kings: [14]
"I will open gates before him,
Gates that will never again be shut. . . ."

> (XLV:1)

The summoning of Cyrus was directly related to the fate of Israel, and its restoration to its land:

I called from the east a ravenous bird [Cyrus];
From a distant land, the man who carries out My purpose.
I have spoken and I will bring it about,

I have formed plans, and will do them.
Hearken unto Me, you faint of heart,
For whom deliverance has seemed distant.
I have brought My victory near and it is no longer far off,
And My salvation will not tarry
And I will bring salvation in Zion
And restore to Israel My splendor.

(XLVI: 11-13)

Yahve did not call Cyrus for Cyrus' sake:

For the sake of My servant Jacob and My chosen one, Israel!
I called you, [O Cyrus,] by your name, I spoke it, even
    though you do not know Me.
I am God and there is no other; besides Me there is no God.
I have girded you with strength, though you have not known Me,
That from the east and from the west people will know that
    nothing takes place except through Me.
I am God and there is no other.
I fashion light and create darkness.
I create peace and I create evil.
I am God Who does all these things.

(XLV: 4-7)

If one asks, Why should Yahve be concerned for the people whose
trespasses had led to their defeat and exile?, the answer comes in
these words:

For My own sake, for My own sake, I do this. . . .
    I have blotted out, as a thick cloud, your transgressions,
    And, as a cloud, your sins.
    Return to Me, for I have redeemed you.

(XLVIII: 11A; XLIV: 22)

The redeemed Israel would have renewal and growth:

I shall pour My spirit on your descendants,
My blessing on your offspring.
They shall spring up like trees amid the grass,*
Like willows by water courses.

(XLIV: 3B-4)

As a consequence, there would be Gentiles who would become proselytes into the Jewish community (quite likely the first expression of this idea):

> This one will say, I belong to God
> And that one will call himself by the name of Jacob.
> This one will enroll himself to God
> And surname himself by the name Israel.
>
> (XLIV:5)

He puts into a single passage the relationship of God and Israel:

> "You are My witnesses," says God,
> "My servants whom I have chosen. . . .
> I, only I, am God, and besides Me there is no redeemer.
> I have declared this and have made it known* . . .
> You are My witnesses," says God, "And I am God."
>
> (XLIII:10A, 11-13A)

The sense in which Israel is God's servant for all mankind is expressed in these words:

> Behold My servant Jacob* whom I uphold,
> Israel My chosen one in whom I delight.
> I have put My spirit upon him, that he bring forth justice
>   to the nations.
> He will not shout nor raise his voice,
> He will not have his voice heard in the street.
> He will not break even a bruised reed,
> Nor extinguish a smoking wick of wax,
> Yet he will bring forth justice in full truth.
> He shall not fail nor shall he be discouraged*
> Until he brings forth justice on the earth,
> And the [known] world waits for his revelation. . . .
> I, God, have called you with righteousness and taken hold
>   of your hand,
> I will watch over you and I will make you a covenant of
>   the people,
> A light to the nations, to open the eyes of those who are blind,
> To bring the prisoner out of his bondage, and those who sit
>   in darkness out of the dungeon.
>
> (XLII:1-4, 6-7)

The prospective return from the Exile never fades from the prophet's mind. He conceives of the return as almost a second Exodus. He does not condemn Babylon for enslaving Israel; rather, he condemns the Bablyonians for their preoccupation with idolatry. He speaks with scorn about the Babylonian processions in which idols were carried (XLVI:1-7) and derides the making of them (XLIV:9-20). Now God is redeeming His people: despite the rigor of the journey across the eastern wilderness, He will bring them to their land:

> I will open rivers on the bare high places
> And fountains in the midst of the valleys,
> I shall make the wilderness into pools of water
> And the arid land into springs of water. . . .
> The wilderness and the arid places rejoice,
> The desert is happy and bursts into flower,
> Like the rose, it bursts into flower,
> It is happy, joyous and singing. . . .
> Water will spring forth in the wilderness,
> And streams in the Araba.
> There will be a road there;
> It will be called the Highway of Holiness. . . .
> The ransomed of Yahve will return,
> They will come to Zion with song,
> And eternal joy will be on their heads. . . .
>
> (XLI:18; XXXV:1, 6B, 10A)

Jerusalem itself would be restored:

> Wake, wake, put on your ornaments, O Zion.
> Don your beauteous clothes, O Jerusalem, sacred city. . . .
> Shake off the dust; stand up, O Jerusalem,*
> The chains about your neck are broken, O captive daughter
> of Zion.
>
> (LII:1A, 2)

He portrays an observer in Judah who looks eastward for the sight of those who are returning:

> How beautiful are his feet!
> When the announcer of good tidings is on the mountains,

> He proclaims peace, He announces that all is well,
> He proclaims redemption, he says to Zion, "Your God reigns!"
>
> (LII:7)

Never again would God forsake or punish His people:

> "For a brief moment I abandoned you, but in great love I
>   gather you.
> In great momentary anger,* I hid My face from you,
> But with everlasting reliability I love you."
> Says Yahve, your Redeemer.
>
> (LIV:7-8)

These selections can at best exhibit only what is typical of Second Isaiah's thought and poetry; it is the actual reading which provides the fullest appreciation of the insight and the beauty and, indeed, of the perceptive mind which the poet-prophet possessed.

There has been, then, a full turn in prophecy, from the thundering words of doom in Amos to the passionate solicitude and solace in Second Isaiah. In the range of these writings, much in the realm of religious thought has become illumined: monotheism and universalism, authenticity in worship, the implication of religious ethics. Above all, the prophetic writers spoke about the meaning of history, and they dared to insist that there is a divine purpose in the flow of events, in disasters and inequities, and in the march of world conquerors. Profundity and beauty are blended together, a joining to my mind miraculous, far beyond the nature miracles which the narrative materials so often present.

It would be too much to expect that prophetic literature after Second Isaiah should retain the loftiness which it reached in him. Our interest in Haggai and Zechariah is much more historical than literary. These two prophets lived in Judah after the return of the exiles, and they were concerned with the rebuilding of the Temple (which Jeremiah had scorned!). In their books there appears the indistinct figure of Zerubbabel, apparently a descendant of David who was expected to be the Jewish governor under the Persians, and who may possibly have led an unsuccessful revolt against the Persians. Such *may* be the meaning of the rebuking verse, Zech. IV:6, "This is God's word to Zerubbabel, 'Not by power and not by might, but by My spirit. . . .'" Not only is the text of Zechariah in rather poor condition—it contains many obscure verses of this kind—but the author deals in symbolic visions which are colorful but unclear.

Malachi is not a man's name; it means "My messenger." Coherence seems lacking in his book. There is a contention that God has shown His love for Judah by His punishment of Edom; there is distress that the priests have failed to live up to the high standards expected of them. The prophet laments a treachery which he asserts exists among the people; he is chagrined at intermarriage with alien peoples; he is unhappy that divorces are taking place. God will come to punish the transgressors, but only after first sending His "messenger"; the divine intent, though, is to purify the people, not to destroy them. An appendix identifies this "messenger" as Elijah, who, we remember from II Kings II:11, did not die but went up to heaven in a storm. Obadiah is very short, and of little consequence; much that is in Obadiah appears also in Jer. XLIX: 7-16. It reflects a frequent post-exilic motif, the hatred of Edom.

In Joel we find, on the one hand, a high level both of idea and content, and, on the other, much that is vengeful, showing a resentment of the injuries which neighboring nations have inflicted. The coming Day of Yahve would be a judgment on them. This resentment is somewhat mystifying. It seems premised on injuries suffered, but we have no knowledge of just what these injuries were. One scholar has suggested the hypothesis that about the year 485 a coalition of neighboring nations attacked Judah, sacked Jerusalem, and destroyed the Temple.[15] Whether the hypothesis is right or not, there is in post-exilic prophecy, and in some of the Psalms, a recurrence of reflections of injury and suffering, and resentment of neighboring peoples.

Perhaps this same suffering also bred new hopes; one such hope was for the revival of the dynasty of David, in the person of an ideal king:

> Then a shoot will arise from the stock of Jesse,
> And a branch will become fruitful from its roots.
> The spirit of God will rest on him . . .
> And he will abstain from judging by what he sees
> Or make decisions [merely] by what he hears. . . .
> Justice will be his belt,
> And integrity the girdle about his loins.
> The wolf will live with the sheep,
> And the leopard lie down with the goat.
> The calf and the lion cub will be together,
> And a little child will lead them. . . .
> They will neither harm nor destroy in all My sacred mountain,
> For the land will be filled with the knowledge of God
> As the waters cover the ocean. . . .
>
> (Is. XI: 1-2A, 3B, 5-6, 9)

Another hope, that of universal peace, is expressed about the remote future, the goal toward which history is moving. This peace
would be fashioned by God, but through Israel. One such expression occurs twice, in Isaiah II and in Micah IV:

> It will happen at the climax of history that the mount of
> Yahve's Temple will be established as the highest of peaks,
> higher than all the hills. Onto it nations will stream.[16] Great
> peoples will arrive, having said, "Come you, and let us go up
> to the mount of Yahve and to the Temple of Jacob's God. He
> will teach us His ways,* so that we shall walk in His paths,
> for divine teaching comes from Zion, and Yahve's word from
> Jerusalem. He will adjudicate among the nations, and give
> counsel to powerful peoples, even those which are distant.
> They will beat their swords into spades and their spears into
> pruning-knives. No nation will raise the sword against an-
> other, and they will never again train for war. Rather, each
> man will sit under his vine or under his fig tree, secure."
>
> (Is. II: 2-4; Mic. IV: 1-3)

Still another hope centered about the fact that the Judeans were
by now scattered all over the world. We cannot be sure when this
scattering took place, whether at the Babylonian conquest, or at
some later time, perhaps unrelated to any incident; of the fact of

the scattering we can be certain, for a number of passages speak eloquently of the ingathering of the scattered:

> It will come about in that future day that Yahve will recover a second time, by His power, the remnant of His people from Assyria, Egypt, Pathros (Upper Egypt), Ethiopia, Elam, Shinar, Hamath, and the sea islands.
>
>> He will raise a signal to the nations,
>> And assemble Israel's forced exiles.
>> And gather in the scattered of Judah
>> From the four corners of the earth. . . .
>>
>> (Is. XI:11-13)

At times the prophecy of the ingathering of the exiles is accompanied, as in Is. XI:14-16, by expressions of vengeance or hostility to other nations. We can be puzzled by the divergent motifs, of a concern for universal peace on the one hand, and a war-like animosity toward nations on the other; if we knew more about the historical events, we might be able to understand such divergencies better. What seems clear, however, is that the prophecies in the post-exilic period are concerned less with what was in the present than with what would be in the future. The feeling seems to pervade such prophecy that the present was tolerable only because one might reasonably hope for a better future. Because so much of the prophecy deals with the better future, scholars use the word "eschatological," from *eschaton*, a Greek word meaning "limit" or "end," for writings which are so oriented. The predictions about the future involve revelations ("apocalypses") of what was believed would some day take place. Such apocalypses were often couched in flamboyant, exotic symbols, and we today fail to understand them.

Distress, desperate hope, and symbolic revelation mark that strange book, Daniel. Fortunately, we possess its historical background. At the time Daniel was written, Judea belonged to some heirs of Alexander the Great, the Syrian Greeks, centered at Antioch. Other heirs of his, the Ptolemies of Egypt, were recurrently at war with the Greeks at Antioch, and Judea, situated as it was between them, was often the battleground. Burdensome taxation brought needed revenues from Judea to Antioch. Antiochus Epiphanes IV of Antioch was returning home in 168 from a defeat at the hands of the Ptolemies, who were helped by Rome. While on his way to Antioch he occupied Jerusalem, and he confiscated the valuables at the Temple and desecrated it. For his own political necessities he had determined to force the Judeans to abandon their religion and to conform to the state religion, hoping thereby to secure his southwestern frontier from hostile attack. The Judeans, led by the family called Hasmoneans (also known as Maccabeans), promptly rose in rebellion. The revolt was partially crushed, but it persisted even into the reign of Antiochus' successors; after some setbacks, Judea successfully achieved increasing measures of independence, and it gained full independence about 142.

The Book of Daniel, based on earlier materials, reached its present form during the Maccabean revolt, probably in the first decade of the struggle, between 168 and 158. Daniel falls into two parts, the first half a series of amusing stories which relate the wisdom of the courageous Daniel, the second half, a series of apocalypses. The stories are depicted as taking place in Babylon and Persia, but seem clearly pointed to the times and misdeeds of the Syrian Greeks of Antioch. The apocalypses are robust and vivid—and not fully comprehensible, especially in details. One apocalypse, Chapter VII, can be paraphrased to illustrate the manner:

> Daniel saw a vision in a dream. Four enormous beasts came out of the stormy Mediterranean, each different from the others. The first, though it looked like a lion, had an eagle's wings; its wings were pulled off, and the beast was set on its feet like a man, and given a human heart. The second beast was like a bear. In its mouth were three bones; it was commanded to eat a great deal of meat. The third beast was like a leopard, but had four wings and four heads; to it was given sovereignty. A fourth beast, terrifying and powerful, had great teeth of iron, and the power to trample things underfoot. This beast had ten horns, among which there presently emerged a small horn, with the result that three of the ten horns were uprooted. That small horn had human eyes and a

mouth which uttered strong words. This fourth beast was killed, and its body burnt up. The other beasts lost their sovereignty but received an extension of life for a season and a half.

In the vision Daniel saw someone, as if a man, coming amid the clouds of the sky, and then brought before the Ancient of Days, to receive sovereignty, authority, and royal dignity, so that all nations and people were to serve him; his sovereignty was to be eternal.

Daniel, troubled by the visions, received the meaning from someone standing about. The four beasts were four kingdoms destined to arise. The fourth beast was an empire; its ten horns were ten kings who would arise; the small horn would humble three of these ten kings. Thereafter the small horn would speak defiance against the Deity, and weary the "holy ones" through tampering with festivals and the laws. This would last for "a season" and "two seasons" and "a half-season." After that, a heavenly court would take away this authority forever, and give it to the "holy ones."

The general meaning here is fairly clear. The first three beasts are the Assyrian, the Babylonian, and the Persian empires,[17] and the fourth is that of Alexander the Great. The small horn which toppled three of the ten horns is the Syrian Greek kingdom of Antioch, which emerged as more powerful, from the standpoint of the Judeans, than the other three kingdoms that arose among Alexander's heirs. The "Ancient of Days" is God; the one, like a man, who came amid the clouds, is figuratively the Judean kingdom.[18] The allusion to altering feast days and laws is a reference to Antiochus' effort to root out Judaism (as related in I. Mac. I: 41-64); the three and a half "seasons" alludes to that period of oppression.

That is to say, this vision was a prediction of the ultimate freedom of the Judeans and their triumph over the Antiochene foes. There is no reason to doubt that the passage was well understood in the age in which it was written, or that it brought great hope to those who suffered under the Antiochenes.

Yet I confess to having little admiration for the literary substance of the Book of Daniel, or for the apocalyptic manner. Granted, the book has historical importance; yet I do not find it in itself edifying, or touching, or moving. Indeed, the way in which the Book has been used by the pious, as if it contains clues to every historical age, makes me wonder if it has not done more harm than good.

In the Hebrew Bible, Daniel is not found in the section of the Prophets, but in the Ketubim, "the [sacred] Writings," probably because by the time Daniel was written and came to be circulated, the prophetic section was already regarded as complete.

Though the post-exilic prophets and Daniel do not equal the pre-exilic and exilic prophets in profundity and literary eminence, they nevertheless served a useful function in their own times. Yet it is the sequence of Amos through Second Isaiah, plus the random later passages we have cited, which give the prophetic literature its literary and religious significance. The denunciations of Amos and Isaiah are expressions of a unique level of standards which the Hebrews demanded of themselves. The first prophets, bound as they were to a covenant idea, rose far beyond the mere covenant itself; then Jeremiah took the step of reinterpreting the covenant to be concerned with the inner heart of man; not external demands. Nowhere in any literature is social responsibility raised to the pinnacle which it reaches in prophetic thought; impractical as Isaiah's counsel on international relations may have been, there is no doubt that his views penetrated deeply into the important matter of national probity. Above all, the prophets turned religion away from matters of external ritual and redirected it toward the ultimates of inner integrity. The course which the totality of prophetic thought ran was from doom to comfort to hope.

The prophetic literature is the glory of the Hebrews, far beyond the military prowess or national triumphs which other books, such as Samuel and Kings, record. For the prophets, national honor was a matter of loyalty to ideals, national attainment was a matter of purity of living, and national triumph was a matter of the translation of the ideals into the pure living.

No one who observes the realities of our day, with east and west rivalries, armaments races, small and large wars, and the threat of nuclear destruction, can avoid some sense of despair, like that the pre-exilic prophets expressed. Yet it is this same prophetic literature which speaks to man of hope, and provides man with purpose and a sense of clear direction to a better world.

Epilogue

What was it—the religion, the literature, or the people—that preserved Scripture into our time? The three, of course, cannot be separated.

Each of us had his own private penchant. What I personally find most glorious in Israel's past is the succession of storytellers and gifted poets, and the profound human and religious insights which they recorded. Whatever else the Hebrews were, they were pre-eminently a race of extraordinarily gifted writers.

The Greeks and Romans taught us how to think, how to be scientists. Theirs has been an easy lesson to learn. The Hebrew effort was more arduous, for they tried to teach how to understand life and how to live.

Bibliography

The Oxford Annotated Bible, Revised Standard Version, ed. Herbert G. May and Bruce M. Metzger, New York, 1965.
The New English Bible with the Apocrypha, Oxford, 1970. An annotated version is under preparation.
The Jerusalem Bible, ed. Alexander Jones, Garden City, N.Y., 1966.
The New American Bible, Confraternity of Christian Doctrine, New York, 1970.
The Torah: The Five Books of Moses, Philadelphia, 1963. In modern English. This Jewish Publication Society translation will ultimately encompass the entire Hebrew Bible.

James Hastings, ed., *Dictionary of the Bible*, revised, New York, 1963. A one-volume work which has been brought up to date.
The Interpreter's Dictionary of the Bible, 4 vols., New York, 1962. An excellent tool which both beginners and scholars can use.
Jerome Biblical Commentary, Englewood, N.J., 1968. A Catholic work of highest caliber. Its ingenious index greatly increases its usefulness.
The Interpreter's One-Volume Commentary on the Bible, New York, 1971.
A. Cohen, ed., *Soncino Books of the Bible*, 14 vols., London, 1945-1952. A Jewish series; the commentary is traditional rather than modern. Excellent for its purposes.

Ira Maurice Price, *The Ancestry of our English Bible*, 2nd rev. ed., by
William A. Irwin and Allen P. Wikgren, New York, 1949. A
good account.

Max L. Margolis, *The Hebrew Scriptures in the Making*, Philadelphia,
1922. In some ways superseded, but still useful.

Max L. Margolis, *The Story of Bible Translations*, Philadelphia, 1917.
Reliable, and also fascinating.

Herbert G. May, ed., *Oxford Bible Atlas*, Oxford, 1964. Inexpensive
in paperback, and excellent.

James B. Pritchard, ed., *The Ancient Near East: An Anthology of
Texts and Pictures*, Princeton, N.J., 1965. A paperback abridge-
ment of two excellent works.

Jack Finegan, *Light from the Ancient Past*, 2nd ed., Princeton, 1960.
A useful summary of archaeology.

Ernst Ludwig Ehrlich, *A Concise History of Israel*, tr. by James Barr,
New York, 1965. Useful for a beginner.

Martin Noth, *The History of Israel*, tr. by S. Godman, rev. by P. R.
Ackroyd, 2nd ed., New York, 1960. Excellent, but possibly too
technical for a beginner.

H. H. Hahn, *The Old Testament in Modern Research*, Philadelphia,
1954. An account of modern biblical criticism.

Otto Eissfeldt, *The Old Testament: An Introduction*, tr. by Peter R.
Ackroyd, New York, 1965. A detailed and technical work, an
indispensable tool for scholars.

Gerald A. Larue, *Old Testament Life and Literature*, Boston, 1968. A
well-written college textbook.

Samuel Sandmel, *The Hebrew Scriptures: An Introduction to Their
Literature and Religious Ideas*, New York, 1963. An introduction for the general reader, it describes each scriptural book.

Yehezkel Kaufmann, *The Religion of Israel*, tr. and abridged by
Moshe Greenberg, Chicago, 1960. A work by a highly original,
and at times erratic, Israeli scholar.

Helmer Ringgren, *Israelite Religion*, Philadelphia, 1966. A well-
balanced work.

Norman Snaith, *Distinctive Ideas of the Old Testament*, New York,
1964. A good survey.

Notes

1. Ancient Jewish interpretation often responded to such passages by so treating them that the abhorrent disappeared. Such interpretation arose only because such passages disturbed those interpreters too.

2. The King James Bible of 1611 is a unique achievement in English literature, but it presents three difficulties. First, English has so changed since 1611 that a modern reader may find the King James unclear, or even, in places, unintelligible. Second, advances in scholarship have made it possible today to revise inaccuracies or correct downright errors in the King James. Third, the King James is everywhere majestic, even in passages in which the Hebrew is folksy, so that the King James is quite often untrue to the tone of the Hebrew. While the King James is the most admired translation ever made into English, and justly so, I regard it as unusable for my present purpose. It is, however, well worth a reader's time to become familiar with it.

1. It is the view of certain other passages too (Josh. XV:63 and I Chron. XI:4) that prior to a specific conquest by David, Jerusalem was known as Jebus, a place from which the Judahites were unable to dislodge the native Jebusites. A passage in a very old nar-

rative, Judges I:8, relates, in contradiction, that the Judahites did take the city before David's time.

2. There is a pun in the Hebrew (Judg. XI:35) which is impossible to reproduce in the English. The play is on *kārā'*, to be prostrate, and *'ākár*, to be in trouble, in distress.

3. Because of this beginning, the book was placed by the Greek translators of the Bible immediately after Judges, and it still holds this position in the usual Christian editions; in Jewish editions, the lateness of the story is attested to by its position in the last of the usual three divisions, *Ketūbĭm* (The [holy] Writings).

4. Like the Gilbert and Sullivan character who sings:

> But when the breezes blow
> I generally go below
>   And seek the seclusion that the cabin grants. . . .

5. The second chapter of Jonah is a psalm, a poetic prayer of thanksgiving for rescue from drowning. To some later author it seemed appropriate for Jonah to have prayed while in the belly of the fish, and he added the poem.

CHAPTER II

1. Scholars in general seem to believe that the utilization of angels represents an influence derived from the Persians. Perhaps this is so, but I see no reason not to regard angels as a natural development in Hebrew thought.

CHAPTER IV
2. *The Mood of the Reader*

1. One can read: Genesis entirely, Exodus I-XX:21; XXIV:1-18; XXXII-XXXIV: Numbers X:33-XVII:11; XXV; XXXIV:1-29; Deut. XXXI:1-29; and XXXIV:1-12.

4. *Creation and Primeval Man*

1. A marginal "gloss" has come into the text (Gen. II:9), adding that "the tree of life and the tree of knowing good and evil" were in the midst of the garden.

5. *Noah*

1. Among Jews 120 years is regarded as the desired span of life; when one wishes another a long life, he phrases it "even up to 120!"

2. In Num. XIII:33, the *Nefilim* are identified as giants, men of great stature. See also Deut. II:10-11 and 20, where these and other primeval giants are mentioned. Perhaps they were gigantic because they "fell" from heaven, in a now-lost folktale.

3. Diverse traditions, one that the rains lasted 40 days and nights, another that they lasted 365 days, have become so intertwined as to resist ready separation. Also, at Gen. VI:18 the author mentions the covenant between the Deity and Noah, anticipating the making of the covenant, which ensues only later, at Gen. IX:9. He distinguishes between pure and impure animals in VII:2, though this distinction is not made until the supposed age of Moses, in Leviticus XI. Other anomalies, too, exist.

4. Perhaps a pun is intended in *Noah*, the *resting* (*va-tānáḥ*) *of the* ark on Mount Ararat, and the resting place (*mānōáḥ*) for the doves.

5. How tragic that this passage about the curse of Ham was to be used to justify the enslavement of Africans in countless subsequent centuries, and that this justification persists among some people to our own time!

6. The many names in this chapter relate to peoples, but in only a few cases are we able to identify these peoples precisely. Among the descendants of Japheth was *Yavan*, a name that came to mean Greece.

7. In the process of this recasting, there has, strangely, been retained a tiny fragment (Gen. X:8-10) of a very ancient legend about a certain Nimrod, the son of Cush, a mighty hunter, the founder of eastern cities in Babylonia and Assyria. Post-biblical Jewish literature abounds in legends about him.

6. Abraham

1. Even under Solomon the borders of the Hebrew kingdom never extended so far. This vast area was perhaps the wish of the post-exilic community, when its territory was only Jerusalem and the environs, an area about the size of an American county.

2. In prophetic writings there are allusions to the wickedness of Sodom and Gomorrah, and to Yahve's punishing destruction: Amos IV:11; Isa. I:9-10; XIII:19; Jer. XXIII:14; XLIX:18 and Zeph. II:9. In none of these passages is either Lot or Abraham mentioned.

3. Pillars of salt abound in that area. Perhaps this incident explains the origin of what may at one time have been a well-known pillar resembling a woman.
4. Some scholars even interpret Ex. XXII:29, "You shall give your first-born son to me" to allude to child sacrifice as a one-time practice among the Hebrews. The rite is mentioned in II Kings XVI:3; XXI:6; Jer. VII:31; XIX:5, XXXII:35, and elsewhere.
5. The manner of the oath, here and in another passage, Gen. XLVII: 29, is strange to our ways. The person sworn put his hand under the thigh, that is, the sex organ, of him who was being sworn. One notes, however, that the Deity is invoked; that is, it is by the Deity that the oath is sworn.
6. There is a trivial loose end or error here. The father, Bethuel, seems to be dead. Later in the chapter he is mentioned as if alive; some scholars believe that this latter mention of Bethuel is a scribe's mistake, and that "*son of* Bethuel" is the correct reading there.
7. There are some minor confusions. By implication, both at the end of the story, and at the beginning, Abraham sends the servant on the mission as if Abraham is on his deathbed; it is to Isaac, not Abraham, that the servant returns. The tent is described in the Hebrew as the tent of *Sarah* whose death was earlier narrated; in the Greek translation it is Isaac's tent.
8. The dictum reads: "There is neither priority nor sequel in Scripture." This interpretive principle was the instrument by which the rabbis handled the chronological discrepancies.

8. *Jacob*

1. Many of the words in the Hebrew passage are obscure; I have greatly simplified the account.
2. We cannot be sure exactly what these were. "Household idols" is a frequent rendering. They were small, as we shall see.
3. The Pentateuch seems to reserve the term "Hebrews" for the period of the Patriarchs and Joseph; "Hebrews" is used in Kings on the lips of aliens as a taunt. To avoid a possible confusion about Israel, we must recall that, after the time of Solomon, the unified kingdom became divided into the southern kingdom of Judah and the northern kingdom of Israel. Hence, "Israel" as a collective term can ordinarily mean all the Hebrews, but it can also at times have the restricted meaning of the northern kingdom.

4. Gen. XXXIV relates an incident at Shechem. In this chapter
   Shechem is also the name of a man, the son of Hamor. Either two
   similar stories have become unified, or else an older story is corrected in a later rewriting. The basic tale is this: Shechem became
   the lover of Dinah, the daughter of Jacob. Thereafter he wished to
   marry her, for which purpose his father Hamor approached Jacob.
   The latter consulted his sons, who proposed that all the people of
   the city of Shechem undergo circumcision. The proposal was accepted, and the circumcision done. On the third day following, the
   twelve brothers fell on the people treacherously, slaughtered many,
   captured flocks, and made women and children slaves.

   Perhaps the early account went along this line, that Shechem seduced Dinah, and then earnestly wanted to marry her, but her
   brothers believed that a defiling act had been committed, and they
   therefore wrought their deceitful vengeance, to the extreme displeasure of Jacob. In the recasting, the seduction seems altrered to
   rape, and only two of the twelve brothers, Simeon and Levi, are
   guilty of the treacherous slaying, for which they are denounced in
   Gen. XLIX:5-7.

   A frequent explanation offered for this story is that through the
   medium of individuals there are portrayed authentic echoes of relations between the Canaanites and the Hebrew tribes. Perhaps this
   is the case.

   We might notice that the liaison between Shechem and Dinah is
   described as a "*nebālāh* in Israel." While the root meaning of the
   word *nebālāh* is folly, it also denotes a crime of concern to the
   total community (Deut. XXII:21; Josh. VII:15; Judg. XIX:23-24
   and XX:6-10). There was as yet, in the presuppositions of the
   story, no collective Israel; hence the phrase here is an anachronism.

5. I Sam. X:2 and Jer. XXXI:15 put the tomb further north, in
   Ramah, in the region belonging later to Benjamin; see Josh. XVIII:
   25.

6. Between this lame ending of the Jacob stories and the first part of
   the Joseph story, there is a strange section, Chapter XXXVI, sum-
   marizing by name the many descendants of Esau. Verse XXXVI:
   31 casually speaks of certain Edomite kings who reigned "before
   any king reigned over the children of Israel." This is one of the
   verses often cited to deny that Moses wrote the Pentateuch, for an
   awareness of monarchy in Israel puts one at a time much later than
   Moses.

9. *Joseph*

1. There are a few doublets; specifically, in some places the leader of
the brothers is Reuben, in some it is Judah. There is an account in
Gen. XXXV:22 of a misdeed of Reuben with Bilhah; perhaps a
redactor preferred to depict Judah as the leader, rather than the
oldest son Reuben, who is denounced in Gen. XLIX:4. The Judah
version makes the passers-by Midianites, the Reuben account Ishmaelites. A harmonization has the Midianites rescue Joseph and
then sell him to Ishmaelites.

There are two extraneous items. The first, integrated into the
long, unified story, is a poem, Gen. XLIX, containing the "blessings" conferred by the patriarch Jacob on his sons. The second
item, Gen. XXXVIII, is totally unrelated. Its ending appears to be
a possible clue to its elusive meaning, for by a pun it explains the
origin of the name of a clan of the tribe of Judah, that of Peretz.
The story, which sounds very ancient, is not very edifying. Judah
had married a Canaanite woman who bore him three sons, Er,
Onan, and Shelah. For his son Er, Jacob arranged a marriage with
a woman named Tamar; Er, however, died childless. Judah thereupon bade Onan to fulfill the levirate, "the brother-in-law requirement," an ancient obligation whereby a brother mated with a
childless widowed sister-in-law so as to provide offspring to carry
on his brother's line. Onan did an unseemly thing (which yields the
English word *onanism*), namely, at the climax of coition with
Tamar, he let his seed spill on the ground rather than within her.
For this action, Yahve slew Onan. It was now incumbent on Shelah
to fulfill the "brother-in-law" requirement, but Shelah was very
young; Judah proposed that the matter be deferred. Tamar returned to her father's home. Somewhat later, Judah, now a wid-
ower, returned to the area where Tamar was living; Shelah had
not met the brother-in-law requirement. Tamar took off her widow's garb and dressed herself as a harlot. Judah approached her,
and she asked as her price a kid from Judah's flock. The price was
agreeable, but he had no kid with him, so he gave her in pledge his
signet ring and his staff. He then had relations with her.

When Judah wanted to redeem the things given in pledge,
Tamar could not be found, and Judah shrugged the matter off. But
Tamar, who had again put on her widow's clothes, was pregnant.
The news came to Judah in the form of a report that Tamar had

become pregnant through looseness. Judah wanted her to be executed by burning. Tamar then showed him the articles he had left
in pledge. Thereupon Judah recognized his own responsibility,
especially in having failed to make Shelah meet his obligation.

Tamar had twins: One began to be born, and on his wrist the
midwife tied a scarlet thread, saying, "This one came out first."
But the hand was withdrawn, and instead the other twin was born
first. The midwife said, "You have made quite a (*péretz*) 'breach,' "
so she named him Peretz. The other twin was named Zérah, "scarlet." Perhaps the story occurs where it does because at this point in
the Joseph story Potiphar's wife tried to seduce Joseph. But the
import of the story is beyond ready explanation; it is well to regard it as a very ancient item a late author discovered and used,
without incorporating it into his running account.

2. A long "blessing" by Jacob of his sons before his death (Gen.
XLIX) is in poetry. It is not as much a blessing as a summary of
the history of the twelve tribes.

3. A P summary informs us that Jacob lived in Egypt seventeen years.
Before his death he put Joseph under oath to bury him with his
fathers in Canaan.

10. *Moses*

1. Presumably, though, Zipporah and the child, or children, returned
to Jethro, as we see from Ex. XVIII:2-4.

2. The P sacred calendar (see Lev. XXIII:5-6) keeps the two near
each other, but separate.

3. I Chron. IV:41-43 relates that in the reign of King Hezekiah the
Amalekites were exterminated.

4. We read (XX:13): "When the trumpet sounds, then they may
ascend." The clear import here is that the people may ascend later;
in verse 23, however, the import is that the people were not to
ascend at all. It is likely that an older account which supposed that
the people ascended the mountain was superseded by a later account in which the people did not, and this discordant verse 13
somehow failed to be omitted.

5. From Ex. XX:21 to Ex. XXIII:33 there is an intrusive legal section.

6. The entire section is somewhat confused in minor details, for the
reason that this most important incident was told and retold, and as
a result it underwent natural variations. Some such variations clus-
ter about the precise people who were to ascend. We are told that

only Moses and Aaron were to do so; in XXIV:1-10, the list is found expanded: Moses, Aaron, Nadab, and Abihu, plus seventy elders. One tradition appears to suppose that Joshua accompanied Moses, either part way or all the way to the top of the mountain (Ex. XXIV:13 and XXXII:17). A more fundamental variation is in the sequence of the details, that is, how many ascents there were, and just what intervened between them. Scholars have tried to sort out all these disparities, and perhaps too neatly.

7. There is given next (Ex. XXXIII:7-10) a brief account of the Tent of Meeting, a portable shrine at which the Deity customarily revealed Himself to Moses. Students of folklore explain the Tent of Meeting as a substitute for, or replica of, the cave on the mountain; Yahve revealed Himself at this cave, but when the Israelites moved on, He revealed Himself at the Tent of Meeting. In P sections this portable shrine is infinitely more elaborate, and is called the Tabernacle.

8. The text here varies between "glory" and "face."

9. The text reads glory. These changes are deliberate, and reflect meditative piety, for generations later than the first recording of the narrative shunned speaking of Yahve's face.

10. There ensues next (XXXIV:17-26) a brief section, legal in tone, the main emphasis of which is the observance of the sacred days, that is, the Sabbath and three pilgrimage festivals. The prescriptions for the sacred days here are less specific than those found elsewhere (such as Lev. XXIII); some scholars feel that this section is very ancient, reflecting a relatively early summary of the sacred days, but others have argued that it is a convenient epitome made in late times.

11. The Hebrew word for radiant is *qéren,* "ray of light." The same word also means horn. Confusion on this word explains why Michelangelo portrayed Moses as horned.

12. Deut. XVII:15ff. provides explicitly for such later prophets. Here, though, the provision is only implicit. One might look also at Joel II:28-29, or in III:1-2 in Hebrew texts.

13. The precise complaint is not given; by inference it is that she is not a Hebrew. Here, Num. XII:1, she is identified as a Cushite, an Ethiopian; earlier, Ex. II:15-21, she was a Midianite named Zipporah. Some interpret the word Cushite as inclusive of the Midianites; others believe that a tradition about a second wife is represented here.

14. The text reads, "the form *of Yahve*."
15. Some scholars conjecture that a P writer has expunged a similar punishment on Aaron.
16. The Hebrew *kāvód* is usually translated as "glory," an acceptable translation provided one understands what is meant by glory, for the term is usually vague to the point of being meaningless. Reference to Lev. IX:23-24, among other passages, clarifies this for us: "The *kāvód* of Yahve appeared to all the Israelites, and fire came forth from Yahve and consumed the burnt offering. . . ." Yahve's glory, then, is His fiery radiance. See also Ezek. XLIII:1-5, and Isa. VI:3.
17. Hormah lay in the south. Some scholars believe that this reflects a dim tradition of an abortive effort to conquer Canaan from the south, rather than the dominant tradition of conquest from the east. See Num. XXI:2-3 and Judges I:17 for other mentions of Hormah.
18. The Reubenites' names are given as Dathan and Abiram, sons of Eliab, and *On ben Peleth*. Only in the first verse is this On mentioned. Again, On is unmentioned in a reminiscence in Num. XXVI:9; there Peleth appears as Pallu. Some scholars wish to omit On and to read here: "the sons of Eliab, who was the son of Pallu"; I think this is right.
19. The priesthood is conceived of in the Pentateuch as hereditary; the ending here emphasizes the exclusive prerogative of Aaron's descendants to the priestly functions. There ensues, Num. XVIII:1-XIX:10, a divine commission to Aaron, and a statement of the different responsibilities of the Priests and Levites in the sanctuary.
20. Allusions, also without Moses' reaction, are found in Deut. I:37 and IV:21. We read, however, in Deut. III:23-27, that Moses implored Yahve to allow him to cross into the land of Canaan and see it, but He said to Moses, angrily, "Enough! Do not speak to Me about this again!"
21. In II Kings XVIII:4 we read that King Hezekiah destroyed this bronze serpent because people were offering sacrifices to it.
22. In Numbers there is a long legal section on sacrifices (XXVIII-XXIX); a chapter on vows (XXX); a proclamation of undying hostility to the Midianites, along with rules for warfare (XXXI); an allotment of land east of the Jordan, as asked for by the tribes of Reuben, Gad, and a portion of the tribe of Manasseh, on the condition that first these would join in the conquest of the area

west of the Jordan (XXXII); a review of the itinerary (XXXIII); a statement of the future boundaries of the Israelite possessions (XXIV); the provision of special cities for the Levites (XXXV: 1-8), cities of safety for refugees from blood feuds (XXXV:9-15), and laws distinguishing between manslaughter (accidental slaying) and murder (XXXV:16-24); and, finally, regulations to retain tribal properties intact (XXXVI). This material appears here as though the author could think of no better place for its inclusion.

CHAPTER V

1. *Deuteronomy*

1. There are some appendices, such as the poems in Deut. XXXII and XXXIII.
2. In 722/21, the Assyrians exiled the inhabitants of the northern kingdom—ten tribes which, in popular extrabiblical tradition, became "lost"—and in 586 the Babylonians exiled the inhabitants of the southern kingdom.
3. The observance of the Sabbath is laconic in Ex. XX:8, and is there introduced by the word "remember"; in Deut. V:12, the introductory word is "observe"—"Observe the Sabbath to keep it holy." In Exodus, the Sabbath commandment concludes by allusion to God's resting on the seventh day (as in Gen. II:1-3), while here there is instead an allusion to the Exodus from Egypt. The tenth commandment, against coveting, reverses the order found in Exodus, having "wife" precede "house," rather than follow it.
4. In the legislative section in Deuteronomy there is no mention by name of the place where Yahve is to be worshiped. The supposition was that at some future time the Tabernacle, which was movable, would give way to a temple, to be located at an undisclosed place which Yahve would choose. That place later became Jerusalem. The prophetic writings, and the books of Judges, Samuel, and Kings, disclose that before and during the monarchy temples to Yahve existed in many places, among them Shiloh and Bethel. A passage in Exodus, XX:24, appears to suggest that many places could be suitable, but Deut. XII:4-14 specifically limits the legitimate worship to the single, undisclosed place which Yahve will choose. Most modern scholars regard this injunction for a single sanctuary to be a late development that was associated with the reformation of King Josiah; see esp. II Kings XXIII:8-19.

4. *Samuel, Saul, and David*

1. The ceremony of raising a commoner to royalty was to anoint him, that is, to pour oil on him. A person "anointed," and hence royal, was in Hebrew a *mashíah*; this word comes into the English alphabet as *Messiah*. The word "anointed" in Greek is *Christos*.

   Originally, *mashíah* meant simply "king." Later, after kingship was ended, the word took on the connotation of that person whom, in good time, God would send miraculously to do wondrous deeds on behalf of the people. That is, in late times, *mashíah* was the king of the far-distant future. The belief arose among Jews in various ages, especially in times of crisis, that at long last the distant future was now near, and hence the *mashíah* was soon to appear.

2. The verse reads: "Saul was ———— years old at his reign (*sic!*) and he ruled Israel for two years." We require a figure before "years" in the first half of the sentence—some guess that it should be fifty; perhaps "reign" is laconic for "beginning of his reign." In the second half of the sentence, we need something before the "two," such as "twenty and."

CHAPTER VI

The Laws

1. The layers are treated by the scholars with a general similarity, but there are differences among them, of course. Thus one scholar believes that there are "seven distinct codes of law . . . within the Pentateuch" (Robert H. Pfeiffer, *Introduction to the Old Testament*, 1941, p. 210). These would be the "Covenant Code," Ex. XX: 22-33—some assign it to E; the "Ritual Decalogue," scattered among Ex. XXXIV:10-26, XXII:28b-29, and XXIII:12, 15-19—some assign this to J; the Twelve Curses, Deut. XXVII:14-26; the Ten Commandments, Deut. V:16-18; duplicated in Ex. XX:1-17; the Deuteronomic Code, Deuteronomy XII-XXVI, the Holiness Code, Lev. XVII-XXVI, and the Priestly Code, encompassing most of Leviticus, but with additions scattered throughout Numbers and the later parts of Exodus. As a general pattern, I suppose there is no harm in this, but I, and others, shrink from what seems to be Pfeiffer's excessive certainty. Moreover, I hold, with others, that the Ritual Decalogue is older than the Covenant Code. Again, significant in context as the Twelve Curses are, I do not regard them as embodying legislation.

CHAPTER VII
CHAPTER VII
Verse and Poetry: Canticles, Lamentations, and Psalms

1. The New English Bible supplies suggestions as to who is speaking, as I have done elsewhere (see *The Hebrew Scriptures*, pp. 311-18).
2. So Psalm XXIX:1-2 demands that the "sons of the gods" praise Yahve's power and glory.
3. These are the eastern gates of the Temple.

CHAPTER VIII
Wisdom Literature: Proverbs, Ecclesiastes, Job

1. III:11B is rendered in the Revised Standard Version: "He has put eternity into man's mind, yet so that he cannot find out what God has done from the beginning to the end." The New English Bible reads: "He has given man a sense of time past and future but no comprehension of God's work from beginning to end." A literal rendering is: "Also the world He put in their heart without the man's finding the deed which God did from the beginning to the end."
2. I omit the last portion of XI:9, "Yet know that God will bring judgment on you for all these things," and the first portion of XII:1, "But remember your Creator in the days of your youth." These seem to me, as they have to others, to be additions from what may be described as an "orthodox" hand. Some scholars prefer to emend XII:1 so as to get to a reading such as "But remember your *grave* in the days of your youth."
3. A slight emendation alters "bones" into "sorrow."
4. The meaning is uncertain but in the context it seems to be, "I run a great risk."
5. The traditional translation of this verse is surely wrong. It runs: "Though He slay me, yet will I trust in Him."
6. When one reads it, he might well follow a minor rearrangement, that of moving verses 7-8 to follow verse 13.
7. It is likely that XL:15-XLI:1-34 is a later expansion of the Deity's reply.
8. XXXII:3 reads: [Elihu's] anger burned against the three friends because they had found no answer, and had condemned *Job*. Standard editions of the Hebrew Bible record that the word Job is a deliberate change, a *tiqqūn sōferím*, an "alteration of the

scribes." That is to say, the text originally read *God*, not Job, but later scribes, out of piety, made the change deliberately.

CHAPTER IX

1. That is, sins in abundance.
2. That is, the poor man borrowed money on his garment. The lender was expected to return it at night.
3. Streams in the near east dry up in the hot summer season. A *constant* stream would not.
4. Since city people would have disappeared, farmers would be summoned to weep at funerals.
5. An allusion to consulting wooden statues or trees as oracles.
6. Sacred prostitutes were a part of Baal worship. The idea behind sacred prostitution seems to be this: The crops were believed to grow through the fertilization by the Baal of the earth (who is so often "mother" earth). When the visitor and the sacred prostitute copulate, the Baal and the earth are presumably moved to copulate in imitation.
7. The following is offered as a tentative list of the authentic words of I Isaiah, and a chronological sequence: I. (before 735): VI:1-13; V:1-25; II:6-IV:1; IX:8-X:4; V:25-30. II. (about 735): XVII:1-14; VII-VIII; XXVIII:1-6. IIIa. (about 710): I, XX; XXX:1-17; XXXI: 1-4, XXXII:9-14, XXII:15-23; X. IIIb. (against Assyria): X:5-15, 27-34. Chapters XXXVI-XXXVIII, which are about Isaiah, not by him, largely duplicate II Kings XVIII:13-XX:19.
8. Where guards were sometimes stationed to frustrate thieves.
9. This vineyard, then, had received special and costly care.
10. The last two lines are a conjectural translation of a corrupt passage.
11. Ancient rabbinic sources record that this verse was deliberately altered to read, as it now does, "*we* are not subject to death." It was believed impious even to suggest Yahve's mortality by mentioning His immortality. The change is one of "the emendations of the scribes."
12. The same words are found in Ps. XXXI:14 Heb., XXXI:13 Eng.
13. For our purposes, I consider Second Isaiah to be primarily in XL-LV, and not in later chapters. I also consider XXXV to be part of Second Isaiah (having been separated by the insertion of a section from Kings, which is now Isaiah XXXVI-XXXIX). Within chap-

ters XXXV and XL-LV there are some short sections which seem
to have suffered some truncation and displacement; I believe that
L:4-11 and LII:13-LIII:12 are by quite another hand The section
called the *"suffering* servant" poem seems to be a fragment of a
longer poem. It depicts a single man who endured suffering and
death as a means whereby sinners, the majority, were redeemed.
The poem is touching, moving, exalted—and unclear. In Christian
tradition the poem has been interpreted as predictive of Jesus.
Passages in the Passion narrative seem based on it:

He was tortured, he was oppressed, but he did not open his mouth.
He was brought to slaughter like a lamb,
Like a ewe dumb before his shearers,
Silent, he did not open his mouth.

(LIII:7)

14. That is, to disarm them.
15. On this hypothesis, passages such as Pss. CXXXVII:7-9, LXXIX,
    LXXXIII, LXXIV, and Is. LXIII:18-64, acquire illumination.
16. This is a choice figure, for water seeks a low level, not a high one.
17. Some, however, interpret these empires as the Babylonians, the
    Medes, and the Persians.
18. A later interpretation of the "one like a man" makes him a person,
    a king, rather than the kingdom. In this late view the person was
    identified as the "Messiah."